Impossible Desires

Perverse Modernities

A series edited by Judith Halberstam

and Lisa Lowe

IMPOSSIBLE DESIRES

Queer Diasporas and South Asian Public Cultures

Gayatri Gopinath

Duke University Press   Durham and London 2005

© 2005 Duke University Press

All rights reserved

Printed in the United States of America

on acid-free paper ∞

Designed by C. H. Westmoreland

Typeset in Bembo by Keystone Typesetting, Inc.

The distribution of this book is supported by

a generous grant from the Gill Foundation.

Library of Congress Cataloging-in-Publication

Data appear on the last printed page

of this book.

for

J. H.

CONTENTS

ACKNOWLEDGMENTS

This book is about home, and I have many people to thank for making me feel at home both intellectually and emotionally in disparate locations, across many coasts and continents. The beginnings of this project date back to the early days of South Asian progressive activism in New York City in the late 1980s and 1990s. I feel privileged to have been part of a community of scholars, activists, and artists that made queer/progressive South Asian culture and politics coalesce during those years. Among them are Ayisha Abraham, Haresh Advani, Faraz Ahmed, Radhika Balakrishnan, Vivek Bald, Tamina Davar, Sharmila Desai, David Kalal, Anita Nayar, and Saeed Rahman. Rekha Malhotra and Geeta Javeri generously shared their passion for and encyclopedic knowledge of South Asian popular music with me. I have benefited from Javid Syed's brilliance as both an activist and scholar; much of my thinking on queer representation in popular Indian cinema is indebted to our joint clip show and lecture presentation, "Desi Dykes and Divas: Alternative Sexualities in Popular Indian Cinema," originally commissioned by the 1997 Lesbian and Gay Film Festival in New York City. Chandan Reddy's friendship and intellectual generosity have greatly enhanced the quality of both my life and work.

Ann Wightman and Indira Karamcheti at Wesleyan University provided me early on with a model of impassioned and committed pedagogy that has stayed with me to this day. As a graduate student at Columbia University, I was enriched by conversations and feedback from John Archer, Marcellus Blount, Sarita Echavez See, Qadri Ismail, Anne McClintock, Rosalind Morris, Robert O'Meally, Hiram Perez, and Tim Watson. I am particularly grateful to Rob Nixon for his consistent support and enthusiasm for this project. During my time in New York, it was my good fortune to come into contact with a remarkable group of scholars in queer studies whose work has influenced and inspired my own, as is evident in the pages that follow. Among them are Jacqui Alexander, Arnaldo Cruz Malavé, Ann Cvetkovich, Lisa Duggan, David Eng, Licia Fiol Matta, José Muñoz, Geeta Patel, and Patty White. Martin Manalansan's pathbreaking work on queer Filipino migration is deeply resonant with my own project; I could not have asked for a more sympathetic and constructive reader of this manuscript.

I was welcomed into a wonderful community of scholars at the University of California at San Diego who managed to make even the most unfamiliar of landscapes feel like home, among them Victor Bascara, Jody Blanco, Rick Bonus, Daphne Brooks, Oscar Campomanes, Rod Ferguson, Tak Fujitani, Grace Hong, Nicole King, George Lipsitz, Curtis Marez, Nayan Shah, Stephanie Smallwood, Shelly Streeby, and Lisa Yoneyama. I received the University of California President's Postdoctoral Fellowship in 1998 and was privileged to work with Lisa Lowe, who served as my faculty mentor. She has been an unfailing source of encouragement, and her work has provided me with a model of rigorous and elegant critical engagement that I can only hope to approximate. Rosemary George has been a generative and challenging reader and interlocutor, as well as a dear friend. Her own work on postcolonial literature and domesticity has greatly influenced my thinking. At the University of California at Davis, I wish to thank my current and former colleagues in Women and Gender Studies, as well as all those who have made UC Davis such a congenial place in which to carry out this project. I feel lucky to have had Rosa Linda Fregoso and Sarah Projansky as mentors during my first several years at UC Davis. Suad Joseph's energy, institutional savvy, and wide-ranging intellect have been a source of awe and admiration. A cohort of scholars working at the intersection of area studies, postcolonial, queer, and ethnic studies—Anupam Chander, Sergio De La Mora, Don Donham, Omnia El-Shakry, Nicole Fleetwood, Beth Freeman, Bishnu Ghosh, Caren Kaplan, Sunaina Maira, Kimberly Nettles, Rhacel Parreñas, Juana María Rodríguez, Karen Shimakawa, Smriti Srinivas, Madhavi Sunder—has provided a sense of intellectual community and collectivity that is very precious to me. I especially thank Lata Mani and Ruth Frankenberg for their friendship and sage advice. In what was far above and beyond the call of duty, Juana Rodríguez read every word of this manuscript even before she was officially my colleague at UC Davis. I hope this book reflects some measure of her deft and incisive reading, and the grace of her own writing and argumentation. In winter 2002, I had the pleasure of participating in a University of California Humanities Research Institute Fellowship on diaspora and popular music convened by Josh Kun at the University of California at Irvine. I thank the members of the research cluster—Raúl Fernández, Herman Gray, Jocelyne Guilbault, Michelle Habell Pallán, Josh Kun, Anthony Macías, and particularly Gayle Wald—for sharing their expertise with me and for teaching me so much. I also thank David Theo Goldberg as director of the UC HRI for having granted me this opportunity.

Friends and colleagues who have lent their support throughout the writing of this book in ways large and small include Paola Baccheta, Falu Bakrania, Allan De Souza, Lalitha Gopalan, Gil Hochberg, Sonia Jabbar, Keri Kanetsky, Sonia Katyal, Amy Kautzman, Amitava Kumar, Ira Livingston, Bakirathi Mani, Richard Meyer, T. Muraleedharan, Katrin Pahl, David Román, Cherry Smyth, Karen Tongson, and Tacy Trowbridge. Kale Fajardo and Manchui Leung have been loving, steadfast allies through some difficult times; I have deeply appreciated their humor, warmth, and affection. I am particularly grateful to Shani Mootoo, Pratibha Parmar, Ian Rashid, and Parminder Sekhon for trusting me enough to write about their work; I thank them for creating art that so beautifully captures the pleasures and dangers of queer lives.

I benefited greatly from the feedback from audiences at many venues where I presented early versions of several chapters. My thanks to Anjali Arondekar, Kandice Chuh, Ashley Dawson, Carla Freccero, Evelyn Nakano Glenn, Jody Greene, Josephine Ho, Gertrude Hughes, Ketu Katrak, Iona Man-Cheong, Dwight McBride, Monika Mehta, Yong Soon Min, Jim Schultz, Sahar Shafqat, Anu Sharma, and Linta Verghese for giving me the opportunity to share my work. Ken Wissoker showed an unflagging commitment to this project from its inception; I owe him a tremendous debt of gratitude for being so wholeheartedly supportive at every stage. I am particularly grateful to the two anonymous readers from Duke, whose detailed reports pushed me to clarify and refine my arguments, and in the end made for a far better book. My thanks to Courtney Berger and Kate Lothman for shepherding the manuscript through its final stages, and to Kara Thompson for so skillfully and efficiently creating the bibliography and index. I also thank Arthi Kharkanis and the National Film Archive of India for helping me to secure the film stills. Financial assistance during the writing of this book was provided by the Faculty Research Grant, the Faculty Development Grant, and the Dean's Book Completion Fund from UC Davis.

I owe more than I can say to Jennie Bauduy, April Cotte, Steve Friedman, Carl Haacke, Gayatri Patnaik, and Damon Wadsworth for their love, friendship, and wisdom. I would like to think this book reflects the ways in which my father, P. Gopinath, has imparted to me the need for care, precision, and endurance in all endeavors. My mother, Bharati Nair, has been a source of beauty, joy, and comfort, and the inspiration for much of what I write; her unwavering support has kept me afloat. Finally, Judith Halberstam has seen this project from its beginning to its end, and the arc of its development reflects how much I have learned from her about what it means to be an engaged intellectual. The passion and fearlessness that she brings to her own work continue to amaze me; her love and belief in me have sustained me through these many years.

Sections of individual chapters have appeared previously in different versions. I thank the publishers for permission to reprint, and the editors for their feedback and advice. Parts of chapters 1 and 6 appeared in "Nostalgia, Desire, Diaspora: South Asian Sexualities in Motion," *positions: east asia cultures critique* 5, no.2 (Fall 1997): 467–89, reprinted in *Theorizing Diaspora*, edited by Jana Evans Braziel and Anita Mannur (Malden, Mass.: Blackwell, 2003): 261–79. A brief section of chapter 4 appeared in "Queering Bollywood: Alternative Sexualities in Popular Indian Cinema," in *Queer Asian Cinema: Shadows in the Shade*, edited by Andrew Grossman (West Hazelton, Penn.: Haworth Press, 2000): 281–95. Chapter 5 appeared in a shorter form as "Local Sites/Global Contexts: The Transnational Trajectories of Deepa Mehta's *Fire*," in *Queer Globalizations: Citizenship and the Afterlife of Colonialism*, edited by Arnaldo Cruz-Malavé and Martin Malanansan (New York: NYU Press, 2002): 149–61. Parts of chapter 5 also appeared in "Homo-Economics: Queer Sexualities in a Transnational Frame," in *Burning Down the House: Recycling Domesticity*, edited by Rosemary Marangoly George (New York: Westview Press, 1998): 102–24.

Impossible Desires

I

IMPOSSIBLE DESIRES

An Introduction

In a particularly memorable scene in *My Beautiful Laundrette* (dir. Stephen Frears, 1985), British Pakistani screenwriter Hanif Kureishi's groundbreaking film about queer interracial desire in Thatcherite Britain, the white, working-class gay boy Johnny moves to unbutton the shirt of his lover, the upwardly mobile, Pakistan-born Omar. Omar initially acquiesces to Johnny's caresses, but then abruptly puts a halt to the seduction. He turns his back to his lover and recalls a boyhood scene of standing with his immigrant father and seeing Johnny march in a fascist parade through their South London neighborhood: "It was bricks and bottles, immigrants out, kill us. People we knew . . . And it was you. We *saw* you," Omar says bitterly. Johnny initially recoils in shame as Omar brings into the present this damning image from the past of his younger self as a hate-filled skinhead. But then, as Omar continues speaking, he slowly reaches out to draw Omar to him and embraces Omar from behind. The final shot frames Omar's face as he lets his head fall back onto Johnny's chest and he closes his eyes.

The scene eloquently speaks to how the queer racialized body becomes a historical archive for both individuals and communities, one that is excavated through the very act of desiring the racial Other. For Omar, desiring Johnny is irrevocably intertwined with the legacies of British colonialism in South Asia and the more immediate history of Powellian racism in 1960s Britain.[1] In his memory of having seen Johnny march ("we *saw* you"), Omar in a sense reverses the historical availability of brown bodies to a white imperial gaze by turning the gaze back onto Johnny's own racist past. The scene's ambiguous ending–where Omar closes his eyes and succumbs to Johnny's caresses—may suggest that Omar gives in to the historical amnesia that wipes out the legacies of Britain's racist past. Yet the meaning and function of queer desire in the scene are far more complicated than such a reading would allow. If for Johnny sex with Omar is a way of both tacitly acknowledging and erasing that racist past, for Omar, queer desire is precisely what allows him to remember. Indeed, the barely submerged histories of colonialism and racism erupt into the present at the very moment when queer sexuality is being articulated. Queer desire does not transcend or remain peripheral to these histories but instead it becomes central to their telling and remembering: there is no queer desire without these histories, nor can these histories be told or remembered without simultaneously revealing an erotics of power.

Upon its release in 1985, *My Beautiful Laundrette* engendered heated controversy within South Asian communities in the UK, some of whose members took exception to Kureishi's matter-of-fact depiction of queer interracial desire between white and brown men, and more generally to his refusal to produce "positive images" of British Asian lives.[2] The controversy surrounding its release prefigured the at times violent debates around queer sexuality and dominant notions of communal identity that took place both in South Asia and in the diaspora over the following decade.[3] In New York City, for instance, the South Asian Lesbian and Gay Association waged an ongoing battle throughout the 1990s over the right to march in the annual India Day Parade, a controversy I will return to later in this chapter. And in several Indian cities in December 1998, as I discuss in detail in chapter 5, Indian-Canadian director Deepa Mehta's film *Fire* was vociferously attacked by right-wing Hindu nationalists outraged by its depiction of "lesbian" sexuality. These various battles in disparate national locations speak to the ways in which queer desires, bodies, and subjectivities become dense sites of meaning in the production and reproduction of notions of "culture," "tradition," and communal belonging both in South Asia and in the diaspora. They also signal the conflation of "perverse" sexualities and diasporic affiliations within a nationalist imaginary, and it is this mapping of queerness onto diaspora that is the subject of this book.

Johnny (Daniel Day-Lewis) and
Omar (Gordon Warnecke) in *My Beautiful Laundrette*
(dir. Stephen Frears, 1985).

Twenty years later, Kureishi's film remains a remarkably powerful rendering of queer racialized desire and its relation to memory and history, and acts as a touchstone and precursor to much of the queer South Asian diasporic cultural production that I discuss in *Impossible Desires*.[4] The texts I consider in this book, following Kureishi's lead, allow us to dissect the ways in which discourses of sexuality are inextricable from prior and continuing histories of colonialism, nationalism, racism, and migration. In Kureishi's film, as in the other queer diasporic texts I examine in this book, queer desire reorients the traditionally backward-looking glance of diaspora. Stuart Hall has elegantly articulated the peculiar relation to the past that characterizes a conservative diasporic imaginary. This relation is one where the experience of displacement "gives rise to a certain imaginary plenitude, recreating the endless desire to return to 'lost origins,' to be one again with the mother, to go back to the beginning."[5]

If conventional diasporic discourse is marked by this backward glance, this "overwhelming nostalgia for lost origins, for 'times past,' "[6] a queer diaspora mobilizes questions of the past, memory, and nostalgia for radically different purposes. Rather than evoking an imaginary homeland frozen in an idyllic moment outside history, what is remembered through queer diasporic desire and the queer diasporic body is a past time and place riven with contradictions and the violences of multiple uprootings, displacements, and exiles. Joseph Roach, in his study of Atlantic-rim performance cultures, uses the suggestive phrase "forgotten but not gone" to name that which produces the conditions for the present but is actively forgotten within dominant historiography.[7] Queer diasporic cultural forms and practices point to submerged histories of racist and colonialist violence that continue to resonate in the present and that make themselves felt through bodily desire. It is through the queer diasporic body that these histories are brought into the present; it is also through the queer diasporic body that their legacies are imaginatively contested and transformed. Queer diasporic cultural forms thus enact what Roach terms "clandestine countermemories" that bring into the present those pasts that are deliberately forgotten within conventional nationalist or diasporic scripts.[8] If, as Roach notes, "the relentless search for the purity of origins is a voyage not of discovery but of erasure,"[9] queer diasporic cultural forms work against the violent effacements that produce the fictions of purity that lie at the heart of dominant nationalist and diasporic ideologies.

Significantly, however, Kureishi's excavation of the legacies of colonialism and racism as they are mapped onto queer (male) bodies crucially depends on a particular fixing of female diasporic subjectivity. The film's female diasporic character Tania, in fact, functions in a classic homosocial triangle as the conduit and foil to the desire between Johnny and Omar, and she quite literally disappears at the film's end. We last see her standing on a train platform, suitcase in hand, having left behind the space of the immigrant home in order to seek a presumably freer elsewhere. Our gaze is aligned with that of her father as he glimpses her through an open window; the train rushes by, she vanishes. It is unclear where she has gone, whether she has disappeared under the train tracks or is safely within the train compartment en route to a different life. She thus marks the horizon of Kureishi's filmic universe and gestures to another narrative of female diasporic subjectivity that functions quite literally as the film's vanishing point. Kureishi's framing of the female diasporic figure makes clear the ways in which even ostensibly progressive, gay male articulations of diaspora run the risk of stabilizing sexual and gender hierarchies.

My Beautiful Laundrette presents a useful point of departure in addressing many of the questions that concern me throughout this book. As the film makes apparent, all too often diasporas are narrativized through the bonds of relationality between men. Indeed, the oedipal relation between fathers and sons serves as a central and recurring feature within diasporic narratives and becomes a metaphor for the contradictions of sameness and difference that, as Stuart Hall has shown, characterize competing definitions of diasporic subjectivity.[10] For Freud, the oedipal drama explains the consolidation of proper gender identification and heterosexual object choice in little boys, as masculine identification with the father is made while feminine identification with the mother is refused. In his 1952 work *Black Skin, White Masks*, Frantz Fanon resituates the oedipal scenario in the colonial context and shows how, for racialized male subjects, the process whereby the little boy learns to identify with the father and desire the mother is disrupted and disturbed by the (black) father's lack of access to social power.[11] Fanon's analysis, which I engage with more fully in chapter 3, makes evident the inadequacy of the Oedipus complex in explaining the construction of gendered subjectivity within colonial and postcolonial regimes of power. While I am interested in identifying how queer diasporic texts follow Fanon in reworking the notion of oedipality in relation to racialized masculinities, I also ask what alternative narratives emerge when this story of oedipality is jettisoned altogether. For even when the male-male or father-son narrative is mined for its queer valences (as in *Laundrette* or in other gay male diasporic texts I consider here), the centrality of this narrative as the primary trope in imagining diaspora invariably displaces and elides female diasporic subjects. The patriarchal and heteronormative underpinnings of the term "diaspora" are evident in Stefan Helmreich's exploration of its etymological roots:

> The original meaning of diaspora summons up the image of scattered seeds and . . . in Judeo-Christian . . . cosmology, seeds are metaphorical for the male "substance" that is traced in genealogical histories. The word "sperm" is metaphorically linked to diaspora. It comes from the same stem [in Greek meaning to sow or scatter] and is defined by the OED as "the generative substance or seed of male animals." Diaspora, in its traditional sense, thus refers us to a system of kinship reckoned through men and suggests the questions of legitimacy in paternity that patriarchy generates.[12]

These etymological traces of the term are apparent in Kureishi's vision of queer diasporic subjectivity that centralizes male-male relations and sidelines female subjectivity. This book, then, begins where Kureishi's text leaves off. *Impossible Desires* examines a range of South Asian diasporic literature, film, and music in order to ask if we can imagine diaspora differently, apart from the biological, reproductive, oedipal logic that invariably forms the core of conventional formulations of diaspora. It does so by paying special attention to *queer female subjectivity in the diaspora*, as it is this particular positionality that forms a constitutive absence in both dominant nationalist and diasporic discourses. More surprisingly perhaps, and therefore worth interrogating closely, is the elision of queer female subjectivity within seemingly radical cultural and political diasporic projects that center a gay male or heterosexual feminist diasporic subject. *Impossible Desires* refuses to accede to the splitting of queerness from feminism that marks such projects. By making female subjectivity central to a queer diasporic project, it begins instead to conceptualize diaspora in ways that do not invariably replicate heteronormative and patriarchal structures of kinship and community. In what follows I lay out more precisely the various terms I use to frame the texts I consider—*queer diasporas*, *impossibility*, and *South Asian public cultures*—as they are hardly self-evident and require greater elaboration and contextualization.

Queer Diasporas

In an overview of recent trends in diaspora studies, Jana Evans Braziel and Anita Mannur suggest that the value of diaspora—a term which at its most literal describes the dispersal and movement of populations from one particular national or geographic location to other disparate sites—lies in its critique of the nation form on the one hand, and its contestation of the hegemonic forces of globalization on the other.[13] Nationalism and globalization do indeed constitute the two broad rubrics within which we must view diasporas and diasporic cultural production. However, the concept of diaspora may not be as resistant or contestatory to the forces of nationalism or globalization as it may first appear. Clearly, as Braziel and Mannur indicate, diaspora has proved a remarkably fruitful analytic for scholars of nationalism, cultural identity, race, and migration over the past decade. Theories of diaspora that emerged out of Black British cultural studies in the 1980s and 1990s, particularly those of Paul

Gilroy and Stuart Hall, powerfully move the concept of diaspora away from its traditional orientation toward homeland, exile, and return and instead use the term to reference what Hall calls "a conception of 'identity' which lives with and through, not despite, difference; by hybridity."[14] This tradition of cultural studies, to which my project is deeply indebted, embraces diaspora as a concept for its potential to foreground notions of impurity and inauthenticity that resoundingly reject the ethnic and religious absolutism at the center of nationalist projects. Viewing the (home) nation through the analytical frame of diaspora allows for a reconsideration of the traditionally hierarchical relation between nation and diaspora, where the former is seen as merely an impoverished imitation of an originary national culture.[15] Yet the antiessentialist notion of cultural identity that is at the core of this revised framing of diaspora functions simultaneously alongside what Hall terms a "backward-looking conception of diaspora,"[16] one that adheres to precisely those same myths of purity and origin that seamlessly lend themselves to nationalist projects. Indeed while the diaspora within nationalist discourse is often positioned as the abjected and disavowed Other to the nation, the nation also simultaneously recruits the diaspora into its absolutist logic. The policies of the Hindu nationalist government in India in the mid- to late 1990s to court overseas "NRI" (non-resident Indian) capital[17] is but one example of how diaspora and nation can function together in the interests of corporate capital and globalization.[18] Hindu nationalist organizations in India are able to effectively mobilize and harness diasporic longing for authenticity and "tradition" and convert this longing into material linkages between the diaspora and (home) nation.[19] Thus diasporas can undercut and reify various forms of ethnic, religious, and state nationalisms simultaneously. Various scholars have pointed out the complicity not only between diasporic formations and different nationalisms but also between diaspora and processes of transnational capitalism and globalization.[20] The intimate connection between diaspora, nationalism, and globalization is particularly clear in the South Asian context, as the example of NRI capital underwriting Hindu nationalist projects in India makes all too apparent.

Vijay Mishra importantly distinguishes between two historical moments of South Asian diasporic formation: the first produced by colonial capitalism and the migration of Indian indentured labor to British colonies such as Fiji, Trinidad, and Guyana in the late nineteenth and early twentieth centuries; and the second a result of the workings of "late modern capital" in the mid- to late twentieth century. Significantly, in addition to producing labor diasporas, colonial capitalism also produced what Kamala Visweswaran terms a "middle-man minority" that served the interests of the colonial power and acted as a conduit between British colonial administrators and the indigenous popula-tions in East Africa and other locations in the British Empire.[21] The legacies of this initial phase of South Asian diasporic formation in the nineteenth century are apparent in the second phase of migration engendered by globalization in the mid- to late twentieth century. Mishra defines this diaspora of "late mod-ern capital" as "largely a post-1960s phenomenon distinguished by the move-ment of economic migrants (but also refugees) into the metropolitan centers of the former empire as well as the 'New World' and Australia."[22] While South Asian migrants in the 1960s were allowed entry into the UK primarily as low-wage labor, the class demographic and racialization of South Asians in the United States was strikingly different. Vijay Prashad has pointed out how the 1965 Immigration and Nationality Act, which shifted the criteria for U.S. citizenship from a quota system to "family reunification," encouraged the immigration of large numbers of Indian professionals, primarily doctors and scientists; this demographic was particularly appealing to the U.S. govern-ment in that it was seen as a way to bolster U.S. cold war technological supremacy.[23] Visweswaran argues that this professional technocratic elite in the United States functions in effect as a latter-day middleman minority, working in collusion with dominant national interests in both the United States and in India. Mishra, Prashad, and Visweswaran thus point to the ways in which South Asian diasporic formations engendered by colonial capitalism (in the form of labor diasporas) and those engendered by globalization and trans-national capitalism (in the form of a bourgeois professional class) function in tandem with different national agendas.

Clearly, then, the cultural texts that emerge from these different historical moments in South Asian diasporic formation must be seen as inextricable not only from the ongoing legacies of colonialism and multiple nationalisms but also from the workings of globalization. Indeed theories of diasporic cultural production that do not address the imbrication of diaspora with transnational capitalism shore up the dominance of the latter by making its mechanisms invisible. In an astute critique of Paul Gilroy's influential formulation of black diasporic culture in *The Black Atlantic*, Jenny Sharpe argues that globalization provides the unacknowledged terrain upon which the diasporic cultural productions that Gilroy celebrates take shape. Sharpe notes that the transnational cultural practices that Gilroy draws on are rooted in urban spaces in the First World: "to consider London and New York as global city centers is to recognize the degree to which Gilroy's mapping of the black Atlantic follows a cartography of globalization."[24] Sharpe's analysis is a particularly useful caution against a celebratory embrace of diasporic cultural forms that may obscure the ways in which they are produced on the terrain of corporate globalization. Thus just as diaspora may function in collusion with nationalist interests, so too must we be attentive to the ways in which diasporic cultural forms are produced in and through transnational capitalist processes.

The imbrication of diaspora and diasporic cultural forms with dominant nationalism on the one hand, and corporate globalization on the other, takes place through discourses that are simultaneously gendered and sexualized. Feminist scholars of nationalism in South Asia have long pointed to the particular rendering of "woman" within nationalist discourse as the grounds upon which male nationalist ideologies take shape.[25] Such scholarship has been instructive in demonstrating how female sexuality under nationalism is a crucial site of surveillance, as it is through women's bodies that the borders and boundaries of communal identities are formed. But as I argue in chapter 5, this body of work has been less successful in fully addressing the ways in which dominant nationalism institutes heterosexuality as a key disciplinary regime. Feminist scholarship on South Asia has also, for the most part, remained curiously silent about how alternative sexualities may constitute a powerful challenge to patriarchal nationalism.[26] Nor has there been much sustained attention paid to the ways in which nationalist framings of women's sexuality are translated into the diaspora, and how these renderings of diasporic women's sexuality are in turn central to the production of nationalism in the home nation.[27] In an article on Indian indentured migration to Trinidad, Tejaswini Niranjana begins this necessary work by observing that anticolonial nationalists in India in the early twentieth century used the figure of the amoral, sexually impure Indian woman abroad as a way of producing the chaste, virtuous Indian woman at "home" as emblematic of a new "nationalist morality."[28] The consolidation of a gendered bourgeois nationalist subject in India through a configuration of its disavowed Other in the diaspora underscores the necessity of conceptualizing the diaspora and the nation as mutually constituted formations. However, as I elaborate in chapter 6, Niranjana's article still presumes the heterosexuality of the female diasporic and female nationalist subject rather than recognizing institutionalized heterosexuality as a primary structure of both British colonialism and incipient Indian nationalism. The failure of feminist scholars of South Asia and the South Asian diaspora to fully interrogate heterosexuality as a structuring mechanism of both state and diasporic nationalisms makes clear the indispensability of a queer critique. A queer diasporic framework insists on the imbrication of nation and diaspora through the production of hetero- and homosexuality, particularly as they are mapped onto the bodies of women.

Just as discourses of female sexuality are central to the mutual constitution of diaspora and nation, so too is the relation between diasporic culture and globalization one that is mediated through dominant gender and sexual ideologies. Feminist theorists have astutely observed that globalization profoundly shapes, transforms, and exploits the gendered arrangements of seemingly "private" zones in the diaspora such as the "immigrant home."[29] But while much scholarship focuses on how global processes function through the differentiation of the labor market along gendered, racial, and national lines, how discourses of sexuality in the diaspora intersect with, and are in turn shaped by, globalization is only beginning to be explored.[30] Furthermore, the impact of globalization on particular diasporic locations produces various forms of oppositional diasporic cultural practices that may both reinscribe and disrupt the gender and sexual ideologies on which globalization depends.

The critical framework of a specifically *queer* diaspora, then, may begin to unsettle the ways in which the diaspora shores up the gender and sexual ideologies of dominant nationalism on the one hand, and processes of globalization on the other. Such a framework enables the concept of diaspora to fulfill the double-pronged critique of the nation and of globalization that Braziel and Mannur suggest is its most useful intervention. This framework "queers" the concept of diaspora by unmasking and undercutting its dependence on a genealogical, implicitly heteronormative reproductive logic. Indeed, while the Bharatiya Janata Party–led Hindu nationalist government in India acknowledged the diaspora solely in the form of the prosperous, Hindu, heterosexual NRI businessman, there exists a different embodiment of diaspora that remains unthinkable within this Hindu nationalist imaginary. The category of "queer" in my project works to name this alternative rendering of diaspora and to dislodge diaspora from its adherence and loyalty to nationalist ideologies that are fully aligned with the interests of transnational capitalism. Suturing "queer" to "diaspora" thus recuperates those desires, practices, and subjectivities that are rendered impossible and unimaginable within conventional diasporic and nationalist imaginaries. A consideration of queerness, in other words, becomes a way to challenge nationalist ideologies by restoring the impure, inauthentic, nonreproductive potential of the notion of diaspora. Indeed, the urgent need to trouble and denaturalize the close relationship between nationalism and heterosexuality is precisely what makes the notion of a queer diaspora so compelling.[31] A queer diasporic framework productively exploits the analogous relation between nation and diaspora on the one hand, and between heterosexuality and queerness on the other: in other words, queerness is to heterosexuality as the diaspora is to the nation. If within heteronormative logic the queer is seen as the debased and inadequate copy of the heterosexual, so too is diaspora within nationalist logic positioned as the queer Other of the nation, its inauthentic imitation. The concept of a queer diaspora enables a simultaneous critique of heterosexuality and the nation form while exploding the binary oppositions between nation and diaspora, heterosexuality and homosexuality, original and copy.

If "diaspora" needs "queerness" in order to rescue it from its genealogical implications, "queerness" also needs "diaspora" in order to make it more supple in relation to questions of race, colonialism, migration, and globalization. An emerging body of queer of color scholarship has taken to task the "homonormativity" of certain strands of Euro-American queer studies that center white gay male subjectivity, while simultaneously fixing the queer, nonwhite racialized, and/or immigrant subject as insufficiently politicized and "modern."[32] My articulation of a queer diasporic framework is part of this collective project of decentering whiteness and dominant Euro-American paradigms in theorizing sexuality both locally and transnationally. On the most simple level, I use "queer" to refer to a range of dissident and non-heteronormative practices and desires that may very well be incommensurate with the identity categories of "gay" and "lesbian." A queer diasporic formation works in contradistinction to the globalization of "gay" identity that replicates a colonial narrative of development and progress that judges all "other" sexual cultures, communities, and practices against a model of Euro-American sexual identity.[33] Many of the diasporic cultural forms I discuss in this book do indeed map a "cartography of globalization," in Sharpe's terms, in that they emerge out of queer communities in First World global cities such as London, New York, and Toronto. Yet we must also remember, as Lisa Lowe and David Lloyd point out, that "transnational or *neo-colonial* capitalism, like colonialist capitalism before it, continues to produce sites of contradiction that are effects of its always uneven expansion but that cannot be subsumed by the logic of commodification itself."[34] In other words, while queer diasporic cultural forms are produced in and through the workings of transnational capitalism, they also provide the means by which to critique the logic of global capital itself. The cartography of a queer diaspora tells a different story of how global capitalism impacts local sites by articulating other forms of subjectivity, culture, affect, kinship, and community that may not be visible or audible within standard mappings of nation, diaspora, or globalization. What emerges within this alternative cartography are subjects, communities, and practices that bear little resemblance to the universalized "gay" identity imagined within a Eurocentric gay imaginary.

Reading various cultural forms and practices as both constituting and constituted by a queer South Asian diaspora resituates the conventions by which homosexuality has traditionally been encoded in a Euro-American context. Queer sexualities as articulated by the texts I consider here reference familiar tropes and signifiers of Euro-American homosexuality—such as the coming-out narrative and its attendant markers of secrecy and disclosure, as well as gender inversion and cross-dressing—while investing them with radically different and distinct significations. It is through a particular engagement with South Asian public culture, and popular culture in particular, that this defamiliarization of conventional markers of homosexuality takes place, and that alternative strategies through which to signify non-heteronormative desire are subsequently produced. These alternative strategies suggest a mode of reading and "seeing" same-sex eroticism that challenges modern epistemologies of visibility, revelation, and sexual subjectivity. As such, the notion of a queer South Asian diaspora can be understood as a conceptual apparatus that poses a critique of modernity and its various narratives of progress and development.[35] A queer South Asian diasporic geography of desire and pleasure stages this critique by rewriting colonial constructions of "Third World" sexualities as anterior, premodern, and in need of Western political development—constructions that are recirculated by contemporary gay and lesbian transnational politics. It simultaneously interrogates different South Asian nationalist narratives that imagine and consolidate the nation in terms of organic heterosexuality.

The concept of a queer South Asian diaspora, then, functions on multiple levels throughout this book. First, it situates the formation of sexual subjectivity within transnational flows of culture, capital, bodies, desire, and labor. Second, queer diaspora contests the logic that situates the terms "queer" and "diaspora" as dependent on the originality of "heterosexuality" and "nation." Finally, it disorganizes the dominant categories within the United States for sexual variance, namely "gay and lesbian," and it marks a different economy of desire that escapes legibility within both normative South Asian contexts and homonormative Euro-American contexts.

The radical disruption of the hierarchies between nation and diaspora, heterosexuality and homosexuality, original and copy, that queer diasporic texts enact hinges on the question of translation. Many of the texts I consider here can be understood as diasporic translations of "original" national texts: for instance, in chapter 5 I read Deepa Mehta's *Fire* against Urdu writer Ismat Chughtai's 1941 short story on which Mehta's film is loosely based. Similarly, in chapter 4, I situate Indian American director Mira Nair's 2001 film *Monsoon Wedding* alongside its earlier manifestation as the Bollywood, Hindi language hit *Hum Aapke Hain Koun . . . !* (Who Am I to You?, dir. Sooraj Barjatya, 1994). In most popular and critical discussions of *Fire* or *Monsoon Wedding*, both within and outside India, the earlier, "indigenous" blueprints of each film are conveniently forgotten and effaced. In restoring the prior text as central to the discussion of the contemporary text, and in tracing the ways in which representations of queerness shift from "original" to "remake," I ask what is both lost and gained in this process of translation. Reading diasporic texts as translations may seem to run the risk of reifying the binary between copy and original; it risks stabilizing the "nation" as the original locus that diaspora merely attempts to replicate. Just as the nation and the diaspora are mutually constitutive categories, by extension so too do the "original" national text and its diasporic translation gain meaning only in relation to one another. Tejaswini Niranjana, in her study of translation as a strategy of colonial subjectification, observes that translation functions within an idiom of fidelity, betrayal, and authenticity and appears "as a transparent representation of something that already exists, although the 'original' is actually brought into being through translation."[36] In the juxtaposition of texts that I engage in, the queerness of either text can only be made intelligible when read against the other.[37] Furthermore, reading contemporary queer representations (such as Mehta's

Fire) through their "originals"(such as Chughtai's short story) militates against a developmental, progress narrative of "gay" identity formation that posits the diaspora as a space of sexual freedom over and against the (home) nation as a space of sexual oppression. Rather, I am interested in how the erotic economies of the prior text are mapped differently within a diasporic context. Translation here cannot be seen as a mimetic reflection of a prior text but rather as a productive activity that instantiates new regimes of sexual subjectivity even as it effaces earlier erotic arrangements.

Finally, in its most important intervention into dominant nationalist and diasporic formations, the framework of a queer diaspora radically resituates questions of home, dwelling, and the domestic space that have long concerned feminist, queer, and postcolonial scholarship. Historians of colonialism and anticolonial nationalism in India have examined in detail the ways in which home and housing were crucial to the production of both a British colonial and Indian anticolonial nationalist gendered subjectivity in the nineteenth century.[38] Partha Chatterjee argues that in late-colonial India, "the battle for the new idea of womanhood in the era of nationalism was waged in the home . . . it was the home that became the principal site of the struggle through which the hegemonic construct of the new nationalist patriarchy had to be normalized."[39] Contemporary nationalist and diasporic discourses clearly bear the marks of these colonial and anticolonial nationalist legacies of "home" as a primary arena within which to imagine "otherness" in racial, religious, national, and gendered terms. The "home" within both discourses is a sacrosanct space of purity, tradition, and authenticity, embodied by the figure of the "woman" who is enshrined at its center, and marked by patriarchal gender and sexual arrangements. It is hardly surprising, then, that the home emerges as a particularly fraught site of contestation within the queer diasporic texts I discuss in this book.

Just as the home has been a major site of inquiry within feminist postcolonial scholarship, queer studies has also been particularly attuned to the home as a primary site of gender and sexual oppression for queer and female subjects.[40] Yet while many lesbian and gay texts imagine "home" as a place to be left behind, to be escaped in order to emerge into another, more liberatory space, the queer South Asian diasporic texts I consider here are more concerned with remaking the space of home from within. For queer racialized migrant subjects, "staying put" becomes a way of remaining within the oppressive structures of the home—as domestic space, racialized community space, and national space—while imaginatively working to dislodge its heteronormative logic.[41] From the two sisters-in-law who are also lovers in Deepa Mehta's film *Fire*, to a British Asian gay son's grappling with his immigrant father in Ian Rashid's short film *Surviving Sabu*, to the queer and transgendered protagonists of Shani Mootoo's and Shyam Selvadurai's novels, home is a vexed location where queer subjects whose very desires and subjectivities are formed by its logic simultaneously labor to transform it.

Historian Antoinette Burton writes of how, in the memoirs of elite women writers in late-colonial India, the "home" itself becomes an archive, "a dwelling-place of a critical history rather than the falsely safe space of the past."[42] Similarly, the queer diasporic texts I discuss throughout this book provide a minute detailing and excavation of the various forms of violence and, conversely, possibility and promise that are enshrined within "home" space. These queer diasporic texts evoke "home" spaces that are permanently and already ruptured, rent by colliding discourses around class, sexuality, and ethnic identity. They lay claim to both the space of "home" and the nation by making both the site of desire and pleasure in a nostalgic diasporic imaginary. The heteronormative home, in these texts, unwittingly generates homoeroticism. This resignification of "home" within a queer diasporic imaginary makes three crucial interventions: first, it forcefully repudiates the elision of queer subjects from national and diasporic memory; second, it denies their function as threat to family/community/nation; and third, it refuses to position queer subjects as alien, inauthentic, and perennially outside the confines of these entities.

Impossibility

Because the figure of "woman" as a pure and unsullied sexual being is so central to dominant articulations of nation and diaspora, the radical disruption of "home" that queer diasporic texts enact is particularly apparent in their representation of queer female subjectivity. I use the notion of "impossibility" as a way of signaling the unthinkability of a queer female subject position within various mappings of nation and diaspora. My foregrounding of queer female diasporic subjectivity throughout the book is not simply an attempt to merely bring into visibility or recognition a heretofore invisible subject. Indeed, as I have suggested, many of the texts I consider run counter to standard "lesbian" and "gay" narratives of the closet and coming out that are organized exclusively around a logic of recognition and visibility. Instead, I scrutinize the deep investment of dominant diasporic and nationalist ideologies in producing this particular subject position as impossible and unimaginable. Given the illegibility and unrepresentability of a non-heteronormative female subject within patriarchal and heterosexual configurations of both nation and diaspora, the project of locating a "queer South Asian diasporic subject"—and a queer female subject in particular—may begin to challenge the dominance of such configurations. Revealing the mechanisms by which a queer female diasporic positionality is rendered impossible strikes at the very foundation of these ideological structures. Thus, while this project is very much situated within the emergent body of queer of color work that I referenced earlier, it also parts ways with much of this scholarship by making a queer female subject the crucial point of departure in theorizing a queer diaspora. In so doing, *Impossible Desires* is located squarely at the intersection of queer and feminist scholarship and therefore challenges the notion that these fields of inquiry are necessarily distinct, separate, and incommensurate.[43] Instead, the book brings together the insights of postcolonial feminist scholarship on the gendering of colonialism, nationalism, and globalization, with a queer critique of the heteronormativity of cultural and state nationalist formations.[44]

The impossibility of imagining a queer female diasporic subject within dominant diasporic and nationalist logics was made all too apparent in the battle in New York City between the South Asian Lesbian and Gay Association (SALGA) and a group of Indian immigrant businessmen known as the National Federation of Indian Associations (NFIA), over SALGA's inclusion in the NFIA-sponsored annual India Day Parade. The India Day Parade—which runs down the length of Madison Avenue and is an ostensible celebration of India's independence from the British in 1947—is an elaborate performance of Indian diasporic identity, and a primary site of contestation over the borders and boundaries of what constitutes "Indianness" in the diaspora. In 1992 the newly formed SALGA applied for the right to march in the parade only to be brusquely turned down by the NFIA. Later that same year, right-wing Hindu extremists demolished the Babri Masjid, a Muslim shrine in Ayodhya, India, setting off a frenzy of anti-Muslim violence. These two events—the destruction of the Babri Masjid in Ayodhya, and the resistance on the part of the NFIA to SALGA's inclusion in the parade in New York City—are not as unrelated as they may initially appear. Paola Baccheta has argued that one of the central tenets of Hindu nationalist ideology is the assignation of deviant sexualities and genders to all those who do not inhabit the boundaries of the Hindu nation, particularly Indian Muslims.[45] Thus, while these two events are certainly not comparable in terms of scale or the level of violence, together they mark the ways in which terrifyingly exclusivist definitions of communal belonging are relayed and translated between nation and diaspora within the realm of public culture, through intersecting discourses of gender, sexuality, nationality, and religion. The literal erasure of Muslims from the space of the (Hindu) nation coincides with the symbolic effacement of queer subjects from a "home" space nostalgically reimagined from the vantage point of the diaspora. Indeed the battle between SALGA and the NFIA that continued throughout the 1990s makes explicit how an Indian immigrant male bourgeoisie (embodied by the NFIA) reconstitutes Hindu nationalist discourses of communal belonging in India by interpellating "India" as Hindu, patriarchal, middle class, and free of homosexuals.[46] This Hindu nationalist vision of home and homeland was powerfully contested by SALGA at the 1995 parade, where once again the group was literally positioned at the sidelines of the official spectacle of national reconstitution. One SALGA activist, Faraz Ahmed (aka Nina Chiffon), stood at the edge of the parade in stunning, Bollywood-inspired drag, holding up a banner that proclaimed, "Long Live Queer India!" The banner, alongside Ahmed's performance of the hyperbolic femininity of Bollywood film divas, interpellated not a utopic future space of national belonging but rather an already existing queer diasporic space of insurgent sexualities and gender identities.

That same year, the NFIA attempted to specify its criteria for exclusion by denying both SALGA and Sakhi for South Asian Women (an anti–domestic violence women's group) the right to march on the grounds that both groups were, in essence, "antinational." The official grounds for denying Sakhi and SALGA the right to march was ostensibly that both groups called themselves not "Indian" but "South Asian." The possibility of Pakistanis, Bangladeshis, or Sri Lankans marching in an "Indian" parade was seen by NFIA members as an unacceptable redefinition of what constituted the so-called Indian community in New York City. In 1996, however, the NFIA allowed Sakhi to participate while continuing to deny SALGA the right to march. The NFIA, as self-styled arbiter of communal and national belonging, thus deemed it appropriate for women to march as "Indian women," even perhaps as "feminist Indian women," but could not envision women marching as "Indian queers" or "Indian lesbians"; clearly the probability that there may indeed exist "lesbians" within Sakhi was not allowed for by the NFIA.

The controversy surrounding the India Day Parade highlights how hegemonic nationalist discourses, produced and reproduced in the diaspora, position "woman" and "lesbian" as mutually exclusive categories to be disciplined in different ways. Anannya Bhattacharjee's work on domestic violence within Indian immigrant communities in the United States, for instance, demonstrates how immigrant women are positioned by an immigrant male bourgeoisie as repositories of an essential "Indianness." Thus any form of transgression on the part of women may result in their literal and symbolic exclusion from the multiple "homes" which they as immigrant women inhabit: the patriarchal, heterosexual household, the extended "family" made up of an immigrant community, and the national spaces of both India and the United States.[47] Sunaina Maira's ethnography of South Asian youth culture in New York City further documents the ways in which notions of chastity and sexual purity in relation to second-generation daughters are "emblematic not just of the family's reputation but also, in the context of the diaspora, of the purity of tradition and ethnic identity, a defense against the promiscuity of 'American influences.'"[48] Both Bhattacharjee and Maira valuably point to the complex ways in which the gendered constructions of South Asian nationalism are reproduced in the diaspora through the figure of the "woman" as the boundary marker of ethnic/racial community in the "host" nation. The "woman" also bears the brunt of being the embodied signifier of the "past" of the diaspora, that is, the homeland that is left behind and continuously evoked. But what remains to be fully articulated in much feminist scholarship on the South Asian diaspora are the particularly disastrous consequences that the symbolic freight attached to diasporic women's bodies has for non-heteronormative female subjects. Within the patriarchal logic of an Indian immigrant bourgeoisie, a "nonheterosexual Indian woman" occupies a space of impossibility, in that she is not only excluded from the various "home" spaces that the "woman" is enjoined to inhabit and symbolize but, quite literally, simply cannot be imagined. Within patriarchal diasporic and nationalist logic, the "lesbian" can only exist outside the "home" as household, community, and nation of origin, whereas the "woman" can only exist within it. Indeed the "lesbian" is seen as "foreign," as a product of being too long in the West, and therefore is annexed to the "host" nation where she may be further elided—particularly if undocumented—as a nonwhite immigrant within both a mainstream (white) lesbian and gay movement and the larger body of the nation-state.

The parade controversy makes clear how the unthinkability of a queer female diasporic subject is inextricable from the nationalist overvaluation of the heterosexual female body; but it also functions in tandem with the simultaneous subordination of gay male subjectivity. Thus throughout this book, I pay close attention to the highly specific but intimately related modes of domination by which various racialized, gendered, classed, and sexualized bodies are disciplined and contained by normative notions of communal identity. The rendering of queer female diasporic subjectivity as "impossible" is a very particular ideological structure: it is quite distinct from, but deeply connected to, the fetishization of heterosexual female bodies and the subordination of gay male bodies within dominant diasporic and nationalist discourses.[49] *Impossible Desires* attempts to track the mutual dependency and intersections between these different modes of domination, as well as the particular forms of accommodation and resistance to which they give rise. Indeed, as my brief discussion of *My Beautiful Laundrette* suggested, and as I elaborate in the following chapters, queer female diasporic subjectivity remains unimaginable and unthinkable not only within dominant nationalist and diasporic discourses but also within some gay male, as well as liberal feminist, rearticulations of diaspora. Thus, in their elision of queer female diasporic subjectivity, gay male and liberal feminist frameworks may be complicit with dominant nationalist and diasporic discourses.

While the phrase "impossible desires" refers specifically to the elision of queer female diasporic sexuality and subjectivity, I also use it to more generally evoke what José Rabasa, in his analysis of the Zapatista rebellion in Chiapas, Mexico, calls "a utopian horizon of alternative rationalities to those dominant in the West."[50] Noting that one of the rallying cries of the movement is "Exigíd lo imposible!" (Demand the impossible!), Rabasa understands the Zapatistas' evocation of pre-Columbian myths combined with a pointed critique of the North American Free Trade Agreement and former president Raúl Salinas's economic reforms as articulating a particular vision of time, history, and national collectivity that runs counter to that of dominant Mexican nationalism. The "impossibility" of the Zapatistas' subaltern narrative, argues Rabasa, lies in its incompatibility with the "modern" narratives of dominant nationalism that relegate indigenous people to the realm of the pre-political and the premodern. The power of the Zapatistas thus "resides in the new world they call forth—a sense of justice, democracy, and liberty that the government *cannot* understand because it calls for its demise."[51] It may initially appear incongruous to begin a study of gender, sexuality, and migration in the South Asian diaspora with an evocation of an indigenous peasant struggle in southern Mexico. However I find the notion of "the impossible," as articulated by Rabasa's reading of Zapatismo, to have a remarkable resonance with the project engaged in throughout this book. The phrase "Exigíd lo imposible!," in relation to a queer South Asian diaspora, suggests the range of oppositional practices, subjectivities, and alternative visions of collectivity that fall outside the developmental narratives of colonialism, bourgeois nationalism, mainstream liberal feminism, and mainstream gay and lesbian politics and theory. "Demanding the impossible" points to the failure of the nation to live up to its promises of democratic egalitarianism, and dares to envision other possibilities of existence exterior to dominant systems of logic.

South Asian Public Cultures

Throughout this book, I attempt to read the traces of "impossible subjects" as they travel within and away from "home" as domestic, communal, and national space. In so doing, I ask how we can identify the multitude of "small acts," as Paul Gilroy phrases it, that fall beneath the threshold of hegemonic nationalist and diasporic discourses.[52] This project of mapping the spaces of impossibility within multiple discourses necessitates an engagement with particular cultural forms and practices that are at the margins of what are considered legitimate sites of resistance or the "proper objects" of scholarly inquiry. The term "South Asian public cultures," in my project, functions to name the myriad cultural forms and practices through which queer subjects articulate new modes of collectivity and kinship that reject the ethnic and religious absolutism of multiple nationalisms, while simultaneously resisting Euro-American, homonormative models of sexual alterity. My understanding of the term builds on Arjun Appadurai and Carole Breckenridge's definition of "public culture" as a "*zone* of cultural debate" where "tensions and contradictions between national sites and transnational cultural processes" play out.[53] It is within the realm of diasporic public culture that competing notions of community, belonging, and authenticity are brought into stark relief. Such an understanding of public culture reveals the intimate connections between seemingly unrelated events such as the India Day Parade controversy and the destruction of the Babri Masjid that I just described. The queer diasporic public culture that is the focus of this book takes the form of easily "recogniz-able" cultural texts such as musical genres, films, videos, and novels that have a specifically transnational address even as they are deeply rooted in the politics of the local. But because queer diasporic lives and communities often leave traces that resist textualization, they allow us to rethink what constitutes a viable archive of South Asian diasporic cultural production in the first place.[54] Thus the archive of queer public culture that I track here also encompasses cultural interventions that are much harder to document, such as queer spec-tatorial practices, and the mercurial performances and more informal forms of sociality (both on stage and on the dance floor) that occur at queer night clubs, festivals, and other community events. This queer diasporic archive is one that runs against the grain of conventional diasporic or nationalist archives, in that it documents how diasporic and nationalist subjectivities are produced through the deliberate forgetting and violent expulsion, subordination, and criminal-ization of particular bodies, practices, and identities. This archive is the storing house for those "clandestine countermemories," to once again use Joseph Roach's phrase, through which sexually and racially marginalized commu-nities reimagine their relation to the past and the present. By narrating a different history of South Asian diasporic formation, a queer diasporic archive allows us to memorialize the violences of the past while also imagining "other ways of being in the world,"[55] as Dipesh Chakravarty phrases it, that extend beyond the horizon of dominant nationalisms.

This different mode of conceptualizing the archive necessitates different reading strategies by which to render queer diasporic subjects intelligible and to mark the presence of what M. Jacqui Alexander terms an "insurgent sex-uality" that works within and against hegemonic nationalist and diasporic logic.[56] Indeed, the representations of non-heteronormative desire within the texts I consider throughout the book call for an alternative set of reading practices, a queer diasporic reading that juxtaposes what appear to be disparate texts and that traces the cross-pollination between the various sites of non-normative desires that emerge within them. On the one hand, such a reading renders intelligible the particularities of same-sex desiring relations within spaces of homosociality and presumed heterosexuality; on the other hand, it deliberately wrenches particular scenes and moments out of context and extends them further than they would want to go. It exploits the tension in the texts between the staging of female homoerotic desire as simply a supplement to a totalizing heterosexuality and the potential they raise for a different logic and organization of female desire. Because it is consistently under erasure from dominant historical narratives, the archive of a queer diaspora is one that is necessarily fractured and fragmented. I therefore employ a kind of scavenger methodology that finds evidence of queer diasporic lives and cultures, and the oppositional strategies they enact, in the most unlikely of places—the "home" being one such key location. As we see in relation to "home," often what looks like a capitulation to dominant ideologies of nation and diaspora may in fact have effects that dislodge these ideologies; conversely what may initially appear as a radically oppositional stance may simply reinscribe existing power relations. In my reading of the British film *East Is East* (dir. Damien O'Donnell, 2000) in chapter 3, for instance, I suggest that it may not be the gay British Asian son who leaves the home, but rather the seemingly straight daughter who remains, who most troubles the gender and sexual ideologies of "home" in all its valences. The daughter is able to effect the disruption of home space through the performance of the hyperbolic femininity embodied by the heroines of Bollywood, as popular Hindi cinema is known. It is this practice of citationality, where the daughter evokes different genealogies of racialized femininity, that marks her as "queer." Queerness in this case references an alternative hermeneutic, the particular interpretive strategies that are available to those who are deemed "impossible" within hegemonic nationalist and diasporic discourses. The category of queer, in other words, names the reading and citational practice that I engage in throughout the book, and that I also identify within the texts themselves.

I employ this queer reading practice in chapter 2, where I consider the ways in which popular music functions as one of the primary manifestations and locations of transnational public culture in the South Asian diaspora. I read the music of British Asian bands of the 1990s through a queer diasporic frame by situating it alongside alternative media and cultural practices that allow us to hear different stories about South Asian diasporic formation in the context of globalization. The valorization by critics and audiences of the recognizably oppositional class and race politics of the predominantly male "Asian Under-ground" music scene allows for a complex picture of racialized masculinities in postcolonial Britain to emerge. Yet it misses the more nuanced contestations of gender, sexuality, race, and nation by queer and female subjects that take place at the margins of this scene and in spaces (such as the home) that may not initially appear as crucial locations where globalization makes itself felt. I therefore counterpose my discussion of the "Asian Underground" with an evocation of other musical, cinematic, and literary representations that pro-vide complex renderings of gendered labor and "home" space in the context of globalization. In her 2003 novel *Brick Lane*, for instance, the British Bangla-deshi writer Monica Ali maps the contours of these marginal spaces through the story of Nazneen, a Bangladeshi immigrant woman garment worker who lives and works in a Tower Hamlets housing project in London's East End.[57] Ali traces in minute detail the domestic landscape of Nazneen's cramped flat that she shares with her husband and two daughters, and that also functions as a work space where she does piecework for a local garment sweatshop. The novel makes evident the way in which the seemingly "private" domestic space functions as a key site of globalization, one that is intimately connected to other national locations where goods are produced by women workers for transnational corporations. The careful attention that Ali pays to the domestic and urban spaces of immigrant London maps an alternative geography to that evoked by the militant, antiracist politics of Asian Dub Foundation (ADF) or Fun'Da'Mental, two of the best known British Asian bands of the 1990s. While Ali situates her novel in the same social landscape of London's East End out of which a band like ADF emerged in the early 1990s, the music is unable to access the domestic geography of gendered labor that Ali so carefully details. Indeed, understanding the interrelation between diaspora and globalization through very particular forms of British Asian music, as various cultural critics have tended to do, rather than through the other musical forms and cultural practices that emerge out of the racialized and gendered spaces mapped by a text such as Ali's, risks replicating a dominant model of diaspora that recenters a heterosexual masculine subject. The chapters that follow attempt to think diaspora outside of this masculinist, heteronormative paradigm.

Chapter 3 elaborates on the interrelations between racialized postcolonial masculinities, South Asian diasporic women's labor, and queer articulations of diaspora as they emerge in the home. I read the configuration of queer postcolonial masculinity in the Indian Canadian filmmaker Ian Rashid's 1996 short film, *Surviving Sabu*, which is set in contemporary London, through and against the depiction of masculine failure in V. S. Naipaul's classic 1961 novel of diasporic displacement, *A House for Mr. Biswas*, set in Trinidad. By juxtaposing these two very different texts, I work against a logic of oedipality that would position Naipaul's modernist fable as emblematic of an "older" diasporic model that is invariably superceded by the "new" understanding of diaspora articulated by Rashid's film. Instead I argue that Naipaul's novel provides a brutally accurate diagnosis of the impact of colonialism on racialized masculinity that is productively taken up and reworked through the queer diasporic imaginary of Rashid's text. Yet Rashid's gay male articulation of diaspora, as in Kureishi's *My Beautiful Laundrette*, is dependent on the erasure of the female diasporic subjectivity and therefore has more in common with Naipaul's text than may initially appear. The splitting of a queer project from a feminist one that we see in *Surviving Sabu* raises the larger question of how to theorize diaspora within both a queer *and* feminist framework. I therefore end the chapter with a consideration of how female diasporic subjectivity—as it emerges in the 2001 British film *East Is East*—intervenes into the masculinist frameworks of both Rashid and Naipaul and provides an alternative ordering of "home" space. *East Is East* is set in Manchester in the early 1970s and follows the trials and tribulations of George Khan, a working-class Pakistani immigrant, his white English wife, and their biracial children. While the film's dominant narrative centers on George's relation to his sons and figures diasporic displacement primarily through the trope of damaged, wounded postcolonial masculinity, I employ a queer reading practice to instead draw attention to the seemingly tangential, excessive moment in the film where George's sole daughter engages in a Bollywood-style song-and-dance sequence. This scene offers a much more complex understanding of gendered diasporic subjectivity and Asian women's labor in the "home" than does the rest of the film, or Rashid and Naipaul's texts. As such, my reading of *East Is East* allows us to resist the troubling conflation of queerness as male and femaleness as straight that even progressive gay male texts such as Rashid's inadvertently enact.

Chapter 4 further explores this splitting of "queer" from "female," and "feminist," as it plays out within the realm of Bollywood cinema and the diasporic routes it travels. I begin by reflecting on the ways in which queer diasporic audiences reterritorialize "home" and homeland through their reception of popular Indian cinema. These audiences exploit the tensions and slippages within the Bollywood text, and particularly the song-and-dance sequence, in order to articulate a specifically queer diasporic positionality, one that recognizes both the text and the viewer in motion. As such, a consideration of queer diasporic engagements with Bollywood forces us to extend and challenge notions of spectatorship and cinematic representation that have emerged out of both Indian film studies and Euro-American queer and feminist film studies. Throughout the chapter, I pay particular attention to representations of women's sexuality in Bollywood cinema, in order to gauge what it means for queer female desire to signify onscreen, given Bollywood cinema's intimate connection with Indian nationalism and the intense investment of nationalist discourse in regulating women's bodies. How does queer female desire trouble dominant notions of national and communal identity that emerge within the heteropatriarchal narratives of Bollywood cinema? Interestingly, it is often in moments of what appears to be extreme gender conformity, and in spaces that seem particularly fortified against queer incursions—such as the domestic arena—that queer female desire emerges in ways that are most disruptive of dominant masculinist scripts of community and nation. Indeed the most enabling and nuanced instances of queer female desire on the Bollywood screen transpire not through the representation of explicitly queer coded, visible "lesbian" characters but rather through evoking the latent homoeroticism of female homosocial space.

The second half of chapter 4 traces the ways in which the idiom of Bollywood cinema and its strategies of queer representation have been translated, transformed, and rendered intelligible for an international market by South Asian diasporic feminist filmmakers such as Mira Nair, Gurinder Chadha, and Deepa Mehta. I focus in particular on Mira Nair's film *Monsoon Wedding* (2001), which received tremendous international acclaim, and which I read as a diasporic translation of the hugely popular Bollywood hit *Hum Aapke Hain Koun . . . !* (Who Am I to You?, dir. Sooraj Barjatya, 1994). Surprisingly, I find that in Nair's ostensibly feminist, diasporic rescripting of the neoconservative, nationalist politics of the earlier film, the queerness of female homosocial space that *Hum Aapke Hain Koun. . . !* renders so distinctly is effaced. By substituting queer male characters for queer female space, *Monsoon Wedding* and other feminist diasporic translations of Bollywood such as Chadha's *Bend It Like Beckham* (2002) and Mehta's *Bollywood / Hollywood* (2002), ultimately evacuate the possibility of queer female representation by splitting apart a queer project from a feminist one. Like Rashid's *Surviving Sabu*, they thus reinforce the impossibility of queer female desire and subjectivity that is at the heart of dominant nationalist and diasporic ideologies.

Chapter 5 turns to Deepa Mehta's earlier, controversial 1996 film *Fire*, in order to examine a diasporic representation of queer female desire and pleasure that does indeed signify on screen. The film and the fractious debates it generated provide a remarkably fruitful case study of the fraught relation between representations of queer female desire and discourses of diaspora and nation. I employ a queer diasporic reading practice that traces the multiple and contradictory meanings of Mehta's film as it travels between different national locations. Just as Nair's *Monsoon Wedding* can be read as a diasporic translation of the Bollywood hit *Hum Aapke Hain Koun . . . !*, so too can *Fire* be productively read as the diasporic translation of another earlier, "national" text, namely the 1941 short story that inspired it, Ismat Chughtai's "The Quilt."[58] Although Chughtai's story was only briefly mentioned, if at all, in the ensuing debates surrounding *Fire*, I reinstate it as a crucial intertext to Mehta's film. Both texts situate queer female pleasure and desire firmly within the confines of the middle-class home, thereby powerfully disrupting dominant gender and sexual constructions of communal and national identity in South Asia, as well as dominant Euro-American narratives of an "out," visible "lesbian" identity. Situating Mehta's film in relation to Chughtai's story critiques the film's apparent intelligibility to a non–South Asian viewing public through developmental, neocolonial constructions of "tradition" and "modernity." Instead it underscores the ways in which both texts produce complex models of female homoerotic desire that challenge a Euro-American "lesbian" epistemology that relies on notions of visibility and legibility. Furthermore, both texts put forth a narrative of marriage and the domestic space that interrogate colonial and nationalist discursive framings of female sexuality in general and female homoeroticism in particular. I place my readings of *Fire* and "The Quilt" within the context of South Asian feminist scholarship on gender and nationalism that, I argue, fails to adequately address alternative sexualities when considering the formation of Indian nationalism or the Hindu right. The *Fire* controversy makes all too apparent the necessity of theorizing alternative sexualities as central to the critique of religious and state nationalisms.

My final chapter examines contemporary queer South Asian diasporic literature that theorizes sexual subjectivity through processes of transnationalism and gendered labor migrations, as well as through the complicated negotiations of state regulatory practices and multiple national sites undertaken by queer diasporic subjects. As such, this literature interrogates our understandings of nostalgia, "home," and desire in a transnational frame. I argue that the Sri Lankan Canadian writer Shyam Selvadurai's 1994 novel *Funny Boy*,[59] and the Trinidadian Canadian Shani Mootoo's 1996 novel *Cereus Blooms at Night*,[60] make a timely intervention into the emerging field of South Asian American studies in that they place sexuality firmly at the center of analyses of racialization, colonialism, and migration. I look closely at how both texts rethink the category of "home" through the deployment of what I would call an enabling nostalgia, one that stands in marked contrast to the conventionally nostalgic structures of "home" and tradition called forth by contemporary state and diasporic nationalisms. Within the novels of Selvadurai and Mootoo, as in Chughtai's text, sexuality functions not as an autonomous narrative but instead as enmeshed and immersed within multiple discourses. In its recreation of "home" space, queer diasporic literature refuses to subsume sexuality within a larger narrative of ethnic, class, or national identity, or to subsume these other conflicting trajectories within an overarching narrative of "gay" sexuality. The novels of Mootoo and Selvadurai, like the other queer diasporic texts I consider throughout the book, do not allow for a purely redemptive recuperation of same-sex desire, conscribed and implicated as it is within racial, class, religious, and gender hierarchies. Indeed, as is so apparent in the scene from *My Beautiful Laundrette* with which I began this chapter, it is precisely from the friction between these various competing discourses that queer pleasure and desire emerge.

The framework of a queer South Asian diaspora provides a conceptual space from which to level a powerful critique at the discourses of purity and "tradition" that undergird dominant nationalist and diasporic ideologies; but it also works to reveal and challenge the presumed whiteness of queer theory and the compulsory heterosexuality of South Asian feminisms. While my book limits itself to the analysis of queer South Asian and queer South Asian diasporic texts, I hope that the insights produced here on the illegibility and indeed impossibility of certain queer subjects and desires also allow for a richer understanding of a whole range of texts that have stood outside of dominant lesbian-gay and national canons. Through the lens of a queer diaspora, various writers and visual artists such as Nice Rodriguez, Ginu Kamani, Audre Lorde, R. Zamora Linmark, Richard Fung, and Achy Obejas (to name just a few)[61] can now be deciphered and read simultaneously into multiple queer and national genealogies. Many of the objects of inquiry in *Impossible Desires* appear to be excessive, tangential, or marginal to recognized traditions; often they are but recalcitrant moments within larger narratives which are deeply invested in conventional gender, sexual, and nationalist ideologies. It is precisely at the margins, however, and in relation to sexuality and desire, that the most powerful and indispensable critiques of dominant formulations of nation and diaspora are taking place. My contention here is that the various regimes of colonialism, nationalism, racial and religious absolutism are violently consolidated through the body and its regulation. When queer subjects register their refusal to abide by the demands placed on bodies to conform to sexual (as well as gendered and racial) norms, they contest the logic and dominance of these regimes. Thus theorists of sexuality, as well as of race and postcoloniality, ignore the interventions of queer diasporic subjects at their own peril.

2

COMMUNITIES OF SOUND

Queering South Asian Popular Music in the Diaspora

At a 1999 performance of queer South Asian art and culture in New York City, the high point of the show came as the stage went dark and the audience heard not the familiar strains of Bollywood songstresses Asha Bhosle or Lata Mangeshkar over the loudspeakers, as one might expect in such a venue, but rather the chilly electronic beat of Madonna's 1998 Hinduism-inspired CD *Ray of Light*. As the lights went on, a spotlight bathed the three South Asian drag queens who appeared center stage in a golden glow. The performers were replete with the henna tattoos, gold bangles, and the upper-caste facial markings popularized by Madonna during her brief bout of Indophilia in the late 1990s. As the largely queer South Asian crowd erupted in enthusiastic applause, the performers launched into a sexy and hilarious rendition of Madonna's faux-Sanskrit techno dance track "Shanti/Ashtangi." How can we read this scene of criss-crossing influences, appropriations, and translations, of South Asian diasporic queers performing Madonna at the height of her "millennial orientalist" phase?[1] This performance and its interpellation of a queer diasporic public culture functions as an ironic commentary on Madonna's penchant for cultural theft and tourism, particularly her appropriation of the cultural forms of queer and racialized subcultures. Furthermore, it reverses the standard circuits of commodification and appropriation whereby subcultural forms are absorbed into mainstream culture. But by returning Madonna's performance of exotic otherness to its roots, so to speak, the drag performers are not making a cultural nationalist claim to authenticity or cultural ownership. Rather, they can be understood as what José Muñoz terms "disidentificatory subjects, who tactically and simultaneously work on, with and against a dominant cultural form."[2] Queer diasporic cultural practices challenge "millennial orientalism" not through an outright rejection of dominant cultural forms but through a highly pleasurable refashioning of them; such practices thus open up a queer counterpublic space that both references and resists the simultaneous absorption and elision of subcultural forms within the dominant public sphere.[3] Crucially, they do so without resorting to the conventional articulations of masculine potency that are apparent in other musical expressions of South Asian diasporic culture.

This drag performance at a small nightclub in New York City offers a glimpse of how queer diasporic cultural practices, as brief and fleeting as they may be, produce a space of public culture that powerfully critiques the racism of dominant U.S. culture and the heteronormativity of hegemonic diasporic and nationalist formations. While performances such as this do not fit easily into analyses of South Asian diasporic music, their double-edged critique provides a critical point of reference for considering the production, performance, and consumption of popular music in the South Asian diaspora. As the critical scholarship and popular attention to South Asian diasporic music has grown over the past decade, the focus has for the most part been on two musical movements: Bhangra, a form of popular music originally from the Punjab in North India that became the basis of a diasporic South Asian youth culture in both Britain and the United States in the late 1980s and early 1990s; and more recently, the post-Bhangra, UK-based "Asian Underground" or "New Asian Dance Music" scene of the late 1990s. The exclusive focus on these particular forms of South Asian diasporic musical production, I will suggest, invariably replicates a notion of diaspora that depends on dominant gender and sexual ideologies, in that it tracks forms of "radical" cultural politics only insofar as they circulate between men and pass literally and metaphorically from fathers to sons. In other words, tracing the contours of South Asian diasporic subjectivities through the soundscapes of only one particular music culture tells only one story of diaspora and its relation to both economic globalization and the nation form.

Conversely, my analysis of contemporary South Asian diasporic music cultures in the United States and the United Kingdom seeks to reconceptualize diaspora outside its conventionally masculinist and heterosexist parameters by paying attention to those cultural practices (such as the drag performance of "Shanti/Ashtangi") that are deemed to be tangential or marginal to the more audible forms of diasporic popular music. We can name these eccentric cultural practices as "feminist" and "queer," and together they constitute a different archive of South Asian diasporic culture that forces us to place gender and sexuality at the very center of our understandings of diaspora, nation, and globalization. This is not simply a call for the inclusion of "other" voices within the critical frameworks that define South Asian musical production. Rather, I am suggesting that ignoring the alternative narratives of gendered and sexual subjectivities that emerge from the margins of dominant cultural forms inevitably results in misreading the complex relation between diaspora, the nation, and the processes of globalization as they impact local sites.

Fathers and Sons:
Bhangra Music and the Engendering of Diaspora

In 1995 I wrote an article on Bhangra music and how its production, circulation, and consumption across national borders created a sonic landscape that mapped imaginary lines of connection from rural Punjab, to the industrial cities of the English Midlands, to the urban centers of London and New York.[4] I argued that a second generation of British Asian musicians that emerged in the late 1980s—exemplified by the Birmingham-reared British-Punjabi artist Apache Indian's musical mix of Bhangra with reggae and dancehall—offered a powerful critique of claims to cultural authenticity by drawing on a wide array of black and Asian diasporic musical influences. In so doing, these artists reversed what I called "the hierarchical relation of the nation to diaspora," where the diaspora is seen in some sense as the bastard child of the nation: disavowed, illegitimate, and inauthentic. In the music of Apache Indian—with its referencing of multiple diasporic locations including the Caribbean, India, the UK, and the United States—the "nation" was displaced from its privileged position as the locus of originary or pure cultural identity and became merely one out of many diasporic locations. The web of "affiliation and affect" (to use Paul Gilroy's influential phrase)[5] that Bhangra produced between these disparate sites in the South Asian diaspora resulted in the nation becoming part of the diaspora just as the diaspora became part of the nation.[6] In other words, a consideration of the way Bhangra traveled and continues to travel across national borders radically shifts the way in which diaspora is traditionally conceived as always and forever being oriented toward a phantasmatic lost homeland; rather, this homeland is revealed to be just as dependent on the diaspora as the diaspora is on the homeland.

This analysis of Bhangra music in Britain—a genre largely performed and produced by men—allowed me to consider both the uses and limits of diaspora as a theoretical framework through which to understand gendered and racial subjectivities in migration.[7] It became clear, in the music of first-generation Bhangra musicians in the 1970s, as well as in the work of later artists such as Apache Indian and the deejay Bally Sagoo in the 1980s and 1990s, that discourses of diaspora may challenge racial and ethnic essentialisms while at the same time being deeply invested in notions of dominant masculinity, genealogical descent, and reproduction. The concept of diaspora, after all, is neither purely disruptive of normative notions of culture and community, nor is it purely "regressive" and conservative. Rather the affective ties of diaspora can be mobilized for competing and contradictory interests simultaneously.[8] In the case of Bhangra, many first-generation musicians rooted in the working-class Asian immigrant communities of Southall in London or the depressed industrial cities in the Midlands articulated a "closed" notion of diaspora, as Stuart Hall defines it, one marked by a sense of exile, displacement, and longing for lost homelands.[9] Second-generation Bhangra musicians, on the other hand, for the most part eschewed notions of redemptive return and instead redefine their relation to questions of home, exile, and origin in an exuberant articulation of what Hall calls an "open" diaspora, one where immigrant subjects "remak[e] themselves and fashion new kinds of cultural identity by drawing on more than one cultural repertoire."[10] Of course, claiming that Hall's model of "closed" versus "open" diasporas maps neatly onto the music of first- versus second-generation Bhangra musicians runs the risk of being overly reductive. Nevertheless, I would argue that one of the defining features of the music of second-generation British Bhangra artists was the challenge they posed to the ethnic absolutism and concomitant longing for lost homelands of conventional diasporic ideologies, as expressed in some of the music of an earlier generation of Bhangra musicians. Their music also challenged the ethnic absolutism and dominant notions of English national identity articulated by "New Right" nationalist discourse under Thatcher.[11]

Interestingly, questions of patrilineal descent, inheritance, and generational conflict were mobilized at various levels: within the lyrics of Bhangra songs, in the relation between first- and second-generation Bhangra musicians, and in the actual form of the music itself. The lyrical content of many early Bhangra songs detailed the hardships of working-class immigrant male existence in a racist, xenophobic Britain, while also commenting on the social rifts that migration produced between fathers and sons. The oedipal dynamics between father and son that were the focus of many early Bhangra songs were played out and negotiated musically by second-generation Bhangra artists in the 1990s in their remixes of first-generation Bhangra classics from the 1970s. For instance the 1974 track by Shaukat Ali titled "Why Did I Come to *Vilayet* [England]?," with its piano, accordion, and tabla instrumentation, dramatized the tense but also humorous dialogue between a father in Punjab and his wayward immigrant son in the UK. Twenty years later, Ali's song was remixed by the deejay Johnny Zee by adding a drum kit, sound effects, synthesizers, tabla, and dholak to the original track.[12] Virinder S. Kalra notes that both the 1974 and 1994 versions of this track, as well as other first-generation Bhangra songs, fit easily into the dominant narrative of "culture clash" and generational conflict that characterizes the "ethnicizing project" of the majority of ethnographic accounts of minorities in Britain.[13] Yet the musical dialogue between first- and second-generation Bhangra musicians, as seen in the dynamic of sampling and remixing, may also point to a more complex representation of immigrant existence than that which is produced within a conventional narrative of generational conflict. Bhangra songs of the 1970s through the 1990s seem to mobilize the recurring motif of generational divides between fathers and sons in order to articulate a pointed critique of the pressures brought to bear on working-class immigrant masculinities in the UK. For instance, one of the best-known Bhangra hits of the 1980s, Kalapreet's *"Us Pardes Kee Vasna Yaaran?"* (What Is It to Live in This Place / Abroad?), details the loss of dignity and self-determination that male migrant workers experience in the face of white racism, having left Punjab for *vilayet* (England).[14] Indeed, in the thematic focus of its lyrics, in the contrapuntal relation between first- and second-generation musicians, and in the aesthetics of the remix, Bhangra music can be seen to represent an extended meditation on racialized immigrant masculinity in the diaspora.

The concern with masculinity that is apparent in Bhangra music, however, is often predictably predicated on dominant gender and sexual ideologies. An analysis of Bhangra makes clear that both the "closed" and "open" models of diasporic identity as articulated by first- and second-generation British Bhangra musicians were invariably organized around patrilineality and organic heterosexuality. Although Bhangra music allowed for a reversal of the nation-diaspora hierarchy in critical ways, I argued in my earlier piece that it also intersected with anticolonial and Hindu nationalist discourses in its deployment of the figure of "woman" and in its ultimate adherence to a particularly masculinist, heterosexual genealogy of diaspora. In first-generation Bhangra songs, for instance, the nostalgic evocation of homeland was mobilized through the fixed, static figure of the female, the emblem of tradition and (sexual and moral) purity. Female agency was again foreclosed in the music of later British Asian artists such as Apache Indian, whose concert performances staged a fluid, syncretic, de-essentialized notion of "Indian" identity only through the ritualized enactment of heterosexual descent and inheritance between father and son.[15]

If my early analysis of Bhangra music made clear the "dangers of positing certain notions of genealogy and patrilineality as the underlying logic of diaspora,"[16] in this chapter I want to ask if we can restore the impure, inauthentic, nonreproductive potential of the notion of diaspora by placing queer and feminist diasporic cultural practices at the center of our analysis. What alternative narratives emerge when we displace those of "generational conflict" and oedipal relations between fathers and sons through which much Bhangra music is structured both thematically and musically? By "queering" a discussion of South Asian popular music in the diaspora, I work against the tendency toward patrilineality, biology, and blood-based affiliation that lies embedded within the term "diaspora" and that is enacted by some South Asian diasporic popular music cultures and the cultural criticism about these cultures. In other words, queering the soundscapes of the South Asian diaspora means highlighting those feminist and queer diasporic cultural practices that give us a way of imagining and hearing diaspora differently, outside heteronormative paradigms of biological inheritance, oedipality, and blood-based affiliation.

Nostalgia, Nationalism, and
Masculinity in Post-Bhangra British Asian Music

By the late 1990s, Bhangra was firmly entrenched as a central aspect of South Asian youth culture in both Britain and the United States.[17] But the diasporic South Asian music scene that was once dominated by Bhangra had also proliferated and taken flight in exciting new directions as well, with British Asian bands and artists such as Cornershop, Fun'da'mental, Asian Dub Foundation, the Kaliphz, Hustlers HC, Echobelly, Talvin Singh, and Nitin Sawhney encompassing musical idioms as diverse as punk, reggae, drum 'n' bass, alternative rock, hip-hop, techno, and electronica. These British bands also produced transatlantic linkages between the UK and the United States through venues such as Mutiny, a nightclub in New York City run by deejay and filmmaker Vivek Renjen Bald and dedicated to featuring the music of many new British Asian artists alongside that of local talent.[18] By examining three of the most visible and highly publicized British Asian bands of the late 1990s— Cornershop, the Asian Dub Foundation (ADF), and Fun'da'mental—I ask how this constellation of British Asian musicians, deejays, and consumers (alternately dubbed the "Asian Underground" or "New Asian Dance Music") replicates or reconceptualizes the masculinist paradigms of diaspora, nation, history, and memory as they were produced during an earlier moment of British Asian music. The trenchant commentary on racialized immigrant masculinities apparent in earlier forms of British Asian music are also evident in the music of newer Asian Underground bands. These new sounds explicitly challenge the pathologization of British Asian masculinity within discourses that position young Asian, particularly Muslim, men as "the 'new' threat to British society, the latest incarnation of the black folk devil."[19] As Claire Alexander notes, the newly discovered Asian Other in 1990s Britain is "best captured in the image of 'the Underclass,' 'the Fundamentalist,' and of course, 'the Gang.'[20] In the tracks of ADF, mass media representations of an unassimilable racialized underclass are transformed into the image of what the band calls the "digital underclass," an imagined revolutionary coalition of sound that unites those outside of white male middle-class normativity.[21] Similarly, in naming themselves as they do, the indie rock band Cornershop and the hip-hop–influenced Fun'da'mental ironically inhabit dominant representations of Asian men as mild and meek owners of local grocery stores or, conversely, as dangerous fundamentalists/

terrorists. Yet, as I will discuss, as with an earlier generation of British Asian music, this powerful and necessary critique of dominant representations of British Asian masculinity also runs the risk of replicating conventional gender and sexual hierarchies.

In the mid 1990s, this conglomeration of musical sounds was heralded by the mainstream media as the coming of age of "The New Asian Kool," a marketing category that signaled the "acceptability" of South Asian diasporic popular culture within mainstream popular culture in Britain. The term "Asian Underground" first came into wide usage in 1997, with the release of Talvin Singh's album *Soundz of the Asian Underground*, which included the various British Asian artists featured at his London nightclub Anokha. Yet many of the bands deemed by the press to be at the forefront of the Asian Underground music scene rejected the label as merely a convenient term used by the mainstream media to package and ghettoize British Asian musicians. Pratibha Parmar's documentary *Brimful of Asia* (1998) turns a critical eye on this politics of labeling and the increasing visibility in general of British Asian sounds, arts, and fashion in 1990s Britain. Parmar's video, while largely a celebratory account of the newfound visibility of British Asian cultural production in the late 1990s, nevertheless reveals a troubling tension between the way in which British Asian artists understood the work that they were doing, and the way their work was incorporated into the mainstream. The British Asian artists interviewed by Parmar very explicitly countered narratives of "culture clash" and "between two cultures" that dominated popular and ethnographic accounts of British Asian communities. Instead they embraced a more complicated aesthetic that they understood to be remaking British national identity through a claiming of diasporic and transnational affiliations. While Parmar's film stops short of fully exploring the contradictions it raises, it becomes evident in the film that the complexities of British Asian self-representations were flattened out when they entered the mainstream. Indeed, the film makes clear how these representations were transformed into dehistoricized markers of otherness and exotica, exemplified by the "millennial orientalism" of Madonna's 1998 album *Ray of Light*.[22]

This new audibility of South Asian diasporic culture, as well as its new visibility in the form of ubiquitous citations of Bollywood cinema in mainstream Euro-American popular culture (which are discussed in greater detail in chapter 4), prompted fierce debate and criticism among popular music scholars in the 1990s. Koushik Banerjea forcefully argued that the embrace of the term "Asian Underground" by the mainstream media points to the insidious effects of "an insatiable and . . . uncritical appetite for multiculture and its richly syncretic produce."[23] Banerjea notes that while newly dubbed "Asian Underground" artists enjoy their fleeting fifteen minutes of fame, the harsh material realities of British Asian immigrant existence remain unchanged: "Eulogizing Talvin Singh on a Sunday afternoon at his club in Brick Lane [a largely Bangladeshi neighborhood in East London] does little to hide white distaste for the large Asian community which actually lives there."[24] Banerjea alludes here to the shifting class demographics of South Asian club culture, as the largely working-class audiences and practitioners of Bhangra music in the towns and cities of the Midlands gave way to hip, multiracial, middle-class urban audiences in London. The new class affiliation of the Asian music scene rendered it more palatable to both middle-class Asian and non-Asian audiences alike. Banerjea goes on to argue that the contemporary dynamics between the Asian Underground and the culture "above ground," so to speak, is marked by the legacies of Orientalism: "Even if Empire has subsided, fascination with 'otherness' has persisted, except that this time round neo-Orientalists need travel no further than Hoxton for their masala mudpie."[25] Similarly, on the other side of the Atlantic, Vijay Prashad documented the ways in which all things South Asian are refracted through "U.S. Orientalism" in the context of U.S. popular culture, so that markers of a mythic, spiritual, dehistoricized, and implicitly Hindu India take the place of more radical subaltern histories of transnational alliances and affiliations between South Asia and the United States.[26] Popular music scholars such as John Hutnyk and Sanjay Sharma echo Banerjea's concerns when they plaintively ask, "In Britain the album *Soundz of the Asian Underground* was so rapidly sucked up into the mainstream, while so much more 'difficult' matter was left aside, that we are left wondering what spaces remain for subaltern cultural creativity and production to flourish and 'succeed' without becoming instant vacant fodder for the style magazines?"[27] In his book-length study of British Asian music, Hutnyk specifies what he means by this "more difficult matter" that remains resistant to the voracious appetite of capitalist commodification: it is the music and uncompromising antiracist politics of the hip-hop bands such as Fun'da'mental and Kaliphz, "*not* characterized as Asian Kool."[28]

While these critiques by Hutnyk, Sharma, and Banerjea usefully point to the legacies of Orientalism in the new moment of visibility and audibility of South Asian diasporic culture, they also tend to reduce the dynamic relation between racialized immigrant subcultures and dominant culture into a simple story of unrelenting appropriation and commodification. As such, they run the risk of replicating conventional Marxist narratives, "whose tendency," as Lisa Lowe and David Lloyd remind us, "is to totalize the world system, to view capitalist penetration as complete and pervasive, so that the site of intervention is restricted to commodification; or, more insidiously, with the result that all manifestations of difference appear as just further signs of commodification."[29] As my example of South Asian drag queens "doing" Madonna attests to, laments about the inevitable co-optation of subcultural production tend to flatten out the complexities of the routes that culture travels. Within such a framework, it is impossible to account for the different meanings and effects of "appropriation" depending on both context and audience. For instance, Vijay Prashad documents the way in which African Americans in the early to mid-twentieth century participated in a dominant "U.S. Orientalism" that fetishized a spiritual India; yet he argues that the meanings of this fetishization were radically different than they were in "the world of white America." For black Americans, Prashad notes, "the strategic deployment of India was far more nuanced, particularly because it was used as a means to undercut racist authority."[30] George Lipsitz traces a similar dynamic of strategic subaltern appropriation in his analysis of the performance of (Native American) "Indianness" by working-class black men during the Mardi Gras celebration in New Orleans. While these enactments by black men of the figure of the Indian "display all the orientalism, primitivism and exoticism that plague so much of popular culture's representations of aggrieved groups,"[31] Lipsitz goes on to show how "the politics emanating from Indian imagery to affirm Black nationalism lead logically to a pan-ethnic anti-racism that moves beyond essentialism."[32] These complicated forms of appropriation that Prashad and Lipsitz document have no place within the framework of inevitable, totalizing corporate commodification that Hutnyk and others map out. The following discussions of Cornershop, ADF, and Fun'da'mental in relation to queer and feminist cultural practices suggest that the dynamics of appropriation and the dialectic between the mainstream and minoritarian popular cultures may be more messy and unpredictable than such an analysis can account for. Moreover, it becomes particularly evident when considering queer diasporic cultural practices such as the drag performance I described at the beginning of this chapter that minoritarian cultures respond to their own fetishization and commodification in strategic and imaginative ways.

The contradictory meanings and effects of South Asian diasporic popular culture's entry into mainstream consciousness were sharply delineated in 1997 when Cornershop, fronted by the British Punjabi singer Tjinder Singh, scored a surprise hit on both U.S. and UK charts with their single "Brimful of Asha." The track remained on Britain's Top of the Pops for the entire year, and the album on which it appeared was named the best new album of 1997 by *Spin* magazine.[33] Cornershop's transatlantic success marked a turning point for British Asian music, which had remained largely inaudible on mainstream music charts despite the Bhangra boom of the 1980s and early 1990s. Bearing in mind the cautions of critics such as Hutynk, Banerjea, and Sharma, I would nevertheless argue that Cornershop's success intervenes into what constitutes both "Asian diasporic" and "British" national culture and national memory in important ways. Indeed Cornershop deploys nostalgia not to evoke lost homelands or a fantasied imperial past but rather to offer a different vision of history, collectivity, and cultural genealogy. Nostalgia in their music functions not to reify the nation, as it does in the work of early Bhangra musicians in the 1970s as well as in the Thatcherite evocation of Britain's "golden age" of empire. Rather nostalgia destabilizes notions of "Britishness" espoused by New Right ideology, while also calling into question the status of South Asia as the locus of an originary, redemptive cultural identity.

An obvious point of departure in discussing new British Asian music's interventionist remembering of national history is Cornershop's rendition of the 1965 Beatles classic "Norwegian Wood." The original Beatles song, with its sitar melody line, marked one of the first times Indian instrumentals were used in mainstream pop. Thus, like the reinvention of Madonna's "Shanti/ Ashtangi" by South Asian drag queens, Cornershop's translation of the Beatles track into Punjabi enacts a neat reversal of musical influences and appropriations. In their remaking of "Norwegian Wood," Cornershop also seems to comment quite explicitly on the wave of nostalgia for a whitewashed British past, evident in the tremendous popularity of "Britpop" bands like Oasis and Blur in the mid 1990s. As Rupa Huq argues, "Britpop bleaches away all traces of black influences in music in a mythical imagined past of Olde England as it never was, whereas [post-Bhangra musics] are rooted in the urban realities of today's Britain."[34] Significantly, members of Cornershop have resisted attempts to read their cover of "Norwegian Wood" as solely an act of protest against cultural appropriation; rather, they insist, the song was meant as homage to the enduring musical influence of the Beatles on their own music. By singing the lyrics in Punjabi but otherwise playing a fairly straightforward cover version of the song, Cornershop manages to pay tribute to the legacy of the Beatles—referencing them as part of their musical genealogy alongside Asian artists and influences—while simultaneously challenging the "Britpop" phenomenon's elision of nonwhite musical traditions and histories.

Indeed Cornershop strategically redeploys nostalgia not to evoke an all-white Britain but rather to recall the histories and cultural imaginary of Asian immigrant communities in the diaspora. The eponymous "Asha" in Cornershop's hit single "Brimful of Asha," for instance, is the legendary Bollywood playback singer Asha Bhosle. While "Norwegian Wood" is Cornershop's tribute to the Beatles, "Brimful of Asha" functions as a tribute to Asha Bhosle, as well as to Lata Mangeshkar and Mohammed Rafi, the two other giants of Bollywood music who are referenced in the lyrics. All three singers dominated the Bollywood music industry from the 1950s to well into the 1980s, but were at the height of their popularity in the 1960s and 1970s. The voices of Asha, Lata, and Mohammed Rafi constitute, in a sense, the soundtrack to the lives of first-generation working-class South Asian immigrants to Britain who worked in the factories in the West Midlands and created ethnic enclaves for themselves in London's Southall and Brick Lane. Apache Indian, for instance, has spoken of hearing Bhosle's songs on his Punjabi parents' turntable while growing up in Handsworth, Birmingham.[35] By evoking these Bollywood legends and other iconic figures and symbols of sixties and seventies India, Cornershop gestures to the alternative genealogy of popular culture that constitutes South Asian diasporic subjectivity and that challenges notions of an "authentic" Englishness.

The spectacle of Cornershop performing "Brimful of Asha" on BBC's Top of the Pops, as hundreds of white British youth sing along to lyrics that celebrate the icons of Bollywood music, makes clear the ways in which Cornershop forces South Asian popular cultural referents into the mainstream of British national culture. John Hutnyk cautions that any celebration of this new visibility of South Asian culture in the mainstream—emblematized by the successes of Cornershop, Apache Indian, or Bally Sagoo—must be tempered with an awareness of the workings of corporate capital as it turns "progressive sounds in one place [into] the agents of capitalism in another."[36] This, however, may be too limited a model of popular music and its effects. Indeed, Cornershop calls forth a new relation between immigrant subcultures and the dominant culture, one that resists being read as merely another instance of the unstoppable effects of corporate hegemony and a rapacious capitalist culture industry. Rather than South Asian cultural signifiers being inserted into mainstream popular culture as dehistoricized fetish objects, as Hutnyk fears, we can also read Cornershop's success as actually forcing a mainstream British audience to be literate in the cultural referents of Asian immigrant communities, and to acknowledge that Asian cultural forms are already an intrinsic part of the cultural landscape of the UK. Cornershop offers a playful yet powerful counterdiscourse to the nostalgic rewriting of sixties Britain as all-white, free of race riots and the rise of the British National Party. In other words, Cornershop demands that South Asian cultural forms be recognized by mainstream culture in ways that do not quite so easily resolve into mere absorption or appropriation. Rather, their music stages an intervention of South Asian diasporic public culture into the national public sphere. Thus Cornershop enacts precisely the nation/diaspora reversal apparent within an earlier generation of British Asian music: as I have argued elsewhere, second-generation interpreters of Bhangra music in the 1980s and 1990s, such as Bally Sagoo and Apache Indian, drew the nation (both the UK and India) into a sonic diaspora, so that it no longer provided the anchor for notions of diasporic return, authenticity, and purity.[37] In a similar move, Cornershop's reworking of "Norwegian Wood," as well as its evocation of alternative immigrant knowledges and psychic landscapes in "Brimful of Asia," resituate both "India" and "England" as equivalent sites within the band's diasporic map. But Cornershop also makes clear that the culture of diasporic immigrants is central to British national identity: thus the diaspora, through their music, is revealed to be intrinsically a part of the (British) nation.

If Cornershop rememorializes British culture by drawing on the popular cultural markers of both post-Independence India and post-imperial Britain, the punk/dub/rock band Asian Dub Foundation offers an even more explicit commentary on questions of nation, nostalgia, history, and historiography. ADF's potent mix of punk, ska, reggae, and jungle with snatches of Qawaali, Bollywood soundtracks, and classical Hindustani instrumentals documents the intersection of multiple immigrant and diasporic communities in London. ADF's lyrics consistently espouse an antiracist politics that draws its inspiration from the anticolonial nationalist struggle and other radical social movements in India. Their track "Assassin," for example, celebrates the Indian nationalist hero Udham Singh, who in 1940 assassinated Michael O'Dwyer, the British colonial official responsible for the infamous Amritsar massacre of 1919.[38] By drawing on an anticolonial nationalist past in India to create an antiracist present in the UK, ADF brings to the surface the continuities between the British state's colonial aggression in India and its current racist practices against communities of color in Britain today. The zone of public culture that their music produces thereby functions both transnationally and cross-historically. Similarly, on a track titled "Naxalite," the left-wing peasant insurgency in Bengal in the late sixties serves as an antecedent for the fight against police brutality in the UK in the 1990s. The Naxalite movement remains one of the touchstones of the left in India; its evocation by a diasporic, East London–based band like ADF opens the band to charges of romanticizing a complicated, historically situated movement. Indeed when I presented an early version of this chapter to an audience primarily made up of South Asianists, a debate erupted over the accuracy of ADF's portrayal of the Naxalite movement.[39]

Clearly, what is significant for my purposes here is not so much whether ADF "gets it right" but rather what happens in the always inaccurate process of translation as the memory of this particular movement travels from the West Bengali village of Naxalbari, the birthplace of the movement, to East London, where ADF originated. In their evocation of the Naxalite movement in "Assassin," ADF does not attempt to provide British Asians some sort of unmediated access to South Asian history; rather the track, and the music of ADF in general, can be seen to produce what Josh Kun suggestively calls "audiotopias." Drawing from Michel Foucault's notion of heterotopias, Kun defines audiotopias as "sonic spaces of affective utopian longings where several sites normally deemed incompatible are brought together not only in the space of a particular piece of music itself, but in the production of social space and mapping of geographical space that music makes possible."[40] The "audiotopic map," as Kun terms it, conjured up by ADF's music brings into discursive proximity disparate geographic spaces and temporalities: ADF's "community of sound" (to borrow a phrase from one of their own songs)[41] encompasses London's East End as easily as it does Naxalbari. This new geography of diasporic public culture also enacts a temporal collapse of past histories of social struggle in South Asia, and contemporary realities of race and class in the UK. In so doing, the question of cultural origins is mobilized in a radically different way from the standard evocations of "homeland" and exile that characterize conventional diasporic ideologies. Like Cornershop's rewriting of the history of 1960s Britain, ADF's imagined sonic community mobilizes an interventionist nostalgia where "India" signifies a history of radical organizing rather than a site of pure, unsullied cultural identity. Furthermore, ADF's evocation of "India" as a site of radical movements for social change directly challenges the "millennial Orientalism" evident in mainstream popular culture, where random Indian cultural markers stand in for a vaguely defined, depoliticized "Eastern" spirituality.[42] Offering a trenchant critique of liberal multiculturalism, ADF rants on their track "Jericho": "We ain't ethnic, exotic or eclectic/ The only 'e' we use is electric/With your liberal minds/You patronize our culture/Scanning the surface like vultures/with your tourist mentality/we're still the natives/You're multicultural/We're anti-racist."[43] ADF's redeployment of "India" as the locus not of a lost originary identity or of a transcendent spirituality but of a rich history of anticolonial and antistate resistance is echoed in the names of the nightclubs in the United States and Britain that showcase new British Asian music, such as *Swaraj* (self-rule) in London, Mutiny in New York, and *Azaad* (freedom) in San Francisco. These instances reveal the ways in which auditory cultural forms and practices powerfully mobilize affective loyalties across time and space. ADF's notion of a "community of sound" is therefore suggestive of ways of organizing collectivity that bypass the realm of the visible. For an earlier generation of British Asian musicians, Bhangra was a powerful means of asserting a specifically "Asian" identity within an obliterating scopic economy organized around a black-white binary.[44] For ADF and other British Asian bands in the 1990s, producing affiliation through sound can be seen as a way of critiquing a logic of the visual, where British Asians are rendered either invisible or hypervisible (as stereotype) within the dominant racial landscape of the UK.

Ashley Dawson's careful and nuanced discussion of ADF provides the local context for the band's transnational address by situating the band's politics within the social and economic conditions of London's East End in the 1980s and 1990s, specifically the area known as the Docklands.[45] Drawing on Saskia Sassen's notion of "global cities,"[46] Dawson observes that the emergence of London as one such global city has been particularly devastating for working-class Asians: "Overwhelmingly concentrated in industries and skill levels which have been on the decline, and living in urban areas hardest hit by the restructuring of the global economy, Asians have been the first to suffer from Britain's economic woes and have yet to reap the rewards of the nation's halting economic revitalization during the 1990s."[47] Dawson provides an invaluable historicization of the increasing impoverishment of white and Asian working-class communities in the Docklands and demonstrates that the concomitant rise in racial violence by long-time white residents against newer Bangladeshi immigrants was a direct result of state policies that effectively converted the Docklands into an "enterprise zone" in the late 1980s.[48] ADF's militant antiracist politics, in Dawson's reading, emerges in response to this explosive nexus of white racism, working-class frustration, and the brutal exigencies of global capital. ADF evokes global antiracist, anticolonial struggles as a way of addressing the very local context of race and class inequalities set in motion and exacerbated by the state policies that facilitate the transformation of London into a global city. Thus, for Dawson, the significance of ADF and other militant hip-hop Asian bands lies in the way their music signals a critique of state racism as well as a "resistance to the inequalities often generated by the globalization of the economy."[49]

It is also crucial to remember, however, that these inequalities generated by globalization are produced along gendered divisions rather than solely along the racial and class lines that Dawson discusses. The same dynamics of globalization that resulted in massive unemployment among young working-class black men in the UK in the 1980s produced a large segment of casualized homeworkers that was overwhelmingly made up of Asian women immigrants.[50] Naila Kabeer, in her comparative study of Bangladeshi women workers in London and Dhaka, notes that the international restructuring of the garment industry in the 1970s and 1980s led to firms subcontracting parts of the production process to low-wage labor in the global south, while also utilizing "domestic outworkers in the 'hidden' economy of the depressed inner city areas of Britain."[51] Bangladeshi immigrant women in the East End of London engaged in home-based piecework became the primary source of low-wage labor in the UK garment industry. Kabeer turns a critical gaze onto "the high visibility of Bangladeshi women workers . . . on their way to and from work on the streets of Dhaka, and the near-invisibility of the Bangladeshi women who worked as domestic outworkers for the [garment] industry in London."[52] Kabeer argues that this invisibility of Asian women homeworkers in the UK was compounded by the silence on the part of the British labor movement to address their needs, and spoke to the dominant view of homeworking as "a logical cultural choice for 'Asian' Muslim women and hence not necessarily a matter for public concern."[53] Swasti Mitter's research on immigrant women workers has further demonstrated that Asian women's labor in the UK only registers in the general public consciousness when a horrific accident (such as the death of workers due to the burning down of an illegal sweatshop, for instance) makes occasional front-page news.[54] Ironically, this literal invisibility of Asian women's labor is discursively replicated in analyses of popular music and globalization that fail to account for the gendering effects of the global economy on local sites such as the East End. Asian women's labor, because it takes place in the seemingly "private" space of the home, is not recognized as a critical component of South Asian diasporic public culture. Thus, while it is clearly necessary to contextualize a band like ADF through an analysis of "the political economy of racism," as Dawson does so thoroughly, the failure to recognize the gendered logic of this economy means that men are once again the tacit subjects and objects of analysis.

Popular music critics such as Dawson, John Hutnyk, and Nabeel Zuberi, all of whom have written extensively on the Asian Underground, are cognizant that the black nationalist politics of Asian Underground bands may valorize a militant, tough Asian masculinity at the expense of female agency. As Zuberi comments, in much militant British Asian hiphop, "the politics . . . are primarily about young men, defined by the homosociality of Asian lads on the street."[55] Similarly, Dawson is careful to note that the black nationalist politics of ADF may indeed marginalize women, but he also usefully resists reductively labeling the band's gender politics as simply regressive or sexist. Instead, he argues that a track like ADF's "*Tu Meri*," while seeming to buttress conventional gender relations, also implicitly responds to the challenges leveled by feminist and queer artists, activists, and academics to gender conventions within the South Asian community. Dawson's insistence on the multiple meanings and effects of the music is well taken, yet other critical commentaries on the gendering of the Asian Underground are not quite so nuanced. In a telling example that is indicative of much of the existing critical commentary on gender in the British Asian music scene, John Hutnyk discusses the rap group the Kaliphz in the following terms: "The Kaliphz often seem caught up in a version of macho Gangsta rapping that is testosterone-fuelled and boyz-in-the-hood aggressive, yet their record in opposition to British fascist groups is considerable."[56] For Hutnyk, here, the music is radical *despite* the sometimes unfortunate conservatism of its gender and sexual ideologies. By simultaneously acknowledging and disavowing the limits of masculinist militancy, Hutnyk in effect subordinates gender as a terrain of struggle to the seemingly more urgent political project of antiracist organizing. One of Hutnyk's main arguments is that the new visibility of particular, easily consumable forms of South Asian culture in the United States and Britain comes at the expense of a more radical politics espoused by bands like Fun'da'mental.[57] But in celebrating the "hard" politics of ADF, Fun'da'mental, and the Kaliphz over the "soft" politics of more mainstream acts that make it on the charts such as Bally Sagoo, Apache Indian, or the Coventry-born rapper Panjabi MC, Hutnyk implicitly valorizes a particular version of "radical" politics over all others. Such a dichotomy—of good versus bad music, good versus bad politics—obscures the pleasures, disruptions, and challenges posed by South Asian diasporic cultural forms and practices that may not announce themselves as "radical" or "oppositional" in ways that are quite so obvious.

The dangers of privileging antiracism as a singular political project that in effect relies on conventional articulations of gendered and sexual subjectivity are particularly apparent when considering the music and politics of the hip-hop–influenced Fun'da'mental. The band's music samples everything from Bollywood dialogue and the Sufi devotional music of Nusrat Fateh Ali Khan to the speeches of revolutionary male leaders such as Louis Farrakhan, Malcolm X, and Gandhi. As such, like ADF, Fun'da'mental works against a conventional diasporic evocation of India as a site of origination or redemptive return. The music conjures forth a militant, male pan-Islamicist identity that rails against the "U.K. Islamophobia," as Nabeel Zuberi phrases it, that followed the controversy over the publication of Salman Rushdie's novel *The Satanic Verses* in 1992 and that emerged with renewed fervor after the September 11, 2001, terrorist attacks in New York and Washington.[58] David Hesmondalgh notes that Fun'da'mental's first single, "Righteous Preacher," contained lyrics which supported the Ayatollah Khomeini's *fatwa* against Rushdie. In an interview in *Melody Maker* that caused great controversy at the time of the single's release, the band member Goldfinger made the following statement: "Even though

I'm Sikh, I agree with my Muslim brothers that Rushdie has to face the consequences of what he has done . . . Until you understand the importance of religion in our culture, you will not understand how much this man has hurt us."[59] Hesmondhalgh takes this statement as a deliberately provocative attempt on the part of the band to challenge assumptions of an easily consumable "multiculturalism" held by the white press. While this may be true, Gold-finger's statement is deeply problematic in its couching of South Asian collective identity, "culture," and "religion" as unitary and homogenous. During the Rushdie controversy, it was precisely against both the multicultural rhetoric of the white liberal press, as well as the claims to a singular cultural identity made by self-appointed male British Muslim community "leaders," that a multi-racial feminist alliance such as Women Against Fundamentalism (WAF) was formed. As Clara Connelly and Pragna Patel have documented, WAF used the Rushdie affair as an occasion to level a powerful multipronged critique of state-sponsored racism and the gendered politics of patriarchal fundamentalism in immigrant communities.[60] The valorization and visibility of the pan-Islamist black nationalist political stance held by bands like Fun'da'mental invariably elides these more nuanced negotiations of gender, race, religion, and multiple nationalisms undertaken by feminist critics, activists, and cultural producers.

"Other Ways of Being in the World": Alternative Narratives of Globalization and Diaspora

My point here is not only to decry the marginalization of non-male, non-heteronormative subjects in much of the critical scholarship on the British Asian music scene, much less to simply dismiss the music and bands themselves as sexist. Rather, I am suggesting that the invisibility of "other" subjects and forms of cultural insurgence in the critical discourses of British Asian music are an inevitable result of the misrecognition, on the part of scholars and critics, of the new mappings of space, race, gender, and sexuality effected by globalization. Saskia Sassen notes that "the global city is a strategic site for disempowered actors because it enables them to gain presence, to emerge as subjects, even when they do not gain direct power."[61] Within Sassen's framework, the global city is a site of contestation between global capital and the vast pool of low-wage labor that sustains it. Sassen forces us to pay attention to the new actors that globalization produces—such as working-class women, immigrants,

and people of color—who are invisible within a top-down narrative of globalization that can only see members of the new transnational professional work
force as viable global agents. Thus, while Dawson is dependent on Sassen's
model of global cities to make his argument about ADF's remapping of urban
space, what remains curiously absent within his framework is the migrant
female work force that Sassen demonstrates is so central to the workings of the
global city. Within the new cartography that globalization produces, much of
this gendered labor occurs not only in the "public" spaces of the factory and
sweatshop but also, as the works of Naila Kabeer and Swasti Mitter document,
in the "private" space of the immigrant home. Hence the "street" (implicitly
codified as male) can no longer be held up as the privileged and singular site of
contestation, as it tends to be by both the music and its critics. Rather, less
visible sites such as the "home" must also be theorized as key locations in the
production of diasporic public cultures and in what Sassen calls "a worldwide
grid of strategic places" where global processes materialize.[62] To use a band like
ADF as the grounds for an analysis of the impact of globalization on local sites is
to inadvertently replicate in discursive terms the historical invisibility of Asian
immigrant women's labor and subjectivity.

The difficulty of making visible and audible the "other" subjects, spaces, and
modes of contestation within British Asian landscapes through an analysis of
the Asian Underground music scene may point to the need to redefine the very
archives that are being identified by this current scholarship on South Asian
diasporic public culture. In other words, the black nationalist and antiracist
politics and self-presentation of some UK British Asian bands may not necessarily be the most fruitful places to look for alternative renderings of diaspora
and globalization. If anticolonial and black nationalist movements provide the
inspiration for much of the more explicitly politicized British Asian music
being produced today, it is worth asking if this particular remembering of
history also inadvertently tends to replicate some of the subordinating tendencies of the very movements it evokes. Critics of black nationalist ideologies in
the United States have long argued that the militant masculinity upheld by the
movement comes at the expense of all those outside of heterosexist, patriarchal
ideals. As Mark Anthony Neal notes, "during the 1960s this violence [of black
nationalism], rhetorical or otherwise, at best trivialized various expressions that
were not in sync with nationalist desires to unify black identity and culture
under a common rubric that would ideally best survive the bombardment of

white supremacist discourses and practices."[63] While the music of bands like ADF or Fun'da'mental clearly works against the ethnic essentialism of conventional diasporic and nationalist ideologies, it nevertheless imagines a male, masculine, militant diasporic subject at the center of its antiracist politics. While the lyrics seldom tip into overt homophobia or misogyny, the militant masculinity asserted by ADF and Fun'da'mental nevertheless forecloses the transformative possibilities initially suggested by their music.[64]

This necessity of rethinking the archives of British Asian cultural production in order to make audible "other" diasporic voices becomes apparent when we consider the ways in which a singular focus on one form of diasporic popular music throws others in shadow. Several critics have argued that the privileging of Bhangra as *the* primary signifier of British Asian youth culture in the 1980s by both the mainstream media and cultural critics meant that other musical cultures in the diaspora were rendered inaudible.[65] For example Giddha, the female equivalent of Bhangra that is sung and performed within all-women's spaces such as weddings and religious ceremonies, never received the same kind of scholarly or popular attention as did Bhangra. Virinder Kalra observes that the live performances of Giddha take place in female homosocial spaces that lie outside the circuits of "written, manufactured and mechanical reproduction" of the male-dominated Bhangra industry.[66] Thus male Bhangra producers have been able, in effect, to "cannibalize" the form by using Giddha lyrics and melodies without acknowledging the Asian immigrant women's culture from which they come.[67] Consequently the pointed, complex reflections on the intersections of class, race, gender, and sexual ideologies that emerge in the lyrics of many Giddha songs remain inaudible to most critics and consumers of British Asian music. Furthermore, what also remains unthinkable within standard approaches to South Asian diasporic music is the way in which a Giddha performance itself, in its production of female homosocial space, may very well allow for forms of female diasporic intimacy that exceed the heteronormative—a question I return to in chapter 4 in my analysis of the Giddha sequence in Mira Nair's *Monsoon Wedding* (2001).

Some of the alternative gendered configurations that Giddha evokes are evident in the music of Mohinder Kaur Bhamra, a renowned female vocalist and one of the few female presences in the largely male dominated Bhangra industry. The lyrics to Mohinder's 1980 track, *"Aiyee Naa Vilayet Kurie"* (Don't Come to England Girlfriend), are worth quoting at length as it is a pointed critique of the regime of racialized gendered labor both in the home and in the factory that awaits female immigrants:

> My *mehndi* (henna) was still on my hands
> When my mother-in-law brusquely said
> Let's put the new daughter-in-law to work.
> Chorus: Don't come to England girlfriend
> If you wish for a life of ease, don't come to England girlfriend . . .
> All lost in the factory life.
> My back doesn't straighten, every day I have to clock,
> All my hopes lost in the depths of my heart.
> Don't come to England girlfriend.
> Intense cold strikes my chest
> When I wake up, On Time, in the morning.
> Like lightning I have to finish the housework
> Put the children in the pram
> Drop them off at strangers, on the way to work.
> Working on the shifts has stripped my good looks
> There's no one to give me any consolation
> I wash my face with tears, who should I cry to?
> [The man] who married me and brought me here on a lie?
> Don't come to England girlfriend.[68]

Significantly, the lyrics of the song were written not by Mohinder herself but by Manjit Khaira, a male Punjabi immigrant who spent years working alongside Punjabi women in factories in the West Midlands in the 1970s.[69] While Virinder Kalra briefly discusses the song as reflecting "the multiple facets of migrant working women's experiences,"[70] he only hints at the complexities of its representation of racialized and gendered labor migration. I would argue that the song can be read as a remarkably astute analysis of what Lisa Lowe terms the "racialized feminization of labor in the global restructuring of capitalism."[71] Lowe reminds us that "the particular location of racialized working women at the intersection where the contradictions of racism, patriarchy and capitalism converge produces a subject that cannot be determined along a single axis of power or by a single apparatus, on the one hand, or contained within a single narrative of oppositional political formation, on the other."[72] Structured as a warning to an unseen and unheard female friend who remains in Punjab, the song conjures forth a "community of sound" that in a sense lies beyond the realm of audibility of ADF's or Fun'da'mental's singular narratives of militant antiracist, anticolonialist politics. The oppositional political formations so powerfully expressed by these bands cannot contain the multiple and intersecting axes of domination articulated by "*Aiyee Naa Vilayet Kurie.*" The particular "feminist audiotopia" imagined by the singer is brought into being through transnational affective bonds that exist between women. As such the song produces an alternative zone of public culture that connects geographic and discursive sites as seemingly disparate as rural Punjab and the West Midlands, the factory and the home, "private" and "public" space.

That the song is a cautionary tale that enacts a diasporic intimacy between women in different geographic locales is particularly significant given that many Asian women in the UK are recruited into factory and sweatshop work through friends and relatives.[73] The song thus performs and signals a refusal to participate in the informal networks that perpetuate the exploitation of racialized gendered labor. The emphasis on time, shifts, and the clock in the lyrics point to the ways in which time itself is a disciplinary mechanism that regulates the rhythms of the female worker's embodied existence. The singer articulates her struggle to adhere to Aiwha Ong's definition of Taylorism, the disciplinary apparatus underlying Fordist production that is "based on 'time-motion' techniques that dictate precisely how each task is to be performed in order to obtain the highest level of productivity within a strict time economy."[74] Indeed Kalra notes that the song is sung "at a breakneck pace, almost as if Mohinder, like the woman in the song, does not have enough time to sing the song before her next shift begins."[75] The song in a sense then registers a rejection of the mechanistic efficiency, the demand to be punctual and "On Time," that is required of the singer's body as it is transformed into an instrument of wage labor. Significantly, the song represents the home as a site that is just as regulated and disciplined by the clock as is the factory: waking up "On Time" in order to finish the housework, the singer experiences the space of the home not as a private space of leisure but rather as one that becomes yet another site of labor within the global economy. The familial relations that the song maps out between husbands and wives, mothers and children, daughters-in-law and mothers-in law are irrevocably marked and defined by the exigencies of transnational capital and the labor migrations that it precipitates: affective bonds between family members are superseded by the demands of home and factory work. Swasti Mitter, in her research on Asian women workers in the West Midlands garment industry in the 1970s and 1980s, observes that for many women who work in what she terms the ethnic sweatshop economy, "the working conditions at the factory are seen as an extension of home life."[76] Mitter notes that the dominant gender ideologies within diasporic communities "create a unique dependency relationship between the women and their ethnic [male] employers, from whom they are often compelled to accept exploitative wage rates, ethnic ties notwithstanding."[77] In other words, as women remain dependent on male employers for payment, job security, and immigration status, the particular hierarchical gendered arrangements of the familial space are replicated on the factory floor. Indeed, in "*Aiyee Naa Vilayet Kurie*" the hierarchies of the domestic space—between husband and wife, mother-in-law and daughter-in-law—are seen as coextensive with the disciplinary regime that governs the factory space.

Interestingly, Mohinder's song bears a startling resemblance to the 1993 testimony of Fu Lee, a Chinese female immigrant garment factory worker in San Francisco, that Lisa Lowe cites in her analysis of Fae Myenne Ng's 1993 novel *Bone*. Lowe reads Fu Lee's testimony as revealing "the manner in which the factory extracted surplus value not only through her 'labor' as an abstract form, but from using and manipulating her body itself."[78] Fu Lee's testimony, according to Lowe, evokes "her conscious, embodied relation to work, [while] it also refuses the isolation of each part as a separate site to be instrumentally exploited."[79] Similarly, in the Giddha song, the female body becomes the primary site on which the different disciplinary regimes of gender, class, sexuality, and race are mapped: the *mehndi* on the singer's hands, which initially marks her as wife, is overlaid with the bodily labor she does in the household as well as in the factory. The cataloguing of body parts—hands, back, chest, face—speaks to the bodily fragmentation that the singer experiences in the process of laboring in both "public" and "private" space. In her naming of herself as daughter-in-law, mother, wife, migrant, and worker, she resists this fragmented, instrumentalized sense of self that is required by the regime of racialized gendered labor and instead insists on the simultaneity of these subject positions. That we can hear the echoes of "*Aiyee Naa Vilayet Kurie*"—released in 1980 and detailing the experiences of Punjabi women workers in factories in the West Midlands—in the 1993 testimony of a Chinese garment worker in San Francisco is not coincidental. Rather, it speaks to the lines of commonality between the experiences of racialized immigrant women workers in various "First World" nations, as transnational corporations shift their primary labor source from export processing zones in developing countries to the vast pools of low-wage immigrant labor in metropolitan locations.[80]

Dipesh Chakravarty's analysis of the way history informs Marx's notion of capital is useful in further unpacking the complicated critique of racialized gendered labor enacted by Mohinder's song. Chakravarty argues that two ideas of history underlie Marx's understanding of capital. The first notion of history, which Chakravarty designates in shorthand as History 1, is "the past that is internal to the structure of capital" and that capital posits as the precondition of its own existence. But, according to Chakravarty, there is another idea of history (or histories) that mobilizes Marx's critique of capital. These pasts, which Chakravarty calls History 2, "do not belong to the 'life process' of capital. They enable the human bearer of labor power to enact *other ways of being in the world*—other than, that is, being the bearer of labor power."[81] As Chakravarty writes, "the idea of History 2 suggests that even in the very abstract and abstracting space of the factory that capital creates, ways of being human will be acted out in manners that do not lend themselves to the reproduction of the logic of capital."[82] The song articulates the "other kinds of pasts" and "other ways of being in the world" embodied by the singer that exceed her instrumental status as merely a bearer of labor power. These other pasts and other histories that "interrupt the totalizing thrusts of History 1," as Chakravarty phrases it, are referenced in the song by the singer's affective relation to a female friend left behind in Punjab. Female friendship, here, is the signifier of those allegiances, desires, yearnings, and memories that literally and metaphorically exceed the boundaries of the factory floor. They bring into the space of the factory life histories and experiences that disrupt capital's demand that the singer/worker be simply "living labor, a bundle of muscles and nerves and consciousness, but devoid of any memory except the memory of the skills the work needs."[83] Chakravarty reminds us, however, that "History 2s are . . . not pasts separate from capital; they inhere in capital and yet interrupt and punctuate the run of capital's own logic."[84]

The way in which these "other kinds of pasts" are not outside the logic of capital but rather are embedded within it is made clear in the depiction of Asian immigrant women workers in the documentary *Bringing It All Back Home* (dir. Chrissie Stansfield, 1987). The documentary, which details the local effects of the global restructuring of capital on working-class communities in the UK in the 1980s, features an interview with a South Asian immigrant woman home-worker in the West Midlands doing piecemeal garment work for London retailers in her home.[85] Here, as in *"Aiyee Naa Vilayet Kurie,"* the bodily and psychic demands that the factory makes on the worker are transported to the home space. The camera focuses not on the woman's face, which remains invisible throughout the scene, but on her hands as they move continuously from the sewing machine to the pile of garments by her feet. The woman's baby daughter sits watching her mother intently from a sofa and mimics her mother's hand movements, an image that again speaks to the ways in which affective ties between family members are cross-cut and overdetermined by laboring relations. The woman, speaking in an English that retains Punjabi intonations barely beneath its surface, poignantly describes the experience of homeworking as "worse than being in a factory; it is like a jail." She continues:

> When you go in the factory, you meet different sorts of people. You get to know about different ideas of people and you talk with them and you feel less depressed. (Voice rising) I feel so isolated and confined in the house. When I'm very busy on the machine I'm gone so deep in thoughts, you know, of my past time, when I used to go to school and college, of my good friends in India. It is really totally different, in the house.[86]

Ironically, the factory is imagined by the woman worker as the site of inter-action and sociability that is unthinkable within her current location in the house. Indeed, she conflates remembered forms of sociability and female homosocial space (the all-girls schools and colleges that she attended in India) with the imagined space of the factory floor. The woman's words reveal the psychic costs of migration and give voice to the deep despair and anguish that the lived experience of racialized gendered regimes of labor produces. Echoing Mohinder's song, the migrant woman worker brings to her current experience of homeworking memories of "past time" and affective ties with other women in other locations. The bringing of these pasts into the present experience of laboring in a sense both interrupts the current experience of work (she is no longer simply an abstract embodiment of "living labor") while simultaneously enabling her to continue with it (conjuring up the past makes her current work more bearable), thus underscoring Chakravarty's caveat that these pasts are not separate from capital but rather inhere within it.[87]

Both "*Aiyee Naa Vilayet Kurie*" and this brief scene from Stansfield's documentary speak to the collapse of "public" and "private" space as the global economy is instantiated in the home and factory through the very body of the female worker. Similarly, Monica Ali's 2003 novel *Brick Lane*,[88] set in the predominantly Bangladeshi borough of Tower Hamlets in London's East End, is inspired by Naila Kabeer's research on Bangladeshi women homeworkers in the garment industry and provides a fictionalized account of their lives. Kabeer's empirical study stresses the need to move beyond generalized stereotypes of "Asian women workers" in popular and academic discourse that imagine such women as simply an undifferentiated and homogenous mass. Instead, Kabeer stresses Bangladeshi women's agency in making labor market decisions and argues that "women workers do not only exist as artifacts of employers' strategies nor is the quality of their lives fully determined by their experiences in the work place."[89] Ali takes up Kabeer's call to illuminate the motivations and decision-making processes of the women themselves by providing us with a finely drawn portrait of Nazneen, the protagonist of the novel who works as a home-based machinist while living in a housing estate in Tower Hamlets. While the Bangladeshi neighborhood of Brick Lane provides the backdrop of the novel, Nazneen's imagined geography extends far beyond its groceries and restaurants to the densely packed streets of Dhaka and the open landscapes of rural Bangladesh. Indeed, Nazneen's narrative of life in working-class, immigrant London is shadowed by that of her sister Haseena in Bangladesh who, having migrated from the country to the city, becomes a worker in one of the numerous garment factories in Dhaka that are subcontracted by transnational corporations. Nazneen and Haseena are thus part of an interconnected labor market of migrant, low-wage, female workers that exists in the cities and free trade zones of the global south as well as in the immigrant enclaves of the advanced industrialized countries of the north. The incorporation of Nazneen and Haseena into the two opposing ends of the international garment industry makes apparent the ways in which both locations are intimately connected through the gendered exigencies of transnational capital. The epistolary, transcontinental relationship between the two sisters evokes the same sense of female diasporic intimacy that animates the Giddha song discussed previously, and acts as a powerful reminder of those "other ways of being in the world" that resist the reduction of complex lives and histories to "living labor." The novel ends with Nazneen's husband returning to Dhaka to fulfill a fantasy of diasporic return, unable to withstand the daily, petty, racist humiliations that he faces as a Bangladeshi immigrant male in the UK. Nazneen, however, courageously decides to stay on in London with her two young daughters, where she eventually becomes part of a sewing cooperative with other Bangladeshi women in the housing estate. She thus collectively produces a new notion of "home" that is no longer organized around a conventional diasporic longing for lost homelands. This new collective home space thereby also breaks with the patriarchal gender arrangements that characterize diasporic nationalism and that situate women as embodiments of communal tradition and the longed-for homeland.

These various musical, cinematic, and literary representations of the "racialized feminization of labor" rarely enter the realm of the visible within standard accounts of globalization, nor do they enter the realm of the audible within standard accounts of diasporic popular music. As such, they force us to revise and expand our understanding of South Asian diasporic public culture as being formed through and against the seemingly "private" space of the home. All three texts—the Giddha song, Stansfield's documentary, and Ali's novel— raise the important question of what knowledges, histories, spaces, and embodiments are seen to inhabit the public culture of the diaspora as it is produced and impacted by economic globalization. The submerged relation of Giddha to Bhangra has particular resonance when we consider the way in which a new moment of British Asian cultural production is being narrativized through the Asian Underground. That a musical form such as Giddha is performed and consumed for the most part outside the "public" spaces of the street, the recording studio, or the concert stage would seem to relegate it to the realm of the "private." But as the lyrics of the song, as well as the testimony of the woman in Stansfield's documentary and her fictionalized counterpart in *Brick Lane* show, the space of the home is hardly private but rather a key site of labor within the global restructuring of capital. Thus in order to fully unpack the ways in which diasporic public culture responds to and is formed by the dynamics of globalization, we must pay careful attention to those cultural practices that seem to exist outside the realm of the "public." It is precisely the cultural practices that emerge from seemingly tangential spaces of cultural production that most profoundly speak to the gendered and racialized effects of globalization on local sites. It is also precisely these cultural practices that are overlooked by many analyses of public culture—and popular music in particular—in the South Asian diaspora. What, then, are the different aural and visual trajectories that become apparent if we turn our attention from the overtly politicized lyrics of ADF to the soundscapes of female British Asian deejays such as the London-based DJ Ritu, or the spontaneous, informal performances of Giddha? Or from the masculinist bravado and posturing of Fun'da'mental to the ephemeral performances of queer femininity that take place at occasional queer club nights in London or New York? Turning to this less visible and less audible archive of South Asian diasporic culture may allow for an alternative understanding of the gendered and sexual landscapes of global cities.

The critical attention paid by critics to the CDs, Web sites, and videos of Asian Underground bands themselves may miss the real "underground" to the Asian Underground, that is, the far more difficult to document cultural practices that occur under the aegis of an Asian Underground event but are not understood as central to the event. These practices suggest the need to ask different questions of dominant, recognizable archives and to rethink what constitutes a viable cultural archive in the first place. For instance, in her ethnography of young British Asian women who are avid club goers in the Asian Underground scene, Falu Bakrania shows that far from simply being passive consumers of a music scene that is still largely produced by men, these young women are actively using club spaces in order to negotiate gendered notions of "Asianness" that are mapped onto their bodies by both patriarchal diasporic and racist English nationalist ideologies.[90] The imaginative consumption strategies that Bakrania documents remain submerged within the dominant discourse of the Asian Underground produced by a body of critical scholarship that privileges more conventionally understood forms of radical political practice. Bakrania also notes that the young women she interviewed strategically use different cultural forms and spaces—such as that of the Asian Underground or Bhangra—in order to challenge racist and patriarchal assumptions at different moments, even as they are simultaneously reinscribed within the very ideologies that they seek to disrupt.[91] Bakrania's research, as well as a consideration of a diasporic musical form like Giddha, raises the following question: how do various forms of South Asian popular music in the diaspora—Asian Underground music, Bhangra, Hindi film music, Giddha, Qawaali—produce distinct social spaces that offer highly particular modes of gendered and sexualized sociability, pleasure, and desire? Such research suggests that each musical form may offer a particular audience different spaces and strategies to negotiate gender and sexual ideologies.

Queer Audiotopias

I have suggested throughout this chapter that theorizing the workings of diaspora and globalization through a singular recognition of particular musical forms (such as Bhangra and the Asian Underground), and the most obvious cultural practices associated with them, misses the crucial ways in which gender and sexual ideologies are foundational to both processes. Diaspora, as it takes shape through these musical forms, is still imagined through an oedipal narrative and a patrilineal genealogy that connects one generation of immigrant men to their second-generation offspring, or through a revolutionary politics that connects men to each other but at the expense of women and alternative forms of masculinity. I want to close, then, with an instance of a queer cultural practice that echoes the drag performance with which I opened this chapter; both instances seem to embody the alternative visions of culture and community that Asian Underground music promises but fails to realize. That such cultural practices are notoriously difficult to document, archive, and preserve speaks to what José Muñoz calls the ephemera of queer life. Writing of the African American drag performer Kevin Aviance, Muñoz understands "queer ephemera" as "the conversations that ensue after [Aviance's] performances, the friends and strangers that approach him on the street, the ads in bar rags, the reviews in local papers, the occasional home video documentation, and the hazy and often drug-tinged memories that remain after the actual live performances."[92] These fleeting cultural practices and memories that are "lost in relation to the space of heteronormativity" are erased from standard representations of the public culture of the diaspora.[93] They may in fact constitute a new mapping of the space of globalization, one that is able to find those bodies, desires, and subjectivities that remain lost within dominant narratives of globalization on the one hand, or diasporic formation on the other.

If for some of the young women Bakrania interviews, the Asian Underground scene seems to offer more possibility for sexual and gender self-definition than does the Bhangra scene, for gay male subjects, the space of possibility that emerges within the more seemingly "traditional" venue of, say, a Qawaali concert may be more useful than an Asian Underground club space.

In order to track the different erotic and affective possibilities opened up by different forms of South Asian diasporic popular music, I return from one global city (London) to another (New York City). Shifting the scene from London back to New York requires that we recognize that different diasporic locations produce their own highly particular forms of resistance to and accommodation with dominant culture.

At an outdoor Summerstage concert in New York City's Central Park in July 1999, the female Sufi devotional singer Abida Parveen's powerful stage presence delighted a large, predominantly South Asian crowd that, for a brief moment, reterritorialized Central Park into a vibrant space of South Asian public culture. While many of the women in the audience remained seated as Parveen's voice soared to ever greater heights of ecstasy and devotion, throngs of mostly working-class, young and middle-aged South Asian Muslim men crowded around the stage, singing out lyrics in response to Parveen's cues, their arms aloft, dancing joyously arm in arm and in large groups. Sufism, a form of Islamic mysticism in which music plays a central role in enabling the individual to commune with the divine, has a long history of homoerotic imagery in its music and poetry.[94] The sanctioned homosociality/homoeroticism of the Qawaali space in effect enabled a group of men from the South Asian Lesbian and Gay Association, gay-identified South Asian men, to dance together with abandon; indeed they were indistinguishable from the hundreds of men surrounding them. In this instance the queer listening and dance practices that revolved around Parveen's performance enabled a male homosocial space to translate quite seamlessly into a homoerotic one. The gay men in the audience (both Muslim and non-Muslim) were able to exploit the "traditional" forms of homoeroticism that lie embedded within a Sufi mystical tradition in order to articulate for themselves a specifically gay male diasporic subjectivity. They were thus producing a "queer audiotopia," to extend Josh Kun's notion of an audiotopia, in that they were conjuring forth a queer sonic landscape and community of sound that remapped Central Park into a space of queer public culture, the locus of gay male diasporic desire and pleasure.

We can perhaps better understand the queer audiotopia fleetingly produced in these moments through Michael Warner's theorizing of "publics and counterpublics."[95] Warner defines both publics and counterpublics as those that "come into being only in relation to texts and their circulation." Publics, Warner writes, are "increasingly organized around visual or audio texts . . .

Often the texts themselves are not even recognized as texts—as for example with visual advertising or the chattering of a DJ—but the publics they bring into being are still discursive in the same way."[96] Warner's notion of a discursively instantiated public that is self-produced (rather than externally, institutionally produced) through the very act of address is particularly suggestive when considering the ways in which music produces queer sociability, belonging, and identification. At the Summerstage concert, Parveen's voice (often described as "manly" and gender non-normative[97]) functioned as the text that enabled the production of a queer counterpublic, one that is discursively produced by virtue of being addressed and that also acts as a "communit[y] and relational chain of resistance that contest[s] the dominant public sphere."[98] José Quiroga, in his study of Latino gay men's relation to the musical form of bolero, argues that the bolero allows for the construction of a "sentimental community" that comes together around the iconic figure of the female bolero singer. For Quiroga, bolero underscores the power of affect in producing a transnational queer community: "the bolero signals the beginning of a new voice that reappears from the past in order to seduce readers again into a transnational (and even meta-Caribbean) space."[99] Similarly, the Summerstage performance created a web of affect that served to bind and connect the queer men in the audience to each other and to Parveen herself.

Such a performance and the remapping of urban space it enables allow us to crucially rework Saskia Sassen's formulation of the ways in which economic globalization produces new political possibilities within the global city. The city, according to Sassen, has "emerged as a site for new claims: by global capital . . . but also by disadvantaged sectors of the urban population" who may indeed create "a new type of transnational politics, a politics of those who lack power but now have 'presence.'"[100] Sassen understands this "new type of transnational politics" that emerges within the transnational geography of the global city as the new forms of organizing and alliances created by those actors within the global economy whose labor is historically rendered invisible: low-wage female and immigrant workers, as well as workers who are U.S.-born people of color. Sassen's invaluable feminist theorizing of globalization thus brings into visibility particular actors that have been systematically devalorized within conventional globalization discourse. But we can also extend Sassen's analysis to bring into visibility, or rather audibility, those actors and forms of political contestation that indeed "lack power" but have "presence," and cannot be seen or heard within a strict materialist framework of political economy that to a certain extent Sassen herself subscribes to. Although the question of alternative sexual subjectivities never enters into Sassen's analysis, we can include the queering of public space that happens in instances such as the one I have described above as constituting one of the new forms of transnational politics that Sassen suggests can emerge from the "new geography of centrality" of the global city.

The Summerstage event thus suggests that different forms of South Asian diasporic music allow for very specific erotic possibilities and mobilize distinct affective loyalties, for particular audiences in particular locations. While Parveen's performance enabled the production of a tremendously powerful form of gay male diasporic intimacy, as I have been arguing, the performance may have had a very different resonance for the women in the audience. Almost all the women remained seated, many with children in tow, and were relegated to being a largely immobile audience for the ecstatic performance of male homosociality/homoeroticism. Indeed, women played a crucial role in enabling this space to come into being: their bodies, voices, and affect (in the form of Parveen as performer) instantiated this space, even while their function as sidelined observers lent the assurance of respectable heterosexuality to the event as a whole. The "queer audiotopia" initiated by Parveen's performance, then, can hardly be seen as a utopian site but rather as one that is contradictory and unstable, imprinted with hierarchical power relations organized along gendered lines. To return to Sassen for a moment, while she fails to acknowledge that queer communities may indeed be among those who "lack power" but "have presence" within the global city, her insistence on revealing the gendered effects of globalization allows us to critique the ways in which "queer" in this instance is predicated on the foreclosure of female agency. In its literal sidelining of female pleasure, desire, and agency, the Summerstage performance of gay male diasporic intimacy thus signals the limits of a "queer audiotopia" and points to the need to consistently use both a queer and feminist lens through which to scrutinize the meanings of diasporic cultural practices. The ensuing chapters more fully examine the dangerous effects of splitting queer from feminist analyses and suggest the necessity of bringing together these rubrics through a focus on queer *female* diasporic subjectivity. The following chapter further explores the ways in which the seemingly "private" space of the immigrant home as a site of racialized gendered labor is crucially remade through queer and feminist interventions, which offer new possibilities for narrativizing diaspora outside of its conventional patrilineal, oedipal logic. It is precisely by making intelligible those queer, feminist cultural practices that are rendered inaudible and invisible within dominant paradigms of nation, diaspora, and globalization, I argue, that we most powerfully intervene into these paradigms, and thereby suggest other ways of being in the world.

3

SURVIVING NAIPAUL

Housing Masculinity in *A House for*

Mr. Biswas, *Surviving Sabu*, and *East Is East*

In *East Is East* (dir. Damien O'Donnell, 2000), a feature film with a screenplay by Pakistani British playwright Ayub Khan-Din, a working-class Pakistani immigrant father in Manchester, UK, in the early 1970s watches in dismay as, one by one, his biracial children slip out of his paternal control. Like *Bend It Like Beckham* (Gurinder Chadha's box-office hit which was released a few years later and to which I turn in chapter 4), as well as some of the British Asian musical forms discussed in the previous chapter, *East Is East* is predictably structured around the narrative of oedipality and the tropes of culture clash and generational divides between parents and children. It thereby reiterates the problematic "between two cultures" thesis that dominates social science and mainstream media representations of Asian immigrant communities in the UK.[1] Yet in a brief, exuberant musical interlude that interrupts the film's conventional diasporic narrative of fathers and sons, the sole daughter in the family pauses from her work in the backyard of the family's fish and chip shop and dazzlingly transforms herself into a picture-perfect replica of a Bollywood film heroine. Dressed in galoshes and a white tunic to shield her clothes from the blood and guts of dead fish, the daughter, Mina, uses a dishrag as a *dupatta* and a broom as a dancing partner as she lip-synchs and dances to the strains of the soundtrack to *Pakeezah* (dir. Kamal Amrohi, 1971), the classic Bollywood film that was released the same year in which *East Is East* is set.[2]

This moment intervenes into dominant conceptualizations of diaspora founded on notions of patrilineal genealogical inheritance and extends the discussion begun in the previous chapter on how female diasporic cultural practices emerge from within regimes of racialized feminized labor. The role of the daughter Mina in *East Is East* is at best secondary; in fact, this is the only scene where the camera is focused exclusively on her, in a departure from the usual glimpses of her as the foil for the central characters and the narratives revolving around the father's relation to his many sons. Indeed, in none of the numerous reviews of the film does this scene even rate a mention, since—like the song and dance sequences from Bollywood cinema that it references and that are discussed in the following chapter—it seems to stand so completely apart from the main events of the film. Moreover, the film's published screenplay curiously excises this moment as well; it is literally unscripted, existing as sound and image and outside the realm of the written. It leaves no textual trace, and can therefore only be read as excessive, marginal, and inconsequential.[3] Yet, as I argued in chapter 2, it is precisely by foregrounding those cultural practices that initially appear tangential to a recognized archive of South Asian cultural production, and that seem to fall outside the realm of diasporic public culture, that we arrive at different narratives of diaspora and globalization. This brief cinematic moment, like queer and feminist engagements with popular music, gestures to alternative narratives that reformulate diaspora outside of the logic of heteronormativity and patrilineality.

In the previous chapter I considered feminist cultural practices that speak to the "racialized feminization of labor" under global capitalism,[4] as well as queer cultural practices that articulate new modes of non-blood-based diasporic affiliation and affect. Both forms of diasporic cultural production are elided within dominant theorizations of diaspora and globalization. This chapter continues to explore the interventions made by queer and feminist diasporic cultural practices into dominant articulations of diaspora, nation, and globalization by looking at three very different texts: *Surviving Sabu*, a 1996 short film by UK-based, queer Indo-Canadian filmmaker Ian Rashid; V. S. Naipaul's 1961 novel *A House for Mr. Biswas*; and O'Donnell's *East Is East*. Situating an experimental film alongside a modernist novel, and reading both against a mainstream feature film, runs the risk of flattening out the radically different ways in which each of these forms circulates diasporically, and of erasing their specific relations to histories of colonialism and postcolonial nationalism. *A House for Mr. Biswas*, for instance, must be situated within a tradition of postcolonial modernist literature; indeed, Rosemary George persuasively reads Naipaul's novel as a postcolonial rescripting of Joseph Conrad's *Almayer's Folly*.[5] We can trace the genealogy of Rashid's film, conversely, to the explosion of experimental Black British filmmaking of the 1980s and early 1990s, such as that of the Sankofa film collective, which powerfully grappled with the legacies of colonialism on racialized, diasporic communities in the UK. However, while the unexpected juxtaposition of texts so disparate in terms of genre and historical context may initially appear disjunctive, identifying the lines of connection between the three allows us to unpack the crucial interrelations between the formation of immigrant masculinities, diasporic women's labor, and queer articulations of diaspora. This alignment of texts also foregrounds the dangers of disassociating a queer project from a feminist one. As I have argued, the progressive antiracist politics of Asian Underground music depends on the inaudibility of female diasporic cultural practices. Similarly, in a text such as Rashid's *Surviving Sabu*, the visibility of gay male diasporic desire is dependent on the invisibility of female diasporic desire and subjectivity. A way out of this binary opposition between "queer" and "feminist," I suggest, is through making female diasporic subjectivity central to a queer diasporic project. By focusing on the seemingly inconsequential scene involving Mina in *East Is East*, rather than on the main plot line revolving around fathers and sons, I hope to dislodge the insistent, obsessive focus on patrilineal inheritance that structures diasporic narratives— even those that are self-consciously gay. This shift in focus—from fathers and sons to the daughters, mothers, wives, servants, and courtesans who fall outside the male lineages that define diasporic and national public cultural spaces— enables us to reconceptualize diaspora through a queer feminist lens.

Fathers and Sons (Again): V. S. Naipaul's
A House for Mr. Biswas and Ian Rashid's *Surviving Sabu*

Frantz Fanon's excavation of colonial masculinity in *Black Skin, White Masks* explores the mechanisms of identification between colonized male subjects and dominant culture. Fanon writes: "Attend showings of a Tarzan film in the

Antilles and in Europe. In the Antilles, the young Negro identifies himself de facto with Tarzan against the Negroes. This is much more difficult for him in a European theater, for the rest of the audience, which is white, automatically identifies him with the savages on screen."[6] Fanon here refers to the complexities of spectatorial identification for the colonized, racialized male subject. Within colonized space, a form of masochistic overidentification between the black male spectator and the white male hero on screen proceeds seamlessly and is central to the creation of colonized subjectivity. In the context of migration to the metropolitan center, however, this mode of identification is abruptly foreclosed: in front of the racist gaze of white spectators in the audience, the black male spectator himself becomes the fetishized "object-to-be-looked-at."[7] We see the imprint of Fanon's masterful theorizing of how ideologies of race, colonialism, and masculinity produce or interrupt spectatorial identification in Rashid's *Surviving Sabu*. A consideration of Rashid's film allows us to trace the contours of a queer postcolonial masculinity but also makes evident the pitfalls of opposing queer and feminist projects in a post-colonial context.

In *Black Skin, White Masks*, Fanon grapples with the meaning and applicability of the Oedipus complex for colonized men. If, for white (male) subjects, the oedipal drama explains how the little boy ascends to the position of the father through the recognition and disavowal of the mother's difference, Fanon asks how "proper" gender and racialized subjectivity is internalized by men of color within a colonial context. He concludes that, "like it or not, the Oedipus complex is far from coming into being among Negroes."[8] As his insight into viewing *Tarzan* in the Antilles makes apparent, because black men are systematically denied phallic power under colonialism, the (black) son's identification with the (black) father cannot take place seamlessly, as it does for white male subjects. Rather within a colonial and racialized schema, identification is produced not between the black son and the black father through a simultaneous libidinal investment in the black mother, but rather between the black son and the white father through the fetishization of the white woman. The black woman, as is apparent in Fanon's own dismissive treatment of women of color, remains outside and apart from this family romance.[9]

It is precisely this fraught relation between father and son as it unfolds within histories of racism and colonialism that is the focus of *Surviving Sabu*. Toward the end of the film, a first-generation Indian immigrant father in a working-

Father and son share a cigarette in *Surviving Sabu* (dir. Ian Rashid, 1996). *Photo courtesy of Liane Harris.*

class London suburb shares a cigarette with his second-generation, gay British Asian son. Father and son sit side by side, thighs just touching, together watching the film adaptation of Kipling's *The Jungle Book* (dir. Alexander Korda, 1942). *The Jungle Book* stars the Indian child actor Sabu, who, we learn, was "discovered" in Mysore, India, by British producer Alexander Korda in the mid-1930s and went on to star in Orientalist vehicles throughout the 1940s and 1950s, first in the UK and then in Hollywood. The paradigmatic figure of Sabu provides the locus around which Rashid interweaves the themes of diasporic displacement, queer desire, and the pleasures and dangers of dominant culture for racialized male subjects. Whereas to the father, Sabu stands as the ultimate symbol of immigrant success (proof that "we *can* make it in the West," as he tells his son), to the son Sabu is nothing more than an anachronistic emblem of Orientalist and colonialist fantasies of perpetually childlike, effeminized "native" men. Like Fanon's young Antillean spectator who suddenly finds himself the fetishized object of the gaze in the European movie house, the son in Rashid's film finds himself uncomfortably aligned with the image of Sabu within a dominant white English imaginary. He thus categorically rejects this image as a way of marking his father's hopeless internalization of colonial logic and asserting his own enlightened politicization.

Yet this particular scene in Rashid's film—where the gay son passes a cigarette from his own lips to his father's, as both watch the image of Sabu's muscular, compact brown body on the Hollywood screen—suggests a more complicated relation between minoritarian subjects and dominant culture. The father's initial masochistic overidentification with the image of Sabu, as well as the son's initial outright rejection of it, gives way in this scene to the representational strategy of disidentification as articulated by José Muñoz. Muñoz's use of the term in effect answers the question posed by Ella Shohat and Robert Stam: "How do we critique dominant Eurocentric media while harnessing its undeniable pleasures?"[10] The disidentificatory strategies of queers of color that Muñoz describes are precisely those which allow for both critique and pleasure in relation to dominant representation. He writes, "Disidentification is the third mode of dealing with dominant ideology, one that neither opts to assimilate within such a structure nor strictly opposes it; rather disidentification is a strategy that works on and against dominant ideology."[11] Indeed, this scene in Rashid's film speaks to an intergenerational queer diasporic desire between fathers and sons that is produced through and against dominant culture.

Rashid's complex, multilayered narrative encapsulates the profound reconfiguration of the space of "home" through the articulation of queer desire that characterizes the queer South Asian diasporic texts that I engage with throughout this book. The film exemplifies the double intervention made by an emergent queer diasporic genre. Queer diasporic texts challenge postcolonial diasporic narratives that imagine diaspora and nation through the tropes of home, family, and community that are invariably organized around heteronormative, patriarchal authority. Furthermore, queer diasporic texts critique standard narratives of gay and lesbian subjectivity that consistently locate the queer subject outside the boundaries of home and family; such narratives thereby elide the complexities of race and migration in the production of queer desires and subjectivities.

Situating Rashid's film alongside V. S. Naipaul's earlier classic tale of failed masculinity and postcolonial homelessness, the 1961 novel *A House for Mr. Biswas*, underscores the challenge posed by queer diasporic texts to conventional postcolonial models of home. In this sense it would be easy to read Rashid's film as representative of what Vijay Mishra terms the "new" diaspora of late modern capital, as opposed to Naipaul's "old" diasporic model of classic capitalism.[12] Yet Rashid's experimental, self-consciously queer film cannot be placed merely in a binary opposition to Naipaul's modernist fable. Instead, I would suggest that the son's relation to his father and to the text of Sabu in Rashid's film parallels Rashid's own relation to Naipaul's text. Naipaul is the father figure, canonized by a Western literary establishment and castigated by postcolonial writers and critics, who casts a long shadow over the field of postcolonial and diasporic literature.[13] His legacy is thus one that must be grappled with when considering the reconstitution of "home" in contemporary diasporic narratives. Instead of simply lauding or rejecting his work, I want to engage his text in a way that enacts a third mode of dealing with the dominant narratives of home, housing, and masculinity that characterize his novel. Reading contemporary queer texts in relation to Naipaul's work allows us to think about the history of diasporic cultural production as shifting and contradictory rather than as an oedipal structure within which later models entirely replace and overturn earlier models. Indeed, following Fanon, both texts by Rashid and Naipaul, and the dialectical relation between the two, suggest the inadequacy of the oedipal narrative as an explanatory device in relation to colonial and postcolonial sexual and racial subjectification. *Surviving Sabu* cannot be read as an outright rejection of Naipaul's novel; rather, Rashid extends, comments on, *and* crucially revises the narratives of housing, paternity, and masculinity evident in *A House for Mr. Biswas.* Thus the title of this chapter, "Surviving Naipaul," borrows from the title of Rashid's film to refer to the often problematic, but also contradictory, legacies of Naipaul's articulations of home and homelessness, immigrant manhood and masculinity, for a new generation of postcolonial diasporic artists.

Surviving Sabu is predicated on the conceit of films set within films. The son is a young gay man, an aspiring filmmaker who wants to make a film of Sabu's life while using his father as both the offscreen narrator and the onscreen talking head. The text that the son wants the father to narrate juxtaposes the historical figure of Sabu alongside the racist realities that have shaped the father's own life history as a first-generation working-class Indian immigrant to the UK. The father is as resistant to his son's queerness as he is to admitting that racism is indeed that which has shaped the limits of his world. Images of Sabu's films, in glorious technicolor, are interspersed with stark black-and-white shots of the father and son in the claustrophobic interior of the immigrant home. The film is structured through a variety of looking relations: between the spectator and the Hollywood image of Sabu, between both protagonists and the Hollywood image, and between the father and the son. Rashid thus carefully delineates the multiple layers of representation at work in the production of queer and diasporic subjects.

The actor Sabu's own diasporic trajectory, from Mysore to London to Hollywood, mirrors the film's meticulous mapping of South Asian diasporic movement. Sabu, we are told, attempted to transform his childhood success in British cinema into adult stardom in Hollywood, only to be plagued by racism within both sites. His career steadily declined in the post–World War II era, and in his penultimate role he was reduced to playing the native "boy" sidekick—at the age of thirty-eight—opposite Robert Mitchum in the 1963 jungle adventure film *Rampage*. Sabu thus remains perpetually frozen as the "wonderful, graceful, frank, intelligent child" who so entranced British film director Michael Powell, who cast him in the lead role in *The Thief of Baghdad* in 1940.[14] Sabu's history eloquently speaks to the peculiar construction of South Asian masculinity within the dominant popular cultural imaginary of both the United States and Britain. The image of Sabu allows Rashid to chart a "Brown Atlantic," to borrow from and rework Paul Gilroy's influential formulation of the Black Atlantic.[15] Such a mapping of South Asian diasporic movement suggests the differences and similarities between the experiences of racialization of South Asian immigrants in North America and the UK. While the film is located in the present day in a working-class London suburb, *Surviving Sabu* sets in motion multiple historical and national frames simultaneously. It contextualizes the vexed relation between the father and son within the history of British colonialism in South Asia and the racist policies of the British state toward the post-Independence wave of South Asian immigrants. The images of Sabu that flicker incessantly across the mental landscapes of the father and son also speak to the complex history of South Asian racialization in the United States and the complicity of Hollywood cinema, in its dissemination of Orientalist cinematic fantasies, with British colonialist ideologies. Vijay Prashad notes that the Sabu films of the 1930s and 1940s played a significant role in the development of U.S. Orientalism, that is, the production of India within the U.S. popular imagination as a "land of ghastly and beautiful mystery," outside of politics or history.[16] The Brown Atlantic framework of *Surviving Sabu* deconstructs British and U.S. Orientalisms by demanding that we place the formation of South Asian diasporic subjectivity at the intersection of the legacies of British colonialism, ongoing U.S. Orientalism, and racist state practices in both the United States and Britain. The film thus epitomizes the ways in which queer diasporic texts enact both spatial and temporal simultaneity: it captures both the local and global dimensions of South Asian racialization and migration, while consistently linking prior histories of colonialism to the present-day realities of racism. Queer desire emerges in the film at the interstices of these multiple historical and national trajectories. Indeed, in a critical intervention into conventional diasporic discourse that calls to mind the pivotal scene from *My Beautiful Laundrette* discussed in chapter 1, queerness in *Surviving Sabu* becomes a way to re-memorialize and re-narrate the past.

In order to understand the full significance of Rashid's intervention, it is useful to refer back to Naipaul's first novel *A House for Mr. Biswas*. Here the traumas of diasporic displacement are figured through the trope of patrilineality, or what gets passed on from the father to the son. The dilemmas and setbacks that befall Mr. Biswas, the novel's protagonist (who is modeled after Naipaul's own father), as he tries and fails to build his own house, mirror the futility of the colonial condition as a whole. Mr. Biswas's travails are representative of the thematic obsessions that run through much of Naipaul's subsequent work: the longing for "home" as a site of both origins and essences and a simultaneous recognition of the inability to recuperate such a space; the lack of a recorded history, both familial and national; the lack of originality and the inevitability of mimicry and failure in individual and collective struggles for independence. As Rosemary George points out in her astute reading of *A House for Mr. Biswas*, Mr. Biswas's struggle to come into subjectivity and individuality is narrated through his quest to build what he calls a "real house, made with real materials" like wood, concrete, and iron rather than with mud, grass, and earth.[17] The obsessive attention paid to the architectures of housing in the novel is matched only by an obsessive cataloguing of the male body and its frailties. The act of constructing a house is simultaneously an attempt to construct a fortified masculinity that can withstand the emasculating power of women and the general chaos of colonial existence. George argues that the psychic and material impoverishment that colonialism produces is primarily figured in the novel through the evocation of masculine failure.[18] Naipaul's framing of Mr. Biswas underscores Fanon's assertion that the oedipal drama fails to hold the same explanatory power for racialized male subjectification given the black father's inability to access phallic power: the hapless Mr. Biswas is consistently characterized as embodying a degraded, weak, and soft masculinity that leaves his son without a model of viable masculinity to inherit. As Naipaul writes, Biswas's son is "a disappointment";[19] Biswas himself possesses a body that is "soft . . . like a woman,"[20] his chest is "hollow,"[21] the flesh of his calves "yields like sponge."[22] He is consistently characterized as emasculated, soft, impotent, neutered, degraded, fragmented and not-whole; he is utterly at the mercy of his wife's family, the Tulsis, and is unable to extricate himself from the chaotic home spaces he is forced to inhabit with them. His first visit to the matriarchal Tulsi household is described as follows: "Mr. Biswas had been overpowered and frightened by Mrs. Tulsi [his mother-in-law] and all the Tulsi women and children; they were strange and had appeared too strong; he wanted nothing so much as to be free of that house."[23]

Naipaul's parable thus narrates the struggle for selfhood in the face of colonialism and its legacies as a contest between the colonized male subject and the emasculating woman. Similarly, for Naipaul the failure to produce a viable and "authentic" masculinity capable of being passed on from father to son is the marker of the debased nature of diasporic existence as a whole. The centrality of a failed or impotent masculinity as a metaphor for the postcolonial condition is also seen in later canonical examples of diasporic literary production such as Salman Rushdie's 1981 novel *Midnight's Children*.[24] The impotence of Rushdie's narrator Saleem Sinai reflects his inability to effect historical change and institute an alternative vision of the nation. Obviously Rushdie's postmodern epic of the birth of the nation is very distinct from Naipaul's modernist articulation of colonialism's legacies; yet both Rushdie and Naipaul remain unable to imagine the nation or the diasporic community outside an evocation of normative masculinity, female abjection, and patrilineal inheritance.

Surviving Sabu can be seen as both a continuation and repudiation of the thematic obsession with masculine failure and patrilineality that characterizes canonical diasporic narratives. In a sense both *Surviving Sabu* and *A House for Mr. Biswas* continue Fanon's exploration of the problematic legacies of colonialism for racialized masculinities. Naipaul's representation of Mr. Biswas both replicates and revises British colonial representations of colonized Indian masculinity as degenerate, weak, and effeminate. The historian Mrinalini Sinha's work has shown that one of the primary ways in which British colonialism sought to naturalize white supremacy in nineteenth-century Bengal was through the production of the concept of "manly" Englishmen, in contrast to the "unmanly" Bengali *babu*, as the class of elite, educated Bengali men were named.[25] While Naipaul's representation of Mr. Biswas clearly bears the traces of this earlier construction of colonized masculinity, it also importantly provides the kernel of a critique of this construction by refusing to produce a triumphalist narrative of potent, empowered masculinity as a response to a prior emasculation. As Rosemary George comments, "In the fiction of the young Naipaul, masculine failure is endemic to the very colonial situation. It is not, as in Conrad's and other imperial romance novels, an outcome of the perennially hot weather of the generic 'tropical land' nor is it simply ascribed to personal or moral weakness."[26] Following George's reading, we can think of *A House for Mr. Biswas* as a brutally accurate anatomizing of the effects of colonial ideology on the psyches of colonized male subjects. Naipaul recognizes that within a colonial system of gender, possessing a viable masculinity is intimately tied to the ownership of property in the form of an idealized domestic space. Naipaul also recognizes that both masculinity and housing are invariably denied to the colonized male subject. Thus *A House for Mr. Biswas* can be read as denaturalizing what Sinha calls "colonial masculinity" even as it capitulates to the terms of colonial ideology in its overt misogyny and reliance on a heteronormative matrix. In his other works, such as his 1967 novel *The Mimic Men*, Naipaul even goes so far as to imply that the colonial order is a hierarchical system which confers inauthenticity upon colonized subjects and elevates colonial rulers to the status of the real.[27] The "mimic" masculinities of colonized men are not so much desperate attempts to become real as they are the only forms of identification available to them.

Surviving Sabu concurs with Naipaul's diagnosis of the ways in which colonial power relations function through discourses of housing and masculinity, but the film also crucially extends and revises that assessment through its representation of queer desire. In Rashid's film, it is queer desire that profoundly reconfigures the tropes of genealogy, normative masculinity, and patrilineal inheritance that structure Naipaul's work as well as other canonical diasporic narratives. Rashid's reframing of the paradigmatic struggle between the immigrant father and the second-generation son refuses to simply reproduce a tradition/modernity binary that would make the straight father the emblem of tradition and "homeland" and the gay son the emblem of modernity and advanced politicization. Rather, the relation between father and son in *Surviving Sabu* is characterized by a complex relay of desire and identification. Rashid's radical rearticulation of the father/son dynamic becomes particularly clear in a key sequence in the film, which opens with a shot of Sabu's body lying prone on a beach, the camera sensuously panning a smooth expanse of glowing brown skin. In this opening shot, Sabu, his eyes closed, is the prototypical "object-to-be-looked at," inviting a fetishizing, voyeuristic gaze that, as the son points out, is simultaneously raced and sexualized. As we see successive shots of Sabu's body in various states of action and undress, we hear the father's voice offscreen narrating as follows: "Sabu had an unnatural natural beauty, such a beautiful body, a muscular, athletic physique. I told my son, 'look at Sabu's body!' That he should exercise and himself look like Sabu. But Amin, he was always reading his books, playing with his dolls, he was never interested in exercise." The father's exhortation for the son to "look at Sabu's body" carries a double valence. On the one hand, as with Naipaul's Mr. Biswas, it is the immigrant father's attempt to pass on normative masculinity to his gender non-normative son (who prefers to read, sing, and play with dolls rather than exercise). Yet in the subsequent sequence, we see that the identification with Sabu that the father seeks to instill in his son has also opened the way to queer desire in the space of the immigrant home. The father's narrative is abruptly forestalled as we are brought back into the present moment: the swelling violin strings that accompany the film images of Sabu is replaced by the tinny sound of the radio the father listens to as he cooks in the kitchen of his cramped home, while his son Amin looks on. The father's reverie on Sabu's body is substituted by Amin's reverie on his father's body, as a shot of Sabu's muscular torso cutting through the water gives way to the voyeuristic gaze of the son as he admires the muscles of his father's shoulders.

This scene reveals how queer desire is produced within the space of the home itself, rather than as exterior to it. If heteronormative diasporic discourse locates queer bodies and desires outside the realm of home as household, community, and nation, homonormative queer narratives consistently place queer desire in exilic relation to home and family. In this scene, however, Rashid overturns both hegemonic queer *and* diasporic discourses. The immigrant home and family function in *Surviving Sabu* not as the prehistory of the queer subject, or as anterior to it, but rather as that which lays the very grounds for queer pleasure and subjectivity. Similarly, diasporic genealogy is evoked not through the inheritance of normative masculinity, as it is in Naipaul's novel, but rather through the passing on of an alternative queer masculinity. Furthermore, in this scene the colonial trope of interracial looking (where the power of the gaze is invariably aligned with whiteness) is transformed into an occasion for homoerotic "intra-racial looking":[28] first as the father in voice-over contemplates Sabu's body and then as the son gazes at the father's body. If the oedipal drama, as David Eng observes, involves "the willful splitting of heterosexual identification from homosexual desire,"[29] *Surviving Sabu* radically reworks this scenario by refusing to replace desire with identification and instead insists on their simultaneity.

The film also reminds us that there is no pure space of desire that transcends the terms of dominant culture. Amin sheepishly averts his gaze as his father catches him looking at his body, and he says accusatorily to the father, "Those movies filmed [Sabu] like he was a woman, and you bought into it . . . You ogle him the same way those films did because he was Asian, and you bought into it." The father responds to this accusation by asking Amin, "And those white boys you take up with, how do they look at you?" The father's stark rejoinder to Amin's accusation that he buys into colonialist fantasies forces Amin to recognize his own co-implication within structures of Orientalism. In this context the film's title is particularly suggestive and multiply inflected. While it most obviously references the ongoing legacies of colonial, Orientalist, and racist ideologies that structure desire and subjectivity in the present, the title also gestures to the survival strategies of minoritarian subjects who labor to "transform a cultural logic from within."[30] Finally, and most suggestively, the film's title references the alternative genealogy set forth by the film: the son is indeed Sabu's survivor or descendent in the sense that he too is marked by hegemonic colonial ideologies that continue to govern homoerotic looking relations between white and brown men. *Surviving Sabu*, then, allows us to trace a queer diasporic genealogy that connects father to son and is produced through and against dominant culture. Queer desire becomes central to a retelling of diasporic history and displaces official diasporic genealogies that rely on the comforting fictions of normative masculinity.

Rashid thus "survives Naipaul" in the sense that he both revisits and redefines the problematic of race, masculinity, and colonialism that Naipaul so carefully delineates. In *A House for Mr. Biswas*, as well as in subsequent works, Naipaul seems to be unable to envision alternatives modes of being and housing other than those predicated on patriarchal domesticity—which, as he is so painfully aware, is always denied to colonized male subjects. Like Fanon's black spectator in the European movie house, Naipaul remains caught between two equally problematic modes of subjecthood, identifying through a white hero or refusing identification with a brown savage. Rashid's film, in contrast, suggests a way out of the trap of identification or counteridentification with hegemonic models of housing and masculinity. At the end of *Surviving Sabu*, father and son move from inside the house to the backyard. As a peace offering to the father, the son sets up a projector in the garden and screens *The Jungle Book* onto the exterior walls of the house. This move from inside to outside the walls of the immigrant home brings into the realm of public culture what has hitherto remained a private ritual of spectatorial identification and desire between an immigrant father and his second-generation son. It also suggests that the protagonists have come to occupy a kind of "third space," as Homi Bhabha terms it.[31] This inside/outside location allows them to stand at a critical distance from the normative familial arrangements that constitute the home, while simultaneously refusing to reject the space of home altogether. By screening Sabu's image onto the exterior walls of the house, Rashid comments on the ways in which dominant ideologies of race and masculinity construct the very architecture of housing while also providing the occasion for alternative imaginings of home, kinship, and collectivity.

The one instance, however, where *Surviving Sabu* remains embedded within hegemonic articulations of diaspora—and thereby shares more with Naipaul's text than it initially appears to—is in the troubling absence of the female diasporic subject. I would argue that the very structure of father-son narratives inevitably precludes alternative stories and subjectivities; in *Surviving Sabu* the centrality of the father-son narrative elides and displaces other possible narratives. Thus the mother's presence in the film is referenced only through the saris that hang to dry in the backyard and that literally provide the backdrop for interactions between the father and son. The mother's ghostly presence is also evoked in the father's comments that she is "at the mosque" or at the "marriage committee," presumably fixing up marriages for "other people's sons." The absent figure of the mother thus becomes the marker of normative tradition, community, and family against which a queer gay male genealogy is formed. Here, as in David Eng's reading of the homosocial/homoerotic bonds between the white male characters in David Henry Hwang's play *M. Butterfly*, "homosociality and its exchange of women gives way to a homosexual economy that no longer, for the moment, requires their presence."[32] Indeed, the mother's absence is precisely what allows the immigrant home to be transformed from a heteronormative space into one where the homosocial bonds between father and son slip into homoeroticism. Thus I now turn to the question of theorizing female diasporic subjectivity in a way that exceeds both the instrumental, curiously disembodied role it plays in *Surviving Sabu*, or the monstrous, emasculating shape it takes in Naipaul's novel.

Female Subjectivity and Queer Diasporas

My interest in marking the elision of female subjectivity in dominant and queer (male) representations of colonial and postcolonial masculinities allies my project with recent scholarship emerging out of queer studies that specifically focuses on racialized masculinities. Important works by scholars such as Kobena Mercer, Robert Reid Pharr, David Eng, and Philip Brian Harper have done much to historicize and theorize the vexed relation between race and masculinity in the "West."[33] Much of this work is attuned to the ways in which a fortified racialized masculine subject comes into being only at the expense of the racialized female subject. In the context of black racial formation in the United States, for instance, Reid Pharr critiques the production of a black nationalist male subject over and against the bodies of women. In his examination of the writings of black male revolutionaries such as Fanon, George Jackson, and Malcolm X, he is struck by their intensely ambivalent relation to the figure of the black mother. He writes, "The phrase 'bad black mama' is a study in redundancy. She is, indeed, the figure who produces the revolutionary, then rushes to cool his ardor, his tendency toward self-destruction. As such, she is perhaps *the* key player in the management of the very American crisis of the black family. She is, therefore, a creature who readily provokes great reverence and icy hot hostility."[34] In the different colonial and postcolonial contexts that concern Naipaul and Rashid, the South Asian diasporic woman/mother similarly evokes profound ambivalence since she functions both as a castrating and emasculating force (as in Naipaul's novel), and as a symbolic marker of "home" whose (absent) presence enables relations of desire and identification between men (as in Rashid's film).

David Eng's incisive study of Asian American masculinity in his book *Racial Castration: Managing Masculinity in Asian America* further points to the ways in which a gay male racialized subjectivity in the diaspora is often constructed at the expense of women of color. Eng analyzes Ang Lee's 1993 film *The Wedding*

Banquet and argues that "queer and feminist discourses are . . . at odds" when we consider the ways in which queer Asian American citizenship in the film is complicit with transnational, patriarchal capitalism and the subordination of Third World women's labor. Thus, Eng concludes, a queer diasporic project may not necessarily be progressive or constitute a challenge to "local and global status quos," but may in fact be antifeminist and fully at the service of corporate capitalism.[35] Furthermore, as Eng and coauthor Alice Hom crucially observe in the introduction to their anthology *Q&A: Queer in Asian America*, between "dominant images of emasculated Asian American men and hyperheterosexualized Asian American women . . . the Asian American lesbian disappears . . . It is precisely mainstream stereotypes of an effeminized Asian American male (homo)sexuality that affect the ways in which the Asian American lesbian goes unseen and unrecognized."[36] Thus, in their effacement of female subjectivity, and queer female subjectivity in particular, seemingly progressive representations of gay Asian men such as in *The Wedding Banquet* in fact acquiesce to and participate in the dominant racial paradigm of Asian masculinity and femininity. This paradigm constructs Asian men as emasculated and effeminized, while situating Asian women within the realm of heterosexuality and domestic labor.

Clearly, as I have argued previously and as my reading of *Surviving Sabu* has shown, the consolidation of a gay male genealogy in the diaspora may very well be dependent on the erasure and invisibility of the female diasporic subject. While Eng's observations provide a necessary caution that tempers a facile celebration of the subversive potential of a queer diaspora, they also raise the question of how we can theorize diasporic queerness in a way that does not simply replicate the violent effacements of conventional diasporic and nationalist formations. How do we clear the theoretical and representational space to imagine a queer subjectivity that is not always already male, or a female subjectivity that is not always already heterosexual? I would argue that one way out of this trap where (male) queerness is counterposed to feminism, and where gay male subjectivity renders queer female desire and subjectivity impossible, is by refusing to privilege gay male subjectivity as the place from which to begin theorizing a queer diaspora. Indeed a queer diasporic project is at odds with a feminist project *only* if we presume the centrality of a gay male diasporic subject. In other words, the apparent incommensurability of queerness and feminism must be radically rethought if we place a female subject rather than a gay male subject at the center of a queer diasporic project. Doing so also demands that we rethink the modes and strategies of resistance used by queer subjects to counter hegemonic diasporic and nationalist claims made on their bodies. To turn once again to Eng's provocative speculations on theorizing queerness and diaspora together, he argues that both queers and Asian Americans have a fraught relation to "home" as both domestic space and the space of the U.S. nation-state since both have historically been figured as exterior and pathological to these spaces.[37] In other words, queerness exists in an analogous relation to diaspora in that queers, like Asian Americans, are always in an exilic relation to home spaces.

If we take queer female diasporic subjectivity as the starting point of our analysis, however, we are compelled to revise this formulation of the relation of queer and diasporic subjects to the space of "home." As is apparent in *Surviving Sabu* as well as in the following discussion of *East Is East*, "home" is not simply or necessarily the place from which the queer subject is evicted or exiled. Rather, "home" is a space that is ruptured and imaginatively transformed by queer diasporic subjects even as they remain within its confines. This queer transformation of the diasporic "home" constitutes a remarkably powerful challenge to dominant ideologies of community and nation in ways that may very well escape intelligibility within a logic of visibility and "coming out." As my reading of *East Is East* makes evident, these queer reorderings of home exist at the interstices and fissures of the most rigidly heteronormative structures. Thus the construction of "queers" being "like Asian Americans" in their alienation from "home" needs to be rearticulated in light of the ways in which queer diasporic subjects—and queer female diasporic subjects in particular— inhabit and transform home space rather than simply existing in exilic relation to it. In short, if the formulation of queerness as male, and femaleness (and feminism) as heterosexual, is a result of privileging gay male subjectivity as the place from which to begin theorizing a queer diaspora, it also misrecognizes the complex ways in which "home" space is remade by queer desire and subjectivity.

In what follows, then, I situate queer *female* subjectivity at the very heart of a queer diasporic project in order to produce a framework that is both queer *and* feminist rather than queer *or* feminist. Such a framework is crucial if we are to have adequate tools with which to theorize and critique the splitting of queerness from femaleness and feminism that is apparent in much recent critical scholarship and cultural production. Eng points to the necessity of this framework when he writes: "Precisely because the feminization of the Asian American male in the U.S. cultural imaginary typically results in his figuration as feminized, emasculated, or homosexualized, we must vigilantly pursue the theoretical connections between queer studies—with its focus on (homo)sexuality and desire—and women's studies—with its focus on gender and identification—in relation to the production of Asian American male subjectivity."[38] One way to avoid continuously reifying this binary between queer studies and women's studies is to understand "queer" not only in relation to male (homo)sexuality but precisely in relation to female sexuality, desire, and gendered agency.

From *Mary Poppins* to Mina: Performing Women's Labor in the Diaspora

A consideration of *East Is East* allows us to flesh out the implications of situating female diasporic subjectivity at the center of a queer diasporic model. The film was marketed in the United States as a light-hearted, nostalgic evocation of South Asian life in Britain in the early 1970s, and it garnered much praise from mainstream audiences in the United States and Britain, no doubt in part because it presents a familiar immigrant narrative of cultural conflicts and generational divides between "traditional" parents and their assimilated offspring. Advertisements for the film in the United States went so far as to proclaim, "he was having the time of his life . . . until his father started picking out his wife," and to bill it as "an outrageous look at what happens when two cultures clash in one family." This tradition/modernity binary allows the film to be rendered intelligible to a mainstream audience, in that such a narrative has come to define mainstream representations of South Asian immigrant existence.[39] However, if we situate *East Is East* within the same matrix of concerns that emerges in Rashid's *Surviving Sabu* or Naipaul's *Biswas*, we can read the film more usefully as an astute representation of racialized masculinity in postcolonial Britain. Furthermore, where *Surviving Sabu* disrupts a familiar generational narrative through its representation of queer desire between father and son, in *East Is East* it is female diasporic subjectivity that stands as the moment of unintelligibility within an otherwise conventional scenario of cultural conflict and generational divides.

East Is East is set in Salford, Manchester, in 1971 and focuses on the biracial family of a Pakistani immigrant man, George Khan (played by Indian actor

Om Puri), and his white working-class English wife, Ella. The background noise to the hybrid British Asian lives of George and Ella's seven children is provided by Enoch Powell's racist calls for the repatriation of immigrants on the one hand, and newscasts charting Pakistan's defeat during Bangladesh's war of independence on the other. In *East Is East*, as in the texts of Rashid and Naipaul, masculine failure is a central feature of postcolonial male subjectivity: the father George's failure as benevolent patriarch is immediately clear in his increasingly desperate and violent attempts to control the lives of his wife and seven children. The film initially seems to replicate the pathologization of Asian families within conventional racist discourse in Britain where Asian families are imagined to be hopelessly enmeshed within "traditional" customs such as arranged marriage. Yet while the character of George appears to conform squarely to stereotypes of backward, patriarchal Asian men who terrorize their hapless wives and children, the film also allows for a denaturalization of this stereotype by contextualizing George's "traditionalism." An investment in patriarchal authority is not portrayed as natural or intrinsic to Muslim immigrant culture; rather it is shown to be an ineffectual response to both the racism of the British state and the undermining of Pakistani nationalism. As the posters of Powell become more and more ubiquitous on the streets of Salford, so too do George's frantic and doomed attempts to pass on "Muslim culture" to his children become more urgent. Similarly, George's response to Pakistan's imminent defeat in the war against India and Bangladesh is to increasingly demand filial and phallic respect from his wife and children.

Indeed, the figure of George embodies the mode of postcolonial patriarchal masculinity that Homi Bhabha outlines in his essay "Are You a Man or a Mouse?"[40] Bhabha recalls this phrase as the question posed insistently to his boyhood self by his attorney father in Bombay, "his barristerish bravura seeking a kind of exclusive, excluding, bonding."[41] For Bhabha, his father's question speaks to the ambivalent and oscillating nature of masculinity itself, in its need to compulsively interrogate itself and act out its power and powerlessness. The question also reveals the "anxious love" between father and son that is linked, Bhabha argues, to the anxious love for the nation that is the basis of nationalist subjectivity. In other words, the father's demand for respect from his son, and his insistence on passing on an empowered masculinity to him, is simultaneously a demand for service and respect to the (masculinist) nation.

Bhabha's scenario of anxious love and phallic respect between father and son is perfectly encapsulated by George's relation to his sons in *East Is East*. George's demand for filial respect is intimately bound up with a demand for respect to the nation (Pakistan) and religion (Islam). Thus he is horrified by his sons' resistance to arranged marriages and their utter disinterest in the teachings of Islam. Again, the sons' rejection of "tradition" and the father's insistence on it fits comfortably within a familiar discourse of "generation gaps" and "cultural conflict" that characterizes conventionally drawn immigrant narratives. And certainly the film is decipherable to a mainstream audience, who may not otherwise be interested or familiar with South Asian immigrant culture, precisely because of its adherence to these conventions. Nevertheless, I would argue that, like Naipaul's rendition of failed postcolonial manhood, *East Is East*'s depiction of an immigrant father's desperate attempts to garner phallic respect from his sons can more fruitfully be read as a dissection of the ways in which state racism, state patriarchy, and immigrant masculinity are mutually intertwined and implicated. In a climactic showdown with one of his rebellious sons, for instance, George states with genuine confusion in broken English, "Son, you do not understand because you don't listen to me. I try to show you a good way to live. You know the English, English never accepting you. In Islam, there is no black man, no white man." Here George articulates an adherence to patriarchal religious orthodoxy as a solution to the racist exclusions of British state.

Such a reliance on seemingly indigenous patriarchal norms as a way out of the traps of state racism must be situated within the context of the immigration debates within the UK in the late 1960s and early 1970s. The Commonwealth Immigrant Act of 1968 and the Immigration Act of 1971 mobilized the notion of "patriality" as a way to distinguish between desirable (white) Commonwealth citizens and undesirable (nonwhite) Commonwealth citizens. Under the patriality laws, only those British passport-holders born in the UK, or with a father or grandfather born in the UK, had access to special immigration rights. Thus, as Anna Marie Smith states, with the concept of patriality "the boundaries of the nation became officially conceptualized in terms of familial [patriarchal] blood ties."[42] The patriality distinction helped to produce the figure of an alien, "unwanted black invader" against which a racially homogenous nationalist collectivity could be defined.[43] Given that British national boundaries were systematically being drawn along the lines of a racist, patrilineal genealogical inheritance, George's response to state racism by resorting to indigenous patriarchy cannot be dismissed as a symptom of anachronistic "tradition" out of synch with "modern" time of the British nation. Instead, George's evocation of patriarchal authority attempts to produce a form of immigrant family that is fortified against the patriarchal, racialized definition of an all-white national family of Britain put in place by anti-immigrant legislation.

In his study of African American masculinity, Philip Brian Harper observes that mainstream U.S. culture "conceives African American society in terms of a perennial 'crisis' of black masculinity whose imagined solution is a proper affirmation of black male authority."[44] Similarly conventional diasporic ideology, as articulated by George in *East Is East*, holds that the only way to resolve the contradictions of migration and racism is through the shoring up of masculine authority. This is precisely the presumption that underlies the impossible question ("Are you a man or a mouse?") posed by the father in Homi Bhabha's meditation on masculinity and paternity. Bhabha, commenting on his boyhood response to his father's question, writes, " 'Do I have to choose?' I remember thinking, in anxious awkwardness, caught impossibly, ambivalently, in between 'two different creeds and two different outlooks on life.' "[45] In *East Is East*, the most powerful rebuttal of such a choice, and the question itself, comes during the brief scene centering on George's half-English, half-Pakistani daughter Mina, with which I opened this chapter. Bhabha ends his essay with a reading of artist Adrien Piper's work as "an instance of feminist 'disrespect' for the hagiography of political father figures."[46] Similarly, Mina's performance constitutes a resounding rejection of the father-son drama of oedipal hatred, rivalry, and anxious love and offers in its stead a joyous enactment of "feminist disrespect" in the face of the phallic respect demanded by father and nation.

In *East Is East* female diasporic subjectivity—rather than gay male desire—provides the greatest challenge to logics of immigrant patriarchy and dominant racist English nationalism. One of the film's subplots follows George's eldest son as he escapes from the family home in Salford on his wedding day, to eventually set up shop as a hip clothing designer in London with a male lover in tow. The son's homosexuality initially appears to be the most obvious site of resistance to the model of normative immigrant masculinity that George seeks to inculcate in his sons. Yet insofar as *East Is East* merely repeats the familiar narrative of queerness emerging only in exilic relation to the (immigrant) home that *Surviving Sabu* so successfully destabilizes, the architecture of home

Mina (Archie Panjabi) as a
tough English schoolgirl in *East is East*
(dir. Damien O'Donnell, 2000).

itself and its structures of gender and sexual normativity are left undisturbed. The space of the immigrant home in *East Is East* is troubled not by the figure of the errant gay son who leaves but by the hybrid diasporic female figure of Mina who remains. This troubling of home space is precisely what makes Mina, rather than the explicitly gay son, the real "queer" character in the film. Queerness can be understood in relation to the figure of Mina as pertaining not simply to sexual identity or even sexual practices. Rather, it speaks to a mode of resistant feminist cultural practice that prevents the reconstitution of patriarchal, immigrant masculinity and that disturbs the space of the hetero-normative home from within.

George translates the loss of his homeland's territorial integrity into an attempt to map out territorial ownership on Mina's body. A tough English schoolgirl with a penchant for torturing her little brother and kicking footballs at Enoch Powell posters, Mina is forced to exchange her bell-bottoms and school uniform first for a *sari*, and then (as Pakistani nationalism mounts) for a *salwar kameez*. The film thus deftly illustrates the ways in which the immigrant woman's body becomes a surface on which competing and shifting notions of home and homeland are screened within the realm of diasporic public culture. As in *Surviving Sabu*, Mina's resistance to and transformation of the multiple discourses inscribed on her body occur through her engagement with dominant popular culture and the structures of looking that it entails. This feminist engagement with popular culture, and Bollywood film in particular, is brilliantly encapsulated in the brief but pivotal scene with which I began this chapter where Mina, dressed in galoshes and white tunic, transforms herself into Kamal Amrohi's classic Bollywood heroine Pakeezah. But Mina's performance references not only the Bollywood genre of courtesan films (of which *Pakeezah* is exemplary) but also a startlingly similar sequence in the film *Mary Poppins* (dir. Robert Stevenson, 1964).[47] Mina's performance, with its citations of the musicals of Bollywood cinema and Disney film, is an intervention into the public cultural space of both the diaspora and the nation; it is through the dual nature of its address that it stages a complex critique of the gendered, sexual, and racial logics of multiple home spaces.

Mina's appropriation of iconic Bollywood femininity in this scene intervenes into two sets of discourses: conventional diasporic ideology with its claims to a fortified patriarchal masculinity, and racist English nationalist discourse with its definition of Britain as an all-white, homogenous collectivity. First, Mina draws on the mode of iconic femininity in *Pakeezah*—a quintessential example of the courtesan genre of popular Hindi cinema—in order to unsettle the place of the properly demure female figure, emblematic of tradition and homeland, that stands at the center of hegemonic South Asian diasporic and nationalist ideologies. Emphatically not "wife" or "mother," the courtesan in Bollywood film, as Sumita Chakravarty argues, is "an ambiguous icon of Indian womanhood," a liminal figure who acts as the repository of Hindu and Muslim high culture and who straddles the line between female moral purity and sexual impurity, the legitimate and illegitimate, the public and the private, belonging and estrangement.[48] *Pakeezah* tells the story of a beautiful but tragic courtesan (played by legendary Hindi film actress Meena Kumari) who is renamed "Pakeezah" or "the pure one" by her lover in an effort to wipe out her past as a dancing girl. Her lover initially sees her asleep in a railway car and is so taken by the loveliness of her feet that he slips a note between her toes that reads, "Your feet are beautiful. Do not let them touch the ground or they will be soiled." The intricately hennaed feet of Pakeezah are the recurring motif of the film, the fetishized markers of her embodied labor as a dancing girl as well as her moral refinement that makes her ultimately unfit for the world of the bazaar and the brothel.[49] The film ends with a climactic sequence in which Pakeezah, broken-hearted and scorned by her lover, dances on broken glass, her bloodied feet staining the white sheets that cover the marble floors of his palace. The figure of Pakeezah in Bollywood iconography, then, embodies a particular form of female masochism in the face of social injustice; the camera's fetishistic gaze on the courtesan's feet references her sexual labor as well as the self-mutilation through which she ultimately proves her essential moral purity.

The film *Pakeezah* occupies a central place within the public culture of the South Asian diaspora; indeed, the actress Meena Kumari's performance has become a staple of drag queen events in diasporic gay male and transgendered spaces. Mina's embodiment of Pakeezah in *East Is East*, however, suggests the uses of camp and the appropriation of iconic, hyperbolic femininity for female diasporic subjects.[50] In a wry commentary on the intense libidinal investment in women's feet in Hindi film,[51] the cinematic focus on Pakeezah's dainty and bejeweled feet in Amrohi's film is cleverly translated in *East Is East* into an opening shot of Mina's thick rubber galoshes stamping time to the well-known beat of "*Inhi Logon Ne*," the first song from *Pakeezah*. In *Pakeezah*, the fetishistic gaze on the courtesan's feet references her sexual labor as well as her inner purity. In contrast, in *East Is East* the shot of Mina's feet encased in galoshes instead speaks to the mundane forms of labor enacted by the diasporic female subject that go unrecognized by either the British state or the patriarchal immigrant family structure. Female labor in both *Pakeezah* and *East Is East* is intertwined with gendered notions of purity, tradition, and propriety. The transformation of Pakeezah's bare and bloodied feet into Mina's feet in galoshes signals Mina's refusal to capitulate to the form of female masochism mythologized in *Pakeezah*, or to abide by the ideologies of female purity on which conventional South Asian diasporic and nationalist discourses rely.

The particular song from *Pakeezah* that Mina performs, "*Inhi Logon Ne*," directly refers to the courtesan figure's capitulation to and critique of these discourses.[52] In the scene from *Pakeezah* that Mina mimics, the courtesan

"The Pure One": Bollywood icon Meena Kumari in *Pakeezah*
(dir. Kamal Amrohi, 1971). *Photo courtesy of the National
Film Archive of India.*

suggestively dances in front of her customers in the public space of the brothel;
she refers to the loss of sexual and moral purity she suffers as a result of
patriarchal social mores as she sings the line, "these people [men] have taken
away my *dupatta* [modesty]." For Mina in *East Is East*, the enactment of
Pakeezah's song and dance becomes a way to critique the various disciplinary
discourses of purity, modesty, and sexual morality that are fixed onto her body
by hegemonic diasporic and nationalist ideologies. Mina utilizes the liminal
status of the courtesan figure, at once the embodiment of high culture and
tradition and that which is rendered abject by normative moral codes, in order
to comment on her own liminal gendered status as English, Pakistani, biracial,
working class, and diasporic. By inhabiting the ambivalent role of the courtesan, Mina lays claim to the undeniable pleasures afforded by the performance
of iconic South Asian femininity. While in *Surviving Sabu*, Sabu as Orientalist
motif emerges as a queer predecessor of contemporary diasporic gay male
masculinity, in *East Is East* Mina reworks the equally ambivalent figure of

Pakeezah into a feminist predecessor of contemporary queer diasporic female subjectivity. In other words, Mina's performance of the hyperbolic femininity of the Bollywood courtesan unharnesses the pleasures of dominant representation from its disciplining and regulatory function. Mina thus enacts a queer reappropriation and citation of Pakeezah, in that she wrests this figure away from its conventional signification within the public cultural imaginary of the diaspora and instead refashions it as emblematic of a resistant femininity.

Second, while Mina's enactment of Bollywood femininity intervenes into dominant South Asian diasporic and nationalist discourses of gender and sexuality, it also intervenes into dominant English nationalist discourses of race, citizenship, and empire. Earlier in the film, Mina takes a road trip with her family to Bradford, with its predominantly South Asian population, in order to view the 1960 classic of Bollywood cinema, *Chaudvin Ka Chand*. This scene of the biracial family in an all-Asian movie theater taking in the lush, color-saturated spectacle of Guru Dutt and Minoo Mumtaz enacting their famous duet makes clear the centrality of Bollywood cinema in producing the public culture of the diaspora. For first- and second-generation British Asians, circuits of pleasure, identification, and desire are routed not through Hollywood but rather through an alternative cinematic tradition. If the white women informants in Jackie Stacey's study of female audiences in 1940s Britain remember Hollywood as their escape from the rigors of daily life during World War II,[53] Mina and her family draw on popular Indian cinema as a means of imagining an "elsewhere" to the strictures of racist, working-class existence in Britain in the 1970s.

Although Mina and her brothers look increasingly bored by the film that clearly entrances their parents, the mode of femininity represented in *Chaudvin Ka Chand* is what provides Mina with the repertoire of gestures that she uses later in the film to produce her own enactment of Pakeezah. Her performance is not so much escapist in the sense that Stacey understands the term,[54] but one that uses the materials available to her to fashion her own relation to multiple national and discursive locations. Mina's citation of *Pakeezah* provides a powerful rejoinder to Enoch Powell's calls for an all-white Britain, in that it evokes an alternative realm of public culture that is available to South Asian immigrants in the diaspora. This space of South Asian diasporic public culture challenges the primacy of "authentic" English national culture and its fictions of racial purity and homogeneity. Mina's intervention takes on particular significance given that the institution of the Immigration Act of 1971, in addition to

instituting the "patriality" distinction, sought to terminate black settler migration and introduce a system of short-term contractual labor that would divest
Afro-Caribbean and Asian workers of citizenship status and render them per-
petual "aliens" in the UK.[55] While George responds to such racist definitions
of British national identity with a demand for filial and phallic respect, Mina
responds with her performance of "feminist disrespect" that rejects indigenous
patriarchal ideology as well as the racist amnesia that would deny the cultural
and economic imprint of colonialism and migration on the national culture
and economy of Britain. As Stuart Hall writes, British racism in the postwar
period "*begins* with the profound historical forgetfulness—what I want to call
the loss of historical memory, a kind of historical amnesia, a decisive mental
repression—which has overtaken the British people about race and empire
since the 1950s."[56] It is precisely this historical forgetfulness that Mina's performance works against, as it forcefully challenges the notion that a South Asian
popular cultural vocabulary is alien or foreign to a British national landscape.

If Mina's evocation of *Pakeezah* stages an implicit critique of the dependency
of postwar Britain on the colonial and immigrant labor that is forgotten within
contemporary British racial discourse, her simultaneous referencing of the
1964 film *Mary Poppins* (dir. Robert Stevenson) further extends this critique.
In a scene from the Disney film that Mina's performance in *East Is East* clearly
echoes, chimney sweeps brandish brooms while singing and dancing in blackface on London rooftops. In Jon Simon's astute reading of this scene in *Mary
Poppins*, he argues that the Disney film must be situated within the context of
two eras of capitalism: the capitalism of 1964, the year of the film's release, and
the capitalism of 1910, the year in which the film is situated.[57] In relation to the
1910 context, Simons suggests that the film reveals the interdependence of
finance capitalism and imperialism in early-twentieth-century Britain: "One
significant consequence of the shift from industrial to finance capitalism is that
the labour that is exploited to generate profit becomes less visible, both because
it appears to be generated by the activity of investment itself and because more
of it is done far away in the colonies."[58] In Simons's reading, the chimney
sweeps are literally rendered invisible by the soot covering their faces and by
the fact that they work on rooftops and in chimneys; their labor represents the
work of colonial laborers whose work is similarly rendered invisible within
British nationalist discourse. Indeed, the chimney sweeps are even mistaken for
marauding "Hottentots" by a vigilant neighbor.

While Simons's reading certainly holds true for the earlier era of capitalism

Mary Poppins (Julie Andrews) and chimney sweeps dance in
blackface in *Mary Poppins* (dir. Robert Stevenson, 1964).

that the film references, I would argue that in the 1964 context the chimney
sweeps refer not only to the invisible labor of colonial and newly postcolonial
subjects in distant lands but also to the invisibility of racialized immigrant labor
within Britain itself. By rendering racial others within the British national
polity as "alien invaders," the chimney sweeps scene in *Mary Poppins* clearly
outlines the contours of the Powellian racism of the 1960s. The racist conception of Britishness in the 1960s, as Anna Marie Smith writes, "renam[ed]
the colonized as 'immigrants,' " thereby rendering "the 'known' colonized" as
" 'unknown' 'strangers' in the land of their own making."[59] Mina's citational
practice, where she reworks *Mary Poppins* via *Pakeezah*, thus demands a remembering of the dependency of postwar Britain on an imperial past and on
the gendered nature of contemporary postcolonial immigrant labor. Mina
parodically inhabits the blackface of the chimney sweep in order to make
visible the racialized immigrant labor—and racialized immigrant women's labor in particular—that is rendered invisible within the dominant British nationalist imaginary but upon which the post–World War II British economy
depends.[60]

"In Search of Some Place Better"

Placing this brief, seemingly tangential, and excessive moment in *East Is East* alongside Naipaul's renderings of debased colonial masculinity and Rashid's tale of postcolonial queer masculinities reveals how both canonical and gay male diasporic narratives may replicate the pathologizing and elision of female diasporic pleasure and subjectivity. Furthermore, such a juxtaposition of texts reveals how the eruption of female diasporic pleasure threatens to undo oedipal narratives of patrilineal descent and conflict on which dominant models of diaspora are based. In situating this image of female diasporic pleasure against the tortured relation between fathers and sons delineated in Naipaul's novel, or against the gay male genealogy mapped out in *Surviving Sabu*, I hope to underscore the need for a diasporic frame of analysis that is at once queer *and* feminist. This queer feminist diasporic framework is produced by foregrounding female diasporic pleasure, cultural practices, and subjectivities, and indeed makes these pleasures, practices, and subjectivities intelligible and meaningful. Without this framework, a moment such as Mina's performance, or the ephemeral queer and feminist cultural practices discussed in the previous chapter, are lost under the weight of conventional diasporic narratives, or are drowned out by the strident sounds of a masculinist, antiracist revolutionary politics.

I have focused with such detail on *East Is East* in relation to *Surviving Sabu* and *A House for Mr. Biswas* because Mina's performance provides a powerful corrective to the effacement of queer female diasporic subjectivity that occurs in both the other texts. At the same time, both *East Is East* and *Surviving Sabu* eloquently point to the ways in which queer diasporic subjects transform the meanings of "home" from within its very confines. Given that leaving, escaping, and traveling to a presumably freer "elsewhere" is not an option or even necessarily desirable for many subaltern subjects, we must take seriously the myriad strategies through which those who remain (out of choice or necessity) conspire to rework the oppressive structures in which they find themselves. In Marlon Riggs's now-classic 1989 video *Tongues Untied*, Riggs recalls his leave-taking from the small, racist, homophobic Southern town of Hephzibah, where he grew up, to the presumed "promised land" of gay male erotic freedom of the Castro in San Francisco. The racism he ultimately encounters in the Castro at the hands of white gay men leads him to conclude, poignantly, "In this great gay mecca I was an invisible man; still, I had no shadow, no substance.

No history, no place. No reflection. I was alien, unseen, and seen, unwanted. Here, as in Hephzibah, I was a nigga, still. I quit—the Castro was no longer my home, my mecca (never was, in fact), and I went in search of some place better."[61] For Riggs, that better place is ultimately a community of black gay men; this is the homecoming he seeks and ultimately finds. Riggs's powerful words resonate profoundly with the ways in which, for the queer diasporic subjects in *East Is East* and *Surviving Sabu*, leaving "home" is no guarantee of freedom from those various forces that curtail their lives. For them, as for Riggs in *Tongues Untied*, the equation of liberation with leaving and oppression with "staying put" cannot be upheld.[62] In rejecting this progress narrative of freedom through exile and the renunciation of home, these texts instead enable a queer reworking of the very space of home itself.

4

BOLLYWOOD/HOLLYWOOD

Queer Cinematic Representation and the Perils of Translation

In an account that echoes *East Is East*'s depiction of George and his Pakistani-English family watching *Chaudvin Ka Chand* in Bradford in the early 1970s, the British Asian writer Ziauddin Sardar recalls growing up in Hackney, East London, in the 1960s and accompanying his mother every weekend to the local Indian movie house. In Sardar's narrative, popular Indian cinema in the Britain of the 1960s provided South Asian audiences with a vital sense of belonging, "home," and "rootedness": "The films testified to the fact that we were all culturally and socially one. We saw them as a universal symbol of our subcontinental identity; a lifeline for the cultural survival of the Asian community. They brought a bit of 'home,' of what my parents had left behind in Pakistan, to us here in Britain and thus provided a sense of belonging not offered by British society."[1] Sardar's reminiscence speaks to the tremendous symbolic power of popular cinema in the making of South Asian public culture in the diaspora and reveals its centrality to diasporic constructions of communal identity. India is the largest film-producing country in the world, and films made in India, particularly in the huge film factories of Bollywood (as the Bombay film industry is known), travel within an ever-expanding network of South Asian diasporic communities throughout South and Southeast Asia, North America, the Caribbean, the Middle East, East Africa, and elsewhere.

Since India's independence in 1947, Bollywood films have also been an important form of pan–Third Worldist cultural exchange between India and East
and South Africa, the Middle East, and Eastern Europe.[2]

   In the previous chapter I engaged with particular renderings of "old" and
"new" diasporas—as represented by the work of V. S. Naipaul and Ian Rashid—
to show that these ostensibly opposing formulations of diaspora in fact coin-
cide in their framing of female diasporic subjectivity as either castrating or
invisible. If Rashid's text relies on the elision of the mother to delineate the
queerness of the bonds between father and son, my reading of *East Is East*
conversely foregrounds female diasporic subjectivity as a way to escape reifying
the equation of queer as implicitly male and femaleness (and feminism) as
implicitly heterosexual. This chapter explores the effects of this split between
queer and feminist as it is reproduced and circulated in the realm of popular
Indian cinema in the diaspora.[3] I begin with an examination of how popular
Indian cinema encodes queer female desire, and how this cinematic genre
becomes available to queer viewing strategies as it travels diasporically. I then
turn to a spate of films by South Asian women diasporic filmmakers that
translate the codes and conventions of popular Indian cinema into a form more
in keeping with the realist demands of Hollywood. In tracing this move from
popular Indian cinema to diasporic cinema, I ask how particular representations of queer female desire and subjectivity shift in the process of translation.
What new forms of queer representation does this translation from a national
to a diasporic cinema enable? What possibilities of queer representation does it
concomitantly efface and shut down? Ultimately what does a consideration of
queer representation, as it migrates from a national to a diasporic cinema, tell us
about the dynamic relation between nation and diaspora?

Diasporic Spectatorship, Queer Spectatorship

Given the vastness of its reach, surprisingly few detailed critical, ethnographic,
or historical works have emerged on the reception, consumption, and distribution of popular Indian cinema within different diasporic locations.[4] In
keeping with Sardar's observations, Vijay Mishra argues that the introduction
of Bollywood films to diasporic locations such as Trinidad in the 1930s was "a
crucial factor in the continuation of culture and in the construction of the
imaginary homeland as a homogenous entity."[5] In a later essay titled "Bombay

Cinema and Diasporic Desire," which stands as one of the few attempts to theorize the diasporic reach of Bombay cinema, Mishra writes:

> In the diasporic production and reproduction of "India" one of the key translatable signs . . . is Bombay (Bollywood) cinema, which (as shown in cinema halls and viewed at home on videos and on cable TV such as ATN in Canada or Sahara TV in the United Arab Emirates) has been crucial in bringing the "homeland" into the diaspora as well as creating a culture of imaginary solidarity across heterogeneous linguistic and national groups that make up the South Asian (Indian) diaspora.[6]

Mishra's essay usefully points to the crucial role of popular Indian cinema in the production and reproduction of diasporic subjectivity through a nostalgically evoked national "home" space. However, I would argue that these texts also circulate in the diaspora in less predictable ways. The audiences that make up the South Asian diaspora may very well be heterogeneous linguistically and nationally, as Mishra observes, but their heterogeneity also extends to their bodily and affective desires and identifications with popular cinema. Because the notion of "desire" in Mishra's analysis remains curiously inert, in that it is imagined as always and everywhere heterosexual, the different uses to which diasporic spectators put popular Indian cinema cannot be adequately explored. A consideration of queer spectatorship challenges us to rethink the ways in which popular Indian cinema circulates in the diaspora. This cinema may in fact provide diasporic audiences with the means by which to reterritorialize the "homeland" by making it the locus of queer desire and pleasure, rather than a site of remembered homogeneity and "unity." Queer audiences can thus be seen to constitute what Janet Staiger calls "perverse spectators," a term she uses to "imply a willful turning away from the norm" that particular spectators of classical Hollywood cinema engage in.[7] According to Staiger, "perverse spectators don't do what is expected";[8] it is precisely the unexpected readings, meanings, and affective power that queer diasporic audiences invest in the celluloid images of popular Indian cinema that concern me here.

My interest in tracing the possibilities of "interpretive interventions and appropriations"[9] by queer diasporic audiences allies my project with recent studies in queer and feminist film theory by Judith Mayne, Patricia White, Chris Straayer, and others who theorize queer and female spectatorship.[10] Mayne comments, "One of the most significant directions in spectatorship studies has investigated the gap opened up between the ways in which texts

construct viewers and how those texts may be read or used in ways that depart
from what the institution valorizes."[11] Queer film scholars such as White and
Straayer have produced useful models of queer spectatorship that are fully
aware of the power of the cinematic apparatus in determining viewing positions, while also being attuned to the strategies by which queer counterpublics
actively read, resist, and reappropriate dominant cinematic representations.
In her study of cross-dressing in classical Hollywood cinema, for instance,
Straayer argues that "those viewers who do not experience pleasure in heterosexuality, or for whom pleasurable heterosexuality does not pacify cross-
gender aspirations, need to resist the traditional narrative thrust and to focus
instead on potentially subversive performance and visual elements."[12] Similarly,
Valerie Traub's analysis of the mainstream Hollywood film *Black Widow* suggests that the appropriations and readings of "lesbian" spectators exceed the
film's strategies of containing lesbian pleasure within a heterosexual matrix:
"Insofar as the film cannot be read separately from the transaction taking place
as it unrolls before an audience, *Black Widow* becomes an event of cultural
production, a moment in which 'lesbian' subjectivities are constructed."[13]

Traub's account of how the process of film viewing produces and shapes
lesbian subjectivity and group identification is echoed in Patricia White's account of "lesbian fandoms." White examines how the lesbian fan's fetishization
of the star image is indicative of the ways in which "minoritarian groups . . .
negotiate a pleasurable response to dominant cultural productions that would
seem to exclude them."[14] Lesbian spectators, White argues, wrest the star
image away from the recuperative operation of a narrative that invariably
replaces homoerotic possibilities with heterosexual resolutions; such viewing
strategies are "a way of claiming power and control when one is literally not in
the picture."[15] Yet White follows Judith Mayne in cautioning against assuming
that all resistant readings are necessarily subversive or politically progressive. As
Mayne notes, "The sheer fact that a spectator or group of spectators makes
unauthorized uses of the cinema is no guarantee that such uses are contestatory."[16] White coins the term "retrospectatorship" as a way of defining a
practice of film reception that guards against an overly optimistic, voluntaris-
tic understanding of spectatorial agency while simultaneously acknowledging
how social and cultural contexts determine viewing positions. "Retrospectatorship," White writes, "also recalls the viewing practice attached to film
retrospectives, through which texts of the past, reordered and contextualized,

are expressed anew in a different filmgoing culture. Classical Hollywood cinema belongs to the past but is experienced in a present that affords us new ways of seeing."[17]

The recent scholarship on queer and female spectatorship that I have briefly outlined above is concerned specifically with classical Hollywood cinema within a U.S. viewing context. I want to build on the insights of this important body of work in order to examine the ways in which queer diasporic viewers negotiate their relation to home and homeland through their consumption of popular Indian cinema. In the context of a queer South Asian diaspora, White's notion of "retrospectatorship" takes on additional significance. Not only can the term be used to name how texts belonging to the past constitute queer subjectivities in the present, but it also speaks to the ways in which diasporic viewers reimagine their relation to an "originary" past national location that is given meaning in the present by being the site of queer desire and identification. This reformulation of past national space through a queer diasporic present is a particularly potent intervention given that hegemonic diasporic and nationalist ideologies imagine the past of the nation through heteronormative evocations of home, family, and community.

If queer and feminist studies of spectatorship have yet to take into account a queer diasporic viewing public, much recent work on popular cinema emerging out of Indian film studies wholly obscures the question of queer representation and spectatorial agency. Scholarship on popular Indian cinema has focused for the most part on popular cinema's complex relation to Indian nationalism, the state, and the production of contradictory notions of "tradition" and "modernity."[18] The groundbreaking studies by Indian film scholars such as Madhava Prasad and Ravi Vasudevan have carefully detailed the conditions of production, narrative form, and generic conventions of popular Hindi cinema but have paid less attention to how various spectatorial strategies may at least temporarily displace or destabilize its ideological project.[19] Prasad astutely observes that the reception studies of popular Indian cinema that do exist, which mostly belong to the field of ethnographic popular culture studies, adhere to familiar neocolonial processes of "othering":

In the west such studies (of reception) are engaged in re-affirming the freedom of the "free individual" and demonstrating the automaticity and inevitability of audience resistance to ideological interpellation. The individual subject is free because she is so constructed as to never completely fit the position that the text offers her. On the contrary, non-western subjects [in ethnographic popular culture studies] are distinguished by being completely at home in their ideological environment, the films they see corresponding exactly to their needs.[20]

Prasad's observation is important to keep in mind when considering the possibility of queer interventions into the dominant ideology of the cinema. While I certainly do not want to replicate the notion that queer diasporic spectators are somehow automatically or inevitably resistant readers, I do want to consider the ways in which these spectators (both within South Asia and in the diaspora) may very well not be completely at home in the ideological space of the cinema and may enact particular viewing strategies in order to remake such a space. Indeed, given its particular structure and generic conventions, popular Indian cinema offers myriad opportunities for queer spectatorial interventions; for instance, many film scholars have pointed out that, in a departure from the realist aesthetic and commitment to narrative integrity that mark classical Hollywood cinema, popular Hindi cinema is instead "distinctly and consistently anti-realist."[21] The "fragmented and episodic" structure of the Hindi film, as Prasad has observed, demotes the status of the narrative to being simply one out of many components that make up the cinematic text, such as the fight scene, the song, the dance, and the comedy track.[22] Vasudevan comments that "the disaggregated nature of the popular form, the various 'niches' and forms of address which compose it, have been used . . . for various types of patriotic address throughout the history of the cinema." However, Vasudevan continues, these modes of address "do not necessarily reinforce each other, resulting in an often suggestive tapestry of images and types."[23] Queer spectators are thus able to seize on the numerous ruptures, slippages, and inconsistencies produced by the cinematic text's heterogeneity in form and address to produce pleasures and identifications that may not necessarily be authorized or condoned within the ideological framework of the text itself. Furthermore, Vasudevan notes that the so-called social films of the 1950s marked the ascendance of the heterosexual couple form as "the idealized emotional unit for a new society";[24] yet as Moinik Biswas points out, the journey from the familial to conjugal space "that is completed in Hollywood films . . . remains largely unfulfilled in Indian popular cinema."[25] The heterosexual couple form does not constitute an autonomous unit within popular Indian cinema but is instead "repeatedly reabsorbed into the parental patriarchal family and is committed to its maintenance."[26] Again, this suggests that the structure of heterosexual coupledom within popular Indian cinematic texts may not be totally impervious to insurgent, alternative forms and organizations of sexual desire.

Reading the codes of Bollywood cinema through a specifically queer diasporic viewing practice allows us to "see" the various articulations of same-sex desire on the screen. Such a viewing practice makes legible nonheteronormative arrangements within rigidly heterosexual structures and reveals how queer articulations of desire and pleasure both draw on and infiltrate popular culture. While queer reading practices alone cannot prevent the violences of heteronormativity, they do intervene in formulations of "home" and diaspora that—in their elision and disavowal of the particularities of queer subjectivities—inevitably reproduce the heteronormative family as central to national identity. This particular viewing practice conceptualizes a viewing public as located within multiple diasporic sites, and the text itself as accruing multiple, sometimes contradictory meanings within these various locations. In other words, a queer diasporic framework allows us to conceive of both the text and the viewer in motion. Cinematic images which in their "originary" contexts simply reiterate conventional nationalist and gender ideologies may, through queer reading practices, be refashioned to become the very foundation of a queer culture both in South Asia and in the diaspora. Judith Mayne's observation of the ways in which particular images in Hollywood cinema become iconic in lesbian culture is useful to keep in mind here: "Some cinematic images have proven irresistibly seductive as far as lesbian readings are concerned . . . [Such images] have been cited and reproduced so frequently in the context of gay and lesbian culture that they have almost acquired lives of their own."[27] Patricia White, building on Mayne's comment, adds that these images "seem to seduce independently of the film texts, which work to contain any lesbian implications through heterosexual narrative resolutions."[28] These observations on the iconic status of Hollywood images in queer culture are particularly relevant when considering South Asian queer diasporic spectatorship. In the context of the material practices that produce the space of queer public culture in the diaspora (such as film festivals, drag performances, Web sites, parades, and parties), particular cinematic images that I discuss in this chapter do indeed acquire "lives of their own," emerging repeatedly as touchstones for shared diasporic identifications.

The song and dance sequence, which is one of the key components of Bollywood cinema, takes on particular significance in the context of queer spectatorship. The fact that most popular Hindi films feature an average of six song and dance sequences suggests that these scenes may need to be taken just as seriously as (if not more so) the film's main plot or narrative.[29] As Vivek Dhareshwar and Tejaswini Niranjana observe, "the song/dance sequence in Indian film has always been a relatively autonomous block, one of the requirements of manufacture rather than a diegetic necessity."[30] The censorship code in popular Indian cinema, a legacy of British colonialism that was formally instituted in the 1950s with the creation of the Central Board of Film Censors, prohibited " 'excessively passionate love scenes,' 'indelicate sexual situations,' and 'scenes suggestive of immorality.' "[31] Interestingly, however, the song and dance sequence is not subject to the same forms of state control as is the rest of the film, as Monika Mehta makes clear in her discussion of the censorship debates that surrounded the hit song "*Choli ke peeche kya hai*" (What is beneath your blouse) from the Bollywood film *Khalnayak* (The Villain, dir. Subhash Gai, 1993). Mehta notes that even while state censors were busy debating the "vulgarity" of the song, it was circulating unimpeded through new technologies that were impervious to state scrutiny. The song was in fact released on audio cassette while the film was still in production, and went on to be shown as a music video on unregulated cable channels—a product of India's liberalization and the advent of satellite television in the early 1990s. The "*Choli ke peeche kya hai*" debate "revealed the limits of state authority" in relation to new technologies such as music videos and audio cassettes: "As a medium which was not subject to state censorship, audio cassettes could circulate and carry potentially subversive . . . or *vulgar* messages freely."[32] Charges of vulgarity, obscenity, and immodesty that are leveled against song and dance sequences, as Mehta points out, invariably involve representations of the female body and female sexuality. Certainly song and dance sequences are the primary arena in which the female body and female sexuality are on display, in a way that may be disallowed in the other components that make up the film text. Shohini Ghosh argues in her discussion of Madhuri Dixit, the leading Bollywood actress and star of *Khalnayak*, "As a space of resistance, song sequences allow female protagonists to masquerade as someone else. Here, heroines can transcend the narrative confines of the script and conventional expectations by indulging in excess, badness, abandon and revelry."[33] I would add that these sequences act as a place of fantasy and excess, not only for the female film star but also for the viewer, that cannot be contained or accounted for in the rest of the narrative. Given that song/dance sequences "allow things to be said which cannot be said elsewhere,"[34] it is not surprising that it is often in these moments of fantasy that queer, non-heteronormative desire emerges.

The song and dance sequence is also the most transnational of all the various components that make up the Bollywood film: often a particular sequence travels across national borders independently from the film in which it originally appeared.[35] We can therefore understand the song and dance sequence as a peculiarly *queer* form: because it falls outside the exigencies of narrative coherence and closure, it can function as a space from which to critique the unrelenting heteronormativity that this narrative represents.[36] Furthermore, the unmoored quality of the song-and-dance sequence—its apparent detachment from the rest of the narrative and its capacity to circulate transnationally separate from the film itself—makes it particularly available for queer viewing strategies. Indeed certain sequences come to occupy iconic status as they are creatively appropriated by queer audiences in different diasporic locations. To cite just one example out of many, the theme song from the classic masala western *Sholay* (Flames, dir. Ramesh Sippy, 1975)—which is sung as a duet celebrating male friendship by the legendary male buddy duo of the seventies, Amitabh Bhacchan and Dharmendra—has become a diasporic gay male anthem of sorts, sung at gay pride parades from New York to London to San Francisco. The song and dance sequence can also be read as a specifically queer *diasporic* form, not simply because of its transnational circulation but also because of its historical function as a discursive space where debates around high and low art, and authenticity and inauthenticity, have been staged. Sumita Chakravarty writes, in her study of nationalism and popular Indian cinema, that following Indian independence in 1947, "much of the debate over classical versus hybrid culture centered around film music and dance, for in the view of many purists, nowhere was the 'bastardization' of the classical arts more apparent than in the realm of film music and dance compositions."[37] This nationalist framing of the song and dance sequence as a debased, bastardized version of "authentic" national culture curiously echoes the discursive production of both "queer" and "diaspora" as similarly degraded forms that act merely as poor copies of the "original," figured in both national and sexual terms. The song and dance sequence, then, becomes the cinematic space where dominant discourses of diaspora and queerness—as inauthentic, illegitimate, and abjected Others to both heterosexuality and the nation—are collapsed, negotiated, and contested.

The homoerotics of the song and dance sequence, which are so imaginatively mined by queer diasporic audiences, are the focus of Thomas Waugh's analysis of the male buddy films of the mid-1990s. Waugh argues that Bollywood knowingly references queer desire and even an emergent Indian gay identity in these sequences, which become one of the primary spaces where *dosti* (male homosocial friendship and bonding) is expressed and articulated.[38] Madhava Prasad notes that the concept of *dosti* functions in Hindi cinema "as the code of fraternity that binds men to a separate society." Prasad writes:

> The code of *dosti* takes precedence over that of heterosexual love and in the case of conflict, the latter must yield to the former. Thus, in a conflict over love between male friends, the woman remains out of the picture, while the two males decide between themselves who will have her . . . The bond of *dosti* is, then, a prototype of the compact among men that institutes the social contract.[39]

Prasad's astute observation makes clear that the idealization of *dosti* within the song and dance sequence may indeed sideline heterosexual narrative resolutions—and make images of male bonding readily available for a queer male viewership—but only through a simultaneous investment in misogyny and patriarchal kinship arrangements. It is important to bear in mind that representations of male homosociality/homoeroticism have vastly different gendered meanings and effects on the Bollywood screen than do representations of female homosociality/homoeroticism. While the song and dance sequence can function as a "space of resistance" for the female film star and the queer (female) viewer, for the male film star and queer (male) viewer it can serve to reinscribe normative gender ideologies through its celebration of *dosti*. The different gendered effects of the song and dance sequence underscore the importance of Janet Staiger's critique of the notion that "doing something different" with the cinema "is necessarily politically progressive." Rather, Staiger suggests, "each act of deviant (*and normative*) viewing requires historical and political analysis to locate its effects and judge its politics."[40]

In the following section, I trace the ways in which popular Indian cinema encodes alternative sexualities and desires between women and makes certain spaces available for their representation. I focus specifically on representations of female same-sex desire because it is precisely this form of desire that is rendered impossible and unimaginable within dominant nationalist and diasporic discourses. Given the close alliance of popular Indian cinema with Indian national identity,[41] what does it mean for Bollywood as a national cinema to register queer female desire on the screen, when such desire is consistently framed within nationalist discourse as antinational, foreign, and inauthentic? If representations of male-male *dosti* often serve to buttress patriarchal and nationalist narratives, do representations of female homosociality/ homoeroticism conversely rupture the dominant nationalist script or are they carefully contained by it? The answers to these questions cannot be approached by looking for "lesbians" in Bollywood, as any such attempt would falsely presume that queer representation in Bollywood film rests on the same logic of visibility as do dominant Euro-American constructions of "gay" and "lesbian" identity. Reading the codes of Bollywood queerly demands that we look not so much for characters who are explicitly marked as sexual or gender deviants, but rather to those moments emerging at the fissures of rigidly heterosexual structures that can be transformed into queer imaginings.

Queer Bollywood:
Female Homosociality/Homoeroticism in Popular Indian Cinema

Bollywood cinema is saturated with rich images of intense love and friendship between women in the context of archetypal spaces of female homosociality, such as brothels, women's prisons, girls' schools, the middle-class home, and the *zenana* (women's quarters in elite Hindu and Muslim homes). As is apparent in the song and dance sequences from a series of films from the 1980s and 1990s, these women-only spaces allow numerous possibilities for female friendship to slip into queer desire. I am interested in identifying some of the visual codes used in popular film to depict this slippage between female homosociality and female homoeroticism that a later film like Deepa Mehta's *Fire* (1996), which I discuss in the following chapter, so productively exploits. Patricia White's discussion of the category of "femme films"—films addressed to female audiences and set in women's spaces—is particularly germane. For White, the invisibility of female homeroticism in Hollywood cinema (mandated by the Motion Picture Production Code's banning of homoerotic content) in fact constitutes a strategy of representation. She writes, "The femme paradigm covers the world of the women's picture: institutions such as schools and prisons and hotels for women, but also the home. . . . My perspective dissociates these sites and practices from an exclusive and exclusionary association with heterosexual femininity."[42] From *Razia Sultan* (dir. Kamal Amrohi, 1983) to Deepa Mehta's *Fire*, spaces of female homosociality in popular Indian cinema enact precisely this dissociation between (hyper)femininity and heterosexuality. As White comments in relation to classical Hollywood cinema, "lesbian visibility is veiled in the feminine display that is the cinema's primary dream language rather than embodied in the cross-gender identifications offered by the invert or the butch."[43] Similarly, in many of the scenes I discuss below, female homoeroticism is signaled through hyperbolic femininity rather than through the figure of the cross-dressing or butch-coded character. While I focus primarily on popular Indian cinema, I also include in my discussion examples of what is known as "middle" or "parallel" cinema, that is, the wave of "socially conscious" films that were made in India between the late 1960s and early 1980s. Parallel cinema was supported by state funding and attempted to chart a middle course between "art" films and the song and dance formulas of popular Hindi film.[44] Including different genres within this discussion allows for an examination of the ways in which each genre both enables and forecloses the possibilities of representing non-heteronormative desires and subjectivities on screen.

   Utsav (The Festival, dir. Girish Karnad, 1984) and *Subhah / Umbartha* (Dawn / Threshold, dir. Jabbar Patel, 1981) are two films from the 1980s that provide useful points of entry for considering the slippage between female homosociality and female homoeroticism on the Bollywood screen. *Utsav* takes place primarily in and around a brothel and *Subhah* in a women's reformatory, and both hint at the alternative forms of sexuality that exist outside the middle-class home. *Utsav* belongs to the genre of courtesan films that plays on the nostalgia for an ancient erotic Indian past.[45] The narrative follows Vasantsena (played by Bollywood icon Rekha), a fourth-century prostitute, as she falls in love with a young Brahmin merchant named Charudutt. Halfway through the film, Charudutt is temporarily shunted out of the narrative by a growing friendship between Vasantsena and his wife Aditi. In a telling scene, Vasantsena and Aditi sing to each other after exchanging clothes and jewelry. This act of making oneself desirable, of dressing and undressing, donning and discarding saris and jewelry in particular, is a sexually loaded trope in popular Indian cinema,

The homoerotics of female homosocial space: Vasantsena (Rekha)
and Aditi (Anuradha) in *Utsav* (The Festival, dir. Girish Karnad,
1984). *Photo courtesy of the National Film Archive of India.*

having connotations of wedding nights and signifying a prelude to heterosexual sex. *Utsav* reworks the typical love triangle of popular film where two women compete for the man's attention; here, it is Charudutt who is sidelined while the two women play erotically together. Interestingly, some feminist analyses of the film have critiqued this scene as merely "playing out the ultimate male fantasy," whereby female bonding between the wife and the courtesan enable the man to "move without guilt between a nurturing wife and a glamourous mistress."[46] Clearly such an interpretation misses the more nuanced eroticism between the two women that a queer reading makes apparent. A queer reading might also allow for the possibility of triangulated desire that does not solidify into "lesbian" or "heterosexual," but rather opens up a third space where both hetero- and homoerotic relations coexist simultaneously.[47] The relation between the two women also hints at the histories of female homoerotic relations that mark the space of the *tawai'if* (courtesan) household, as Veena Talwar Oldenburg's ethnography of courtesans in 1970s Lucknow, North India, documents.[48]

The reversal of the standard heterosexual triangle that is evident in *Utsav* is also apparent in the 1981 film *Subhah*, starring Smita Patil. Firmly situated within the realist aesthetic and thematic concerns of the middle cinema genre, *Subhah's* framing of female sexuality makes apparent how the realism of middle cinema frequently proves less productive for queer viewership than the excess and fantasy of the Bollywood genre. Upon its release, *Subhah* was heralded as a feminist fable, in that it followed the struggles of Savitri, a middle-class house-wife, to leave the confines of middle-class domesticity and become the warden of a women's reformatory. As the film's alternate title (*Umbartha*, or Threshold) suggests, Savitri's process of individuation is figured in terms of movement, with her leaving behind the gendered, hierarchical familial arrangements of the middle-class household and entering instead the confines of the all-women's reformatory. The film ends with a familiar image in "middle cinema" women's films, with Savitri on a train, embarking alone on an unspecified journey after having left both her family and the reformatory behind. Rosemary George usefully situates *Subhah* alongside the literary genre of "domestic fictions" of the 1980s written by and about elite Indian women and their "desire for a feminine/ feminist self that will be a viable *counter* position to the gendered roles of daughter, mother and wife."[49] George reads Savitri's ultimate rejection of middle-class domesticity and her decision to extricate herself from the family scene as significantly altering the terms of the domestic plot, which often resituates the elite Indian woman within the confines of the home.

While the film certainly makes important changes to the script of domestic fiction, as George argues, it is crucial to note that it does so only through the familiar move of pitting queerness (or more specifically, lesbianism) against feminism. *Subhah* is distinguished from the other so-called women's films of the era (as well as the literary domestic fictions that George analyzes) in that it explicitly references female same-sex eroticism: two of the female inmates in the reformatory that Savitri supervises are named as "lesbian" through the use of the English word.[50] Predictably, the "lesbianism" of the inmates is framed in opposition to the burgeoning feminist consciousness of the film's heroine: Savitri labels the two inmates as pathological even as she tries to defend them to her superior. The physical and psychic movement of the feminist subject, then, is opposed to the fixity of the "lesbian" characters, who remain firmly situated within a narrative of sickness and pathology. On a narrative level, the film is unable to articulate female desire and sexuality—let alone female same-sex desire—in terms other than pathology; Savitri herself is shown repeatedly refusing sex with her husband but never actively desiring anyone else.

Feminist autonomy at the expense of "lesbians" in *Subhah* (Dawn, dir.
Jabbar Patel, 1981). Smita Patil as Savitri. *Photo courtesy of the National
Film Archive of India.*

Yet one instance in *Subhah* exceeds its own narrative trajectory and hints at
an alternative narrativization of female same-sex desire. Significantly, the scene
is the only song and dance sequence in the film, again confirming the cinematic depiction of the song and dance sequence as a fantasy space removed
from the exigencies of the social realist narrative. The inmates are seen celebrating a festival, and the camera cuts repeatedly from the face and body of one
of the "lesbian" characters to that of the other, who gazes at her adoringly. The
scene reworks the familiar triangulation between characters in song and dance
sequences in popular Indian film, where two women dance for the male
character whose appraising gaze orchestrates the scene. In *Subhah*, however, a
triangulated relation forms between the two "lesbian" characters and Savitri,
who is drawn into the circuit of exchange of looks between the two, both
returns and receives their admiring and curious glances. The scene is interesting in that it also implicates the viewer within this exchange of looks
and, however briefly, articulates female desire outside the realm of pathology in a way that the rest of the narrative is unable to do. Instead, it hints
at the particular forms and organizations of female same-sex desire that are

Hyperbolic femininity in *Razia Sultan* (dir. Kamal Amrohi, 1983).
Hema Malini is in the title role. *Photo courtesy of the National Film
Archive of India.*

produced within the homosocial spaces beyond the private domestic space of
the middle-class home; and these forms exist, surprisingly, even when those
spaces are thoroughly saturated by the state's patriarchal authority.

The ultimate pathologizing of "lesbian" desire in *Subhah* suggests that narratives that explicitly name female same-sex desire as "lesbian" may be less
interesting than those moments within the narrative that represent female
homoeroticism in the absence of "lesbians." Such a moment is particularly apparent in the Bollywood historical epic *Razia Sultan*, director Kamal Amrohi's
elaborate portrayal of the life of the first female ruler of the Delhi Sultanate in
the thirteenth century. The famed Bollywood actress of the 1970s, Hema
Malini, plays the Mughal princess who pines for her male lover while being
comforted by her lady-in-waiting (Parveen Babi) in the space of the *zenana*, or
women's quarters. The *zenana*, as Antoinette Burton reminds us, is a particularly fraught site within Indian colonial and nationalist discourse and had
emerged by the 1930s as an emblem of "traditional India" for both British
colonialists and Indian nationalists. Burton writes, "As sati had been a century
earlier, the zenana—and the purdahnashin [secluded women] with it—was one
of the chief ideological sites through which power was sought, negotiated and

contested in the two decades before Indian independence."[51] Within British colonial discourse, the *zenana* concretized all that was "primitive" and "backward" about Indian "culture." Indian nationalist evocations of the *zenana*, in contrast, revalorized it as a vanishing sign of authentic and traditional India. In *Razia Sultan*, the *zenana* is portrayed in terms that borrow from both of these contradictory colonial and nationalist constructions, in that it is imagined as a lushly opulent, nostalgically evoked site of female pleasure, leisure, and eroticism. In this sense, the *zenana* space in the film brings to mind Malek Alloula's dissection of the harem in the colonial imaginary. In his analysis of French colonial photographs of Algerian women in the early twentieth century, Alloula finds that the harem is portrayed as "a universe of generalized perversion and . . . the absolute limitlessness of pleasure."[52] A key element of that perversion is what Alloula terms "oriental sapphism," or the titillating promise/threat of lesbianism that shadows all-female space.[53] In one of the most famous scenes in *Razia Sultan*, both actresses are sumptuously dressed in high femme regalia as they recline in a small, swan-shaped boat that is being rowed around a palace lake by two young girls. The spectatorial gaze in the scene is allied with that of the girls who knowingly watch over the antics of the women. Razia lies languorously, her face turned toward the camera and away from her lady-in-waiting, who ostensibly sings to her mistress about her absent male lover while she caresses Razia's hair, face, and body. The scene closes with the lady-in-waiting turning Razia's face toward her and finally bending down to kiss her as a large white feather strategically blocks the gaze of the spectator. The illicit nature of what is taking place behind the feather is registered by a reaction shot in which one of the young girls collapses in giggles as the other cautions her to be quiet. This sequence is a brilliant reworking of the visual conventions of the Bollywood historical epic, explicitly referencing a scene from the classic film *Mughal-e-Azam* (The Great Mughal, dir. K. Asif, 1961), where the hero Dilip Kumar kisses the heroine Madhubala while passing a white feather in front of their faces.[54] While *Razia Sultan*'s use of this fetishistic masking device can be attributed to the prohibition on kissing in Indian cinema, it also speaks to the ways in which female homoeroticism is visually encoded within popular cinema: female homoerotic desire and pleasure are often mediated by and routed through heterosexuality as well as class and generational difference. Just as *Razia Sultan* disassociates hyperfemininity from heterosexuality, so too does it disassociate queer female desire from a visible "lesbian" subjectivity.

Patricia White reminds us that "what is prohibited by the [Motion Picture

Production] Code or ideologically excluded from dominant representation, what is unnamed, may nevertheless signify on screen."[55] The limits of visibility and the uses of invisibility that are so clear when contrasting *Subhah's* "lesbians" with *Razia Sultan's* lack of them are also apparent in the vastly popular *Khalnayak*, the controversial 1993 film that made actress Madhuri Dixit the reigning Bollywood star of the 1990s. Monika Mehta notes that while advocates in favor of censoring the film's infamous hit song "*Choli ke peeche kya hai*" cited the need to protect Indian women from gross displays of "vulgarity," such arguments cannot account for the film's popularity among middle-class urban Indian women. Many of these women delighted in the song's overt representation of female sexuality: "In an atmosphere where the consequences of any sexual expression are sexual violation or harassment, many of Dixit's middle-class female fans find her performances pleasurable because they associate sexual agency with these performances."[56] While Mehta is no doubt correct in her suggestion that female fans access the overt sexuality of Dixit through modes of identification, I would also hold open the possibility that modes of desire are also at work between the female spectator and Dixit's image on the screen. "*Choli ke peeche kya hai*," after all, is staged as a scene where two women (Madhuri Dixit and Nina Gupta) engage in a highly eroticized duet as they ostensibly sing and dance for the male hero (Sanjay Dutt). As in *Razia Sultan,* the erotic interplay between the two women is routed through class hierarchy: the voice of the heroine Ganga (played by Dixit) is alternately interrupted and joined by the rougher, less schooled voice of her dance partner, who embodies a particular class stereotype of free, unbridled low-class/caste sexuality. The possibility of female homoerotic desire is both suggested and apparently foreclosed: the women never share the same frame, and the camera repeatedly interrupts their dance sequence by cutting from shots of their bodies to Dutt as he gazes at the women appreciatively. Hence Dutt's spectatorial pleasure and admiring gaze seem to orchestrate the erotic circuits of the scene.

Yet we can also read the scene as setting up a structure of female homosociality, where, following Eve Sedgwick's formulation of erotic triangles, female homoerotic desire between Dixit and Gupta is routed and made intelligible through a triangulated relation to the male hero.[57] As the song progresses, Dutt's authority as privileged spectator is consistently undercut: rather than embodying a virile and potent masculinity, he appears oddly ineffectual, offering Dixit money only to have her throw it in his face and then grab it back when he least expects it. Not only does the sexual availability of the two women elude Dutt's monetary control but it spins out of his spectatorial control as well. Although the male hero looks on, he becomes peripheral to the scene of desire as it takes shape between the two women, who are clearly more engaged with each other than with him. The song's chorus, repeated suggestively by the gyrating heroines, translates from Hindi as "what's under your *choli* (blouse), what's under your *chuniri* (scarf)." This phrase initially seems to reference a sexual economy of secrecy and disclosure, a promise of the truth of sex that lies underneath the *chuniri* and *choli*, waiting to be uncovered. However, the song also refuses to grant the listener/viewer scopic satisfaction, and ends by answering its repeated question with the line: "My heart is in my blouse, my heart is under my *chuniri*, I'll give this heart to my lover." This apparently anticlimactic ending gestures to an economy of desire and pleasure that exceeds fixed framings of sexuality within dominant regimes of visibility.

Both *Razia Sultan* and *Khalnayak*, then, speak to the ways in which particular representations of queer female sexuality escape and confound the realm of the visible even as they take shape in the most visual of registers (the Bollywood screen). Scenes such as the ones I have discussed here suggest alternative formulations of female homoeroticism that cannot necessarily be produced in popular film under the sign of "lesbian." These scenes become eminently available for a queer diasporic viewership because they encode female homoeroticism outside the logic of visibility and, therefore, homophobia. Indeed the possibility of a fully sexualized form of female-female desire that films such as *Razia Sultan* or *Khalnayak* hint at comes to fruition, in a sense, in the uses to which these films have been put by queer diasporic South Asians. In the 1990s, for instance, the song "*Choli ke peeche kya hai*" became a staple at parties and in drag performances within South Asian queer spaces in multiple diasporic locations. And in the landmark documentary *Khush* (dir. Pratibha Parmar, 1991), which traces an emerging diasporic South Asian queer movement in the late 1980s and early 1990s, British Asian director Parmar intercuts the realism of talking-head interviews of lesbians and gay men with a striking fantasy sequence where two women, both clad in Bollywood-inspired finery, watch old Hindi movie extravaganzas as they stroke each other's hair. In a direct citation and homage to *Razia Sultan* (which in turn cites *Mughal-E-Azam*), the final shot of *Khush* depicts one of the women turning the face of the other toward her as she bends

Queering the *zenana* in *Khush* (dir. Pratibha Parmar,
1991). *Photo courtesy of Women Make Movies.*

down to bestow a kiss on her lips. Parmar here cleverly reframes the kiss
between Parveen Babi and Hema Malini: her translation of the scene into a
queer diasporic context refuses to block our spectatorial gaze and instead
acknowledges the pleasures afforded by dominant representations of hyperbolic femininity and female homosociality to queer viewers, while rendering
explicit their homoeroticism. The masking device of *Razia Sultan* is transformed in Parmar's queer imagination into a screen on which images from
Bollywood cinema are projected and which acts as a backdrop to the inter-
action between the two women. By aligning the look of the spectator with that
of the women in the film, Parmar interpellates a South Asian diasporic lesbian
viewing public that is literate in the cinematic codes that are being referenced.

As this moment in *Khush* suggests, given that explicit gender transgression in women is definitively (and sometimes violently) resolved into heterosexuality on the Bollywood screen,[58] it may be more useful for queer purposes to draw on those moments in Bollywood cinema where extreme gender conformity encodes female homoeroticism, and as such allows queer sexuality to erupt at the interstices of heterosexuality.

Queer viewing strategies, then, make good on the potential queerness of female homosocial space as it is represented in popular Indian cinema. They do so by fetishizing those moments where female homosociality slips seamlessly into female homoeroticism; thus such strategies offer a way to bypass the censure, punishment, and disciplinary power that overt and explicitly marked representations of "deviant" bodies and desires inevitably entail. The queer diasporic circulation of the song and dance sequences from *Razia Sultan* or *Khalnayak* speak to what Patricia White terms "cut and paste fetishism," the acts of appropriation and recontextualization through which lesbian spectators resolve "the contradiction between desire and denial, delectable image and depressing story."[59] As these images travel transnationally, they serve to provide a common visual vocabulary for queer spectators in disparate diasporic locations, one that reconciles not only the contradiction between queer image and heterosexual narrative, as White suggests, but also the contradiction between the space of the nation as implicitly heterosexual and the space of diaspora as foreign, inauthentic, and indeed "queer." Through the fetishizing of particular scenes and images from Bollywood cinema, queer diasporic spectators lay claim to the "home" space of the nation by reading queerness back into national space. The nation is thus remembered and reframed as the locus of queer desire, pleasure, and identification.

Translating Bollywood:
Feminist Filmmakers of the South Asian Diaspora

The early years of the new millennium were marked by an explosion of interest in Bollywood cinema in the West, from Bollywood-inspired works by non–South Asian directors,[60] as well as South Asian diasporic filmmakers,[61] to the success of Bollywood films like *Lagaan* (Land Tax, dir. Ashutosh Gowariker, 2001). The global reach of Bollywood is hardly a new phenomenon, but what is new at this particular historical moment, and therefore worth interrogating, is the popularity of the Bollywood idiom among mainstream non–South Asian audiences in North America and Europe. One could argue that the newfound popularity of Bollywood cinema outside its usual national and diasporic audiences marks but the latest phase of "U.S. Orientalism," to once again use Vijay Prashad's phrase: along with yoga and *mehndi* (henna), the aesthetics of Bollywood is part of the most recent manifestation of Indophilia, where decontextualized markers of exotic otherness elide more complex histories of colonial and postcolonial power relations.[62] But this interpretation is complicated by the fact that the ubiquity of the language and aesthetics of Bollywood in the West to a significant extent has been due to the mainstream success of films by South Asian diasporic women filmmakers such as Mira Nair's *Monsoon Wedding* (set in contemporary New Delhi), Deepa Mehta's *Bollywood/Hollywood* (set in Toronto), and Gurinder Chadha's *Bend It Like Beckham* (set in London). All three films, to a greater or lesser degree, use not only the Bollywood genre but specifically the Bollywood wedding film as their aesthetic and thematic template. How then is Bollywood cinema's particular lexicon of queer representation transformed in the process of translation? I want to illuminate how these diasporic translators of Bollywood use a feminist idiom to "modernize" Bollywood form and content—a feminist framework that, surprisingly, requires a homophobic subtext. Not surprisingly, perhaps, the feminism and homophobia in these films are played out through the medium of dance: in particular the song and dance sequence that is so emblematic of the Bollywood genre.

Mira Nair's *Monsoon Wedding* demands particular scrutiny as the film garnered overwhelmingly positive reviews from North American and European critics and was the first Indian film in forty-four years to win the top prize at the Venice International Film Festival. Interestingly, the film was mislabeled by non–South Asian critics and audiences as a conventional "Bollywood" offering when in fact it strategically evokes Bollywood while clearly residing within the genre of independent cinema geared toward an international film festival circuit.[63] Indeed, it is the telling differences between *Monsoon Wedding* and the template of the Bollywood film that concern me here. Nair's film also warrants particular attention for mobilizing narratives around gender, sexuality, and "home" space that are replicated in the films by Mehta and Chadha. Briefly, *Monsoon Wedding* centers on the wedding celebrations in an elite Punjabi family in contemporary New Delhi. Predictable complications ensue as the family converges in a luxurious upper-middle class Delhi home from various points in the diaspora: the groom arrives from Houston, where he works as an engineer, while other relatives arrive from Australia. Nair has stated that while the film evokes the generic conventions of Bollywood cinema, it is her attempt to make a Bollywood film her way, by representing in particular what it means to be an affluent single woman in a globalized and cosmopolitan India.[64] *Monsoon Wedding* is very self-consciously "feminist" in its depiction of the women of the family as (hetero)sexually autonomous subjects: the bride-to-be, for instance, is no virginal innocent but rather is carrying on a torrid affair with a married older man. In this sense Nair's film may initially appear as a radical feminist reworking of the rash of Bollywood films of the mid 1990s, aptly dubbed "neo-conservative romances" by Thomas Waugh.[65] *Monsoon Wedding* can in fact be seen as a relatively direct translation of the immensely popular film *Hum Aapke Hain Koun . . . !* (Who Am I to You?, dir. Sooraj Barjatya, 1994). *Hum Aapke Hain Koun . . . !* (or HAHK as it is popularly referred to) was hailed by its director as "a tribute to the traditional Indian joint family."[66] Like *Monsoon Wedding*, it focuses on the wedding rituals in an elite North Indian family while it celebrates the conspicuous consumption of the newly formed transnational capitalist class which emerged with India's embrace of economic liberalization in the 1990s. *Monsoon Wedding* replicates HAHK's attempt, as Patricia Uberoi puts it, "to meld haut bourgeois lifestyles seamlessly with religiosity and with traditionalism in rituals—thereby legitimizing affluence as a value in itself."[67] Nair's film clearly replays the familiar binary opposition of tradition versus modernity, even as it claims to transcend it. The reification of this binary is made particularly clear in Nair's production notes for the film, which describe it in the following terms: "Set in today's globalized Delhi, *Monsoon Wedding* interweaves the ancient and the modern, the old fashioned and the irreverent, the innocent and the sexual, to tell a modern Indian story . . . for many viewers, *Monsoon Wedding* will be their first glimpse of contemporary Indian society and Punjabi culture."[68] By mobilizing these categories of tradition and modernity, and by promising the non–South Asian viewer a kind of ethnographic realism that offers unmediated access to a heretofore hidden and unknowable world, Nair functions as native informant and tour guide who traffics in the production of "authenticity" for the global marketplace. Indeed, Nair stresses in the production notes that the film depicts a "true knowledge" of an upper-class, cosmopolitan, urban milieu in

India, one that is captured in all its "authenticity" on hand-held sixteen milli-meter film.[69]

What are the effects, then, of moving from Bollywood as a national cinema to Bollywood as a product of diasporic consumers and producers, from Hindi to English, from a staunchly conservative, nationalist narrative of Hindu pa-triarchal relations to an ostensibly feminist, diasporic celebration of familial harmony? The film critic Roger Ebert, in a glowing review of *Monsoon Wed-ding*, wrote that the film's dialogue, which alternates between English, Hindi, and Punjabi, means that "we [a non–South Asian viewing public] have the pleasure of seeing a foreign film and the convenience of understanding almost everything that is said." In the same review, Ebert notes approvingly that the film is more in line with the conventions of the Hollywood musical than the Bollywood film: "There is a lot of singing and dancing in *Monsoon Wedding*, but all of it emerges in a *logical* way from the action, as it might in a Hollywood musical" (my italics).[70] We need to ask, then, what is lost and gained in this process of translating the Bollywood film into terms that seem "logical" and "conveniently understandable" to a non–South Asian viewing public. In trac-ing this translation from Bollywood to Hollywood, I do not mean to suggest that they exist in a strictly binary relation: Bollywood has always promis-cuously absorbed, transformed, and indigenized Hollywood genres to suit local needs and expectations.[71] Nevertheless it is worth asking who pays the price for this new intelligibility of Bollywood to audiences more accustomed to the conventions of Hollywood.

The answer lies in the changing meaning and function of the song and dance sequence as we move from Bollywood to Hollywood. A closer look at *HAHK* in relation to the representational strategies discussed in the previous section makes particularly apparent how the song and dance sequence constitutes a moment of excess that cannot be contained within the narrative trajectory of the Bollywood film and hence is available for queer viewing purposes. It is critical to note that the popular press attributed the tremendous and sustained popularity of *HAHK*—the largest-grossing film in the history of popular Indian cinema on its release in 1994—to its return to "family values," a phrase which apparently referred to the film's rejection of the sex and violence formulas of other popular Hindi movies. However, this phrase speaks more to the ways in which the film works within Hindu nationalist discourses of the nation by articulating a desire for a nostalgic "return" to an impossible ideal, that of sup-posedly "traditional" Hindu family and kinship arrangements that

Family togetherness in *Hum Aapke Hain Koun . . . !* (Who Am I to You?, dir.
Sooraj Barjatya, 1994). *Photo courtesy of the National Film Archive of India.*

are staunchly upper middle class and heterosexual. Furthermore, several critics
have argued that its immense popularity is due to its seamless reconciliation of
the tensions between India's economic liberalization of the early 1990s and
"traditional" Indian/Hindu values by reconstituting conventional patriarchal
gender relations in the context of a newly globalized Indian middle class.[72] The
film, then, functions as a crucial node in the production of public culture as a
space where (to return to Appadurai's and Breckenridge's definition) the contradictions between the transnational and the national most clearly emerge and
are negotiated.[73] Vijay Mishra also situates the film in the context of the
cataclysmic destruction of the Islamic mosque, the Babri Masjid, in Ayodhya,
northern India, by Hindu nationalists in 1992. Mishra writes that the film
"started a whole new trend about narratives built around the idyllic extended
family order that interweaves the Ramayana [a central text in Hinduism] into
the fabric of the text. The film presents the Ramayana as central to the ethos of
tolerance and liberalism albeit within a dominant patriarchal Hindu order
where a woman's sexuality is circumscribed by respectable social norms."[74]

Yet *HAHK*'s most famous song and dance sequence (the staging of its hit song

"*Didi tera devar divana*" ("Sister, your brother-in-law is crazy") constitutes a moment of rupture and queer incursion into the film's dominant Hindu nationalist, patriarchal ideology. Significantly, the film received substantial critical attention from Indian film scholars, who read it as indicative of the complicity between transnational capital and Hindu nationalist ideology in the context of India's increasingly global economy. Curiously, however, the gendered and sexual dynamics of this particular scene in the film were, for the most part, left unremarked.[75] The scene takes place during an all-female celebration of an upcoming birth; into this space of female homosociality enters Rita (a female relative) cross-dressed as the film's male hero in an identical white suit, who proceeds to dance suggestively with the heroine Nisha (played by Madhuri Dixit) and with various other women in the room. What follows is an elaborate dance sequence where the cross-dressed woman and Dixit engage in a teasing, sexualized exchange that parodies the trappings of the conventional middle-class Hindu family arrangements of marriage, heterosexuality, domesticity, and motherhood. Halfway through the song, however, order is apparently restored as the cross-dressed interloper is chased out of the room by the "real" hero (played by Salman Khan). The cross-dressed character disappears from the scene and Khan proceeds to claim his rightful place opposite Dixit.

This moment constitutes precisely what Roger Ebert would call the illogic and unintelligibility of the Bollywood song and dance sequence: the cross-dressed character never appears again and the entire scene is never referenced in the remainder of the film. Yet this scene of female cross-dressing was seized on by queer audiences both in South Asia and in the diaspora as disrupting, if only for a moment, the otherwise extremely conservative marriage plot and consolidation of heteronormativity in which the rest of the film is so heavily invested. Shohini Ghosh, in her reading of the film, suggests that "this seemingly innocent family drama presents a large canvas of erotic possibilities."[76] Behind the central romance and courtship between the film's hero and heroine hide numerous other erotic permutations—between brothers and sisters-in-law, mothers and fathers-in-law, cousins and nieces, servants and masters—not all of which are necessarily heterosexual and some of which cut across class and generational lines. Significantly, the scene also speaks to the ways in which queer audiences are able to exploit the slippages between homosociality and homoeroticism that occur in representations of gender-segregated spaces on the Bollywood screen. As Ghosh notes, "the woman only setting of the func-

Nisha (Madhuri Dixit) glances coquettishly at the cross-dressed interloper (whose
gaze is the spectator's) in *Hum Aapke Hain Koun . . . !* (Who Am I to You?, dir.
Sooraj Barjatya, 1994). *Photo courtesy of the National Film Archive of India.*

tion provides occasion for 'deviancy' that would otherwise be quite impossible."[77] Thus queer female desire and pleasure, in an ostensibly rigidly conservative film like *HAHK*, is that which permeates home space rather than being
extrinsic to it. The incursion of female homoerotic desire into this ultracon-
ventional Hindu marriage plot—both suggested and contained by the scene
between Dixit and her cross-dressed partner—threatens the presumed seamlessness of both familial and nationalist narratives by calling into question the
functionality and imperviousness of heterosexual bonds.

   Elizabeth Freeman's insightful study of the wedding in Euro-American tradition may be helpful in understanding the apparent contradiction between the
queer valence of this particular scene and the conservativism of the rest of the
narrative. Freeman suggests that the wedding as a ritual offers possibilities of
queer kinship and alliance that are effaced by the marriage it ostensibly inaugu-
rates. The disconnect between the wedding and the marriage, Freeman argues,
is what queers and others outside of normative heterosexuality can productively exploit. While Freeman focuses specifically on the wedding ritual in

twentieth-century American literature and film, her argument can productively be applied to the ways in which the wedding plot functions in Bollywood cinema. As the *"Didi tera devar divana"* sequence makes apparent, the wedding and its rituals open up numerous possibilities of desire and affiliation that, as Freeman asserts, the institution of marriage itself shuts down.

How then does Nair's *Monsoon Wedding*—which can be read as a diasporic "remake" of HAHK—deal with the generic requirement of the song and dance sequence and translate it into a form that is more intelligible and "logical" for non–South Asian viewers? Patricia Uberoi suggests that HAHK was received as good, clean family fun in part due to its "sanitization of a bawdy folk tradition of women's songs, making them fit—or almost fit—for mixed viewing, and for representing Indian culture and tradition."[78] According to Uberoi, HAHK's representation of the wedding and its rituals was deemed to be in "good taste" and was made palatable to a middle-class audience through the purging of "obscenity" that marks women's marriage songs as "a specifically female form of expression and protest."[79] Nair's feminist rescripting of HAHK in a sense seeks to restore to the all-female wedding ritual its characteristic irreverence and ribaldry. Significantly, however, Nair's attempt to reinstate a feminist valence to the representation of female homosocial space requires another effacement in turn: the queer possibilities opened up by the space of female homosociality in HAHK are abruptly foreclosed in *Monsoon Wedding*. Indeed, the moment of queer gender and sexual transgression in HAHK is rescripted in *Monsoon Wedding* into one of straight female bonding. Using Elizabeth Freeman's terms, we could say that the queer potential of the wedding in HAHK has been replaced by the primacy of the marriage in *Monsoon Wedding*.

This becomes particularly apparent in a sequence in which the women in the family gather together during the all-female *mehndi* ceremony and sing bawdy, sexually suggestive songs with and to each other. The scene opens with a shot of the women clapping and beating time on the *dholki* (drum) as Madhorama Pencha, a well-known Punjabi folksinger, begins singing a wedding song. The hand-held, vérité-style camera pans from Madhorama to the other women in the family, both young and old, as they sing and dance with each other in a performance of Giddha, the all-female Punjabi song and dance ritual that often takes place during wedding festivities. The scene culminates with the mothers-in-law telling each other sexually suggestive jokes as they reminisce about their own wedding nights. The beauty of this scene lies in its depiction of the easy intimacy between women, the rituals of touch, grooming, affection, and pleasure that are sanctioned in gender-segregated spaces and expressed through all-female cultural practices such as Giddha. The color scheme that Nair utilizes is particularly striking: the hues of green and orange that imbue the space with a rich, sensuous feel are the national colors of India. By marking this scene as quintessentially "Indian," Nair "nationalizes" and thus naturalizes this space of female homosociality. One of the women conspicuously holds a cell phone as she dances, signaling (somewhat heavy-handedly) the apparently easy coexistence of Indian "tradition" and culture with a globally wired modernity. The scene seems to deliver most dramatically on Nair's promise that the film offers non–South Asian viewers "their first glimpse of contemporary Indian society and Punjabi culture." The use of the hand-held camera forces the spectator to relinquish the distanced role of the voyeur and in effect become a participant in the scene, privy to the intimacy of a hidden, all-female world that exists off the beaten track of the usual tourist itinerary.

Nair's framing of this scene of female homosocial intimacy curiously echoes Antoinette Burton's discussion of representations of the *zenana* in late colonial India. "House and home," Burton writes, "had long been highly charged ideological categories in the context of the Raj."[80] The *zenana* in particular came to occupy iconic status in that it was positioned by both British imperialists and Indian nationalists as a synecdoche for "traditional" India as a whole. Burton analyzes the writings of Cornelia Sorabji, an elite Oxford-trained Indian woman barrister in the early twentieth century, who responded to Indian nationalist anxieties about the passing of the "traditional Indian home" by positioning herself as the authoritative historian–tour guide for a British readership. Her construction of the *zenana* as evidence of an "authentic" vanishing India, Burton argues, enabled Sorabjee to position herself as a cosmopolitan, modern nationalist subject. Burton notes, "According to the *British Weekly*, reviewing her 1934 autobiography, *India Calling*, Sorabji 'opens a door and lets us see a world that is known to very few.' For those who were interested in what she called 'The Inside' of the high-caste Hindu or Muslim home, Sorabji was celebrated as its most authoritative guide."[81] There exists a striking continuity between Sorabji's self-representation as authoritative tour guide to "the subcontinent's most intimate spaces" in the 1930s, and Nair's self-representation over seventy years later as a latter-day tour guide who grants an international viewership access to "The Inside" of the modern Indian home.[82] Sorabji, Burton notes, staged the *zenana* as "a souvenir for consumption by a variety of imperial and colonial publics."[83] Similarly, Nair's framing of female homosocial space in *Monsoon Wedding* positions it as iconic of a newly globalized India, where past and present seamlessly converge. Nair is thus able to construct herself as an authoritative, cosmopolitan diasporic subject who traverses the insides and outsides of different cultural and national spaces with ease. As Nair herself states in the production notes to the film, "We relied on friendships and our true knowledge of the world we were depicting . . . It was a combination of the deeply personal and deeply professional, and it made for an authenticity that is absolutely visible in the finished film."[84] Nair's diasporic translation of the *zenana* space speaks to the ways in which the project of translation is deeply embedded within histories of what Tejaswini Niranjana calls "colonial subjection/subjectification." Niranjana's study of the translation of Indian texts into English by colonial administrators and missionaries illuminates the way in which the process of translation is a key site in colonial structures of domination: "By employing certain modes of representing the other—which it thereby also brings into being—translation reinforces hegemonic versions of the colonized, helping them acquire the status of . . . representations, or objects without history."[85] *Monsoon Wedding* bears the marks of these earlier colonial practices of translation, in that Nair functions to a certain extent as (post)colonial translator, making transparent and natural that which is in effect produced through the very act of translation itself.

Significantly, homoeroticism is clearly positioned at the boundaries of Nair's diasporic feminist reimagining of "authentic" nationalist space, in a way that disturbingly mimics Hindu nationalist discourses of female sexuality. The line between female homosociality and female homoeroticism, which remains so porous in representations of homosocial space in a neoconservative Bollywood romance such as *HAHK* or the other films discussed in the previous section, is strictly policed in the ostensibly feminist *Monsoon Wedding.* In its representation of Giddha, this particular scene makes audible and visible precisely those female cultural practices that, as I suggested in chapter 2, remain inaudible and invisible within standard accounts of South Asian diasporic public culture. Yet it does so at a cost: the film guards against any significant gender or sexual transgression by carefully maintaining the line between homosociality and homoeroticism. This is accomplished in this scene in particular, and indeed throughout the film, by making the bride's younger brother Varun the place-holder of all queerness. The younger brother figure, as some critics have noted, is a stock figure in Bollywood film and is often the repository of gender or sexual transgression.[86] In *Monsoon Wedding* Nair borrows this trope from Bollywood cinema but makes the implicit queerness of this figure explicit. Varun is a pudgy adolescent with a passion for choreographing dance numbers and watching cooking shows, and he is perpetually hounded by his father, Lalit Verma, the patriarch of the family, for being insufficiently manly. The fact that Varun loves dancing and cooking fuels Lalit's relentless attempts to mold his son into proper gender behavior and heightens his fears that Varun may in fact be "funny." By rendering Varun's love of dance a primary marker of his deviance, Nair also makes explicit the way in which the song and dance number functions queerly in Bollywood cinema.

Initially, this subplot involving the deviant son appears to be indicative of Nair's feminist framing of the family scene: on a narrative level, her depiction of the relation between the father and son reveals how familial "harmony" is predicated on strict forms of gender disciplining of unruly bodies. Yet on another level we see that Nair's seeming critique of patriarchal power, and her "outing" of the queer codes of Bollywood cinema, ultimately work in the service of dominant gender and sexual hierarchies. The film quickly cuts from the scene of female homosocial intimacy of the *mehndi* ceremony to one where Varun, who literally occupies the margins of the all-female celebration, is being chided by Lalit for his enjoyment of this feminine ritual. The figure of the brother, then, functions purely instrumentally: by displacing all signs of queerness onto the body of the adolescent brother, the film manages to make the space of female homosociality safe for heterosexual femininity. In other words, the film's depiction of the joys and pleasures of female homosociality is dependent on aggressively disavowing the possibilities of female homo-eroticism that the scene simultaneously opens up. By in effect placing female homoeroticism outside the realm of the naturalized/nationalized space of the all-female ritual, the film replicates dominant nationalist discourse that defines queer female sexuality as unnatural, inauthentic, and alien to the sanctified spaces of home and nation. Thus Nair's insistence that she offers the non–South Asian viewer "an authenticity that is absolutely visible in the finished film" is precisely dependent on rendering *invisible* and *inauthentic* all signs of female homoeroticism.[87]

By shifting queerness away from the bodies of adult women (where it resides in HAHK) and onto that of the adolescent boy, *Monsoon Wedding* relegates queerness to the realm of immaturity and couches it as merely a stage that precedes the responsibilities and requirements of proper adulthood. Thus the queer valences of the wedding, so clearly apparent in a film like HAHK, are effaced in Nair's diasporic reimagining. Here the wedding becomes simply the paradigmatic ritual through which all forms of aberrant desire are corrected and set on the path to respectable, socially sanctioned, reproductive hetero-sexuality. In a parallel subplot, for instance, Lalit's single niece Ria remains conspicuously unmarried not due to any lesbian proclivities, as one may ini-tially suspect, but rather because, as we learn, she remains traumatized after having been molested as a child by a distant male relative. Nair stages a moment of feminist self-determination where Ria confronts her former molester and is then reinstated into the family with the loving support of Lalit as the benign patriarch. Once again this scene appears to speak to Nair's feminist sensibility in revealing the institutionalized violence against women and girls that under-lies the warmth, comfort, and placidity of extended family relations. Yet this instance of feminist consciousness, where Ria speaks the unspeakable and challenges patriarchal authority, stands in sharp contrast to an earlier scene where the "deviant" brother Varun attempts to challenge Lalit's patriarchal authority and to resist being shipped off to boarding school to become a "real man." The film closely follows the effects of Ria's rebellion on the family, and the viewer's sympathies are closely aligned with her as a character. The charac-ter of Varun, on the other hand, is left stranded after his outburst against his father: he literally disappears from the frame and only makes a strategic re-appearance in the film's ending sequence.

This ending, which had viewers at the Venice film festival dancing in the aisles, restages the "family carnivalesque" of HAHK where "hierarchies of social classes break down as domestic help, cooks and other employees of the house-hold participate in the revelry."[88] Similarly in *Monsoon Wedding*, the final scene is a moment of "carnivalesque egalitarianism" that involves all the members of the household taking part in a riotous dance number in torrential monsoon rain.[89] This moment seems to offer a joyous resolution to all the conflicts around class, gender, and sexuality that the film initially sets in motion. The uncomfortable class divide is briefly bridged as the servants join in the celebra-tions; the bad girl bride has given up her married lover and happily sinks into the arms of her prosperous NRI (non-resident Indian) groom; we see Ria "cured," and in the film's final moments she suggestively eyes a handsome male cousin through a shower of raindrops and marigold petals. Significantly, the film corrects the thwarted, damaged, or wayward heterosexuality of the female characters at the expense of the queer male figure. While Varun is shown dancing happily with his relatives in the film's final moments, he conspicuously remains the sole figure who is not coupled up or whose dilemma is not resolved by the film's carnivalesque ending. Indeed, we see here a crucial element of Nair's translation of Bollywood convention into Hollywood convention. Rather than framing queerness as that which permeates home space (as it does in *HAHK*), Nair utilizes the younger brother figure as the quintessential "supporting character" of the Hollywood genre, on whose body all queerness resides. As Patricia White writes:

> The vast majority of "queer-coded" characters in Hollywood film are in fact in supporting roles. They are unsuitable to heterosexual romance and the marriage plot (the organizing principle of the Hollywood universe) and must be assigned other functions . . . Their in-between narrative status frequently resonates with gender liminality: effeminate men and masculine women are conjured up at the boundaries of the model gender behavior of the stars.[90]

Nair's depiction of the younger brother in *Monsoon Wedding* fits squarely within this Hollywood convention of the queer-coded "supporting character": Varun's deviance establishes the ultimate gender and sexual normativity of the film's other characters, and indeed of the film itself as a whole. The result of this translation from the homoerotics of homosocial space and the queer spectacle of the song and dance sequence of Bollywood film to the queer-coded supporting character of Hollywood convention is that the film aggressively equates queerness with male masculinity, and equates femininity with normative heterosexuality. This equation makes queer femininity or queer female desire literally impossible and unimaginable within the logic of the film. It is this elision and containment of queer female desire that makes the film "logical" and "intelligible" to an international audience as a feminist rescripting of Bollywood excess.

It should be noted that this elision of queer female desire through the displacement of queerness onto a male figure is a formula that is repeated in the other films by avowedly feminist South Asian diasporic filmmakers, such as Deepa Mehta's *Bollywood/Hollywood* and Gurinder Chadha's *Bend It Like Beck-*

ham. These films by Mehta and Chadha curiously replay many of the central tropes of *Monsoon Wedding*, albeit modified to fit their diasporic contexts: Mehta's film is set in the rich enclaves and lower-middle-class housing estates of Toronto, while Chadha's film is set in the South Asian immigrant communities of Southhall and West London. Mehta's *Bollywood/Hollywood* fared well at the box office in Canada, while Chadha's film was a huge hit in the UK, leading the box office over more mainstream Hollywood fare for months. If in *Monsoon Wedding* the wedding ritual is what stands as the irreducible marker of national difference, the place where "ancient (Hindu) tradition" and the new "dot.com" modernity of a globalized India seamlessly come together, in *Bollywood/Hollywood* and *Bend It Like Beckham* the wedding stands as the marker of irreducible immigrant difference in a hegemonic white, Christian landscape. It is not surprising that both Mehta and Chadha use the wedding as a primary backdrop: as Karen Leonards's ethnographic work on immigrant South Asian communities in California has shown, marriage and its attendant rituals are particularly loaded signifiers in South Asian diasporic communities.[91] Both Mehta and Chadha quite explicitly point to the ways in which the wedding within diasporic communities becomes the paradigmatic performance of communal belonging and "tradition" along patriarchal lines. Hence the wedding must be rejected by the ostensibly feminist heroines, who shy away from the gender hierarchies it implies. Both films figure their female protagonists as prototypical feminist nationalist subjects who gain entrance into the modern space of the nation (Canada in *Bollywood/Hollywood* and Britain in *Bend It Like Beckham*) by leaving behind the stultifying space of the immigrant home. The films thus remain firmly embedded within the dichotomous logic of tradition and modernity, where the former is embodied by the immigrant marriage and its rituals, and the latter by autonomous couplehood and feminist self-determination.

In *Bollywood/Hollywood*, for instance, the film opens with the male lead, Rahul, a second-generation wealthy Toronto-based businessman, being enjoined to uphold the family line by his dying father. Rahul thus hires an escort, Sunita, to pose as his fiancée, with whom he predictably falls in love. As in HAHK, *Monsoon Wedding*, and *Bend It Like Beckham*, in *Bollywood/Hollywood* the main character's sister's wedding functions as the backdrop to the action. The radicalness of the heroine Sunita and her rebellion against the "family" and its gender requirements are illustrated through her rejection of arranged marriage and the other gendered rituals of immigrant life. The film very self-consciously deploys a Bollywood idiom of high melodrama, farce, romance, and musical numbers, all the while providing tongue-in-cheek Indian-English captions that name the various components of the Bollywood-inspired script. Thus the romantic song and dance sequence is captioned as "Romantic Couple Song," while the phrase "please to bless happy couple" underwrites the requisite closing shot of the hero and heroine speeding off into the sunset. This conceit interpellates a hip, South Asian diasporic audience literate in Bollywood codes while it simultaneously reassures a non–South Asian audience that a knowing presence at work behind the camera is guiding them through possibly unfamiliar territory.

Bollywood/Hollywood thus makes explicit the kind of translation work that a film like *Monsoon Wedding* also engages in. If *Monsoon Wedding* translates the homosocial/homoerotic space of the all-female wedding ritual into one of straight female bonding, *Bollywood/Hollywood* does away with gender-segregated spaces altogether. Both the traditionally male-only celebration, as well as the female-only *sangeet*, are staged in *Bollywood/Hollywood* as aggressively heterosexual spaces. As in *Monsoon Wedding*, the potential for queerness infiltrating home space is foreclosed by solidifying queer identity on the body of a supporting male character. In this case the actor Ranjit Chowdhury plays the seemingly loyal, self-effacing servant who, we learn, has a double life as a female impersonator on the local drag queen circuit. Mehta stages one of the film's several song and dance sequences as a drag performance in what is presumably a local gay bar, although the space remains curiously decontextualized and free-floating. Here we see a painfully stiff Chowdhury, replete with sari, heavy make-up, and hairy forearms, surrounded by glamorous drag queens as s/he lip synchs to a Bollywood number. Solidifying queerness on the body of the servant/drag queen figure has two key effects. First, it dislodges queerness from contaminating the home space by keeping it safely contained within the gay bar space. Second, as in *Monsoon Wedding*, it functions as a foil to the heroine Sunita's gender transgressions by holding them safely within the realm of normative heterosexuality.

This displacement of queerness from the space of the home and the bodies of female characters to the space of not-home and the bodies of gay male figures again plays out in British Asian filmmaker Gurinder Chadha's *Bend It Like Beckham*. Chadha's film was an unprecedented commercial success in Britain where, on its release in April 2002, it topped box office charts and was heralded as "the best British film after *Bridget Jones' Diary* to come out in years."[92] It also had significant box office success when it was released in the United States later that year. The film's lead character is Jess, a second-generation British Asian teenager growing up in West London and obsessed with football, in contrast to her older sister's contentment with arranged marriage and motherhood. The film's climactic ending involves Jess escaping from her sister's wedding festivities in order to take part in a key football match. So-called traditional Indian values, represented by the wedding, the family, and concomitant gender conformity, are contrasted to Englishness, football, and gender rebellion. The film closes with Jess reconciling these apparently irreconcilable elements, as she scores the goal *and* makes it back to her sister's wedding celebration in time. The final scene in *Bend It Like Beckham* shows Jess and Jules, her white counterpart, at Heathrow Airport bidding farewell to their respective families as they head to the promised land of California on a football scholarship. That Jess must ultimately leave the space of home, community, and nation in order to realize her ambitions indicates that Chadha mobilizes a conventional framing of home as a space of racial and gender subordination that stands in contradiction to a presumably freer elsewhere (here the United States). In his cogent analysis of *Bend It Like Beckham,* Michael Giardina notes that the film's ending "reduces the solution to the problems of cultural difference to simply getting out, as both girls leave Britain for the so-called greener pastures of the collegiate soccer fields in the United States."[93] By figuring the resolution as "getting out" rather than "staying put," the film in a sense concedes the space of "home" as one of gender and racial fixity and oppression.

Giardina suggests that the film's tremendous popularity can be attributed to the way in which its multicultural ethos and apparently progressive racial and gender politics mask a conservative aesthetic that comfortably conforms to Prime Minister Tony Blair's mythical "Cool Britannia."[94] I would add that the film also renders its brand of liberal feminism palatable through a strategic containment of queer female sexuality. While *Bend It Like Beckham* draws far more heavily from Hollywood realism and its genre of multicultural "ethnic" comedies than from Bollywood fantasy,[95] the film nevertheless replays the splitting of queerness and feminism that renders *Monsoon Wedding* or *Bollywood/ Hollywood* intelligible to its non–South Asian audience. In her press notes, Chadha states that her film is an attempt to rethink gender roles and to widen

the framework of what constitutes proper masculinity or femininity. She further explains that the metaphor of "bending" in the film's title references not
only English footballer David Beckham's kicking style but also the way in
which, as she puts it, "girls 'bend' the rules rather than 'break' them so they can
get what they want."[96] Yet the metaphor of "bent," of course, also references
queerness: this remains the unspoken valence of the term that Chadha chooses
to ignore in favor of its feminist connotations. Indeed, the film predicates its
feminist assertion of girl power on the containment of the specter of lesbianism
that women's sports invariably conjure up. Chadha acknowledges the charge of
lesbianism that haunts female athletes by working it into a comedic plot line
of multiple misrecognitions. The film situates the queer potential of female
homosociality not in the immigrant home but rather in the girls' locker room,
which is imagined as a space of British multicultural (racial and gender) egalitarianism.[97] Yet *Bend It Like Beckham* ultimately reassures viewers that football-
loving girls are indeed properly heterosexual by once again using the gay male
figure as the "real" queer character in the film. When Jess reveals to her best
friend and male sidekick Tony that she is in love with her white, Irish coach, he
reveals his own sexual transgression and discloses that he is gay, to which Jess
replies in disbelief, "But . . . you're Indian!" Chadha here humorously overturns
the notion that Indian/Punjabi and gay identities are mutually exclusive, but
the film once again reproduces the equation of queerness as male and female-
ness/feminism as straight by abruptly shutting down the possibility of queer
female desire.

The pitting of feminism against male queerness in all three films points to the
ways in which this new crop of South Asian diasporic filmmaking may ironically offer less to queer viewers than either the Bollywood neoconservative
romances of the mid-1990s or the earlier representations of female homoeroticism in films such as *Utsav*, *Razia Sultan*, and *Khalnayak*. The situating of
queerness solely on the bodies of male supporting characters—the brother, the
servant, the best friend—rather than on the central female characters becomes a
crucial mode through which the filmmakers successfully accomplish the translation of a Bollywood idiom into a Hollywood idiom. By sanitizing and het-
erosexualizing female homosocial space, these translation strategies efface the
ways in which insurgent queer female sexualities trouble, disrupt, and refigure
"home" space from within. Thus in these diasporic feminist translations of
Bollywood, queer female desire and subjectivity remain just as unimaginable as

they do within the gay male framings of diaspora that I referenced in the previous chapter. This critical failure to adequately carve out a theoretical or representational space for queer female diasporic subjectivity and desire is perilous when it is precisely queer female subjectivity that is so aggressively disavowed by both dominant nationalist and diasporic discourses. The Hindu nationalist furor over Deepa Mehta's earlier film, *Fire* (1996), which is the focus of the following chapter, makes frighteningly clear the deep investment of religious nationalist ideology in the impossibility of this particular subject position. That Mehta's *Bollywood/Hollywood*, made five years after *Fire*, so definitively effaces the possibility of queer female desire that *Fire* forcefully tackles makes all too clear the chilling effects of Hindu nationalist violence on queer and diasporic cultural production.[98]

By contributing to the effacement of queer diasporic female eroticism, then, ostensibly progressive texts unwittingly collude with dominant nationalist and diasporic ideologies. Thus it is precisely from the vantage point of the impossible position of a queer diasporic female subjectivity that we can and must imagine diaspora and nation differently. Mehta's *Fire* and Ismat Chughtai's 1941 short story "The Quilt," the texts that I turn to in the following chapter, suggest precisely this alternative imagining of diaspora and nation by placing queer female desire at the very heart of the "home" as domestic, communal, and national space. As such they offer powerful counternarratives to the sanitizing of "home" space within the Bollywood translations that have concerned me here. In so doing, as we will see, *Fire* and "The Quilt" make apparent the ways in which alternative forms of desire can be both seamlessly absorbed by *and* radically disrupt the normativity of multiple "home" spaces.

5

LOCAL SITES/GLOBAL CONTEXTS

The Transnational Trajectories of *Fire* and "The Quilt"

In early December 1998, movie theaters in Bombay, New Delhi, and other major Indian cities were stormed by dozens of activists from the Shiv Sena, the Hindu right-wing organization that formed the militant wing of the BJP-led Hindu nationalist government then in power. The activists were protesting the screening of *Fire*, the 1996 film by the Indian Canadian director Deepa Mehta which depicts a lesbian relationship between two sisters-in-law in a middle-class, joint-family household in contemporary New Delhi. Screenings were forcibly stopped, film posters burnt, and property vandalized. The Shiv Sena justified its actions by claiming that the film's depiction of lesbianism was an affront to Hinduism and "alien to Indian culture."[1] Significantly, the fact that Mehta was a diasporic filmmaker was repeatedly cited as evidence of her lack of knowledge about the erotic and emotional lives of "real" (Hindu) Indian women. This critique of Mehta as diasporic, and therefore not authorized to speak about "Indian culture," came not only from right-wing Hindu nationalists but also from moderate and leftist commentators in India. The mainstream national newspaper *The Hindu*, for instance, opined that "*Fire* has very weak links to the true Indian milieu."[2] Similarly Madhu Kishwar, a well-known feminist writer and activist, penned a scathing attack of the film in the feminist journal *Manushi*. Framing Mehta somewhat contradictorily as simultaneously both "foreign" and a member of the indigenous Indian elite, Kishwar dismissed the film in the following terms: "the director lacks an understanding of family life and emotional bonds in India . . . I wanted to ignore [the film] as an exercise in self-flagellation by a self-hating Hindu and a self-despising Indian—a very common type among the English educated elite in India."[3] These critiques of Mehta from commentators from across the political spectrum as foreign and therefore ignorant of Indian "reality" brings into sharp relief the conflation of both "queer" and "diaspora" as inauthentic and alien within nationalist discourse.

Interestingly, over fifty years earlier, a similar outcry had greeted the publication of Urdu writer Ismat Chughtai's 1941 short story "The Quilt," on which (according to Mehta) *Fire* is loosely based.[4] Chughtai's story centers on the curious relationship between a sequestered wife and her female maidservant in an upper-class Muslim household, as observed by the young girl who narrates the tale. Every night, the girl is alternately fascinated and alarmed by the energetic contortions of the two women under the quilt; curious sounds and smells emanate from there. The quilt becomes the organizing metaphor of the story, and its shifting surfaces suggest the mobile relations of erotic pleasures that Chughtai weaves throughout the text. In a gesture that was to be reproduced by the Shiv Sena almost six decades later in response to *Fire*, Chughtai was charged with obscenity by the Indian colonial government in 1944. Chughtai, in a 1983 interview in *Manushi*, recalls the event: "In 1941, three months before my marriage, I wrote a story called *Lihaf* (The Quilt). In 1944, I was charged with obscenity by the Lahore government. A summons arrived : 'George the Sixth versus Ismat Chugtai.' I had a good laugh at the idea that the king had read my story. So we went to Lahore to fight the case."[5] As Geeta Patel's reading of Chughtai's story points out, the obscenity charges were leveled specifically at Chughtai's representation of *female* homoeroticism, although the story quite clearly maps out male homoerotic relations as well.[6] That the Indian colonial government, alerted by members of the elite Muslim community in Lahore, deemed Chughtai's representation of female homoeroticism a far greater threat to public decency than her representation of male homoeroticism speaks volumes about the tremendous symbolic and discursive weight attached to female bodily desires and practices. The controversies surrounding both Chughtai's "The Quilt" and Mehta's *Fire* make startlingly clear the ways in which discourses of women's sexuality are mobilized in the service of imperial, national, and communal projects. Indeed, as Susie Tharu and K. Lalitha note in their

Radha (Shabana Azmi) and Sita (Nandita Das) in *Fire*
(dir. Deepa Mehta, 1996).

analysis of the obscenity charges directed at the work of the eighteenth-century female Telugu poet Muddupalani, when it comes to women's sexuality and artistic production, "the interests of empire and of nation, and the ideologies that ground them, are not always so clearly in contradiction."[7]

In my reading of *East Is East* in chapter 3, Mina's "staying put" within the home signals not her capitulation to the law of the father but rather her defiant claiming of pleasure in the most unlikely of spaces. Similarly, in the Bollywood song and dance sequences discussed in the previous chapter, female homoeroticism suffuses home space rather than existing in exilic relation to it. By reading *Fire* alongside "The Quilt," this chapter further examines the ways in which queer female pleasure and desire remake the home as domestic and national space. Both texts place female homoerotic desire squarely at the center of multiple home spaces in a manner that is unimaginable within the logic of diasporic feminist translations of Bollywood. *Fire* and "The Quilt" thus ask us to consider the interrelation between heteronormative structures of gender and sexuality, and religious and nationalist constructions of community and nation. Tracing the continuities and dissonances between the two texts also allows for a further exploration of the circulation, translation, and transformation of queer representations as they travel between diaspora and nation.

I place Mehta's film and Chughtai's short story within the larger context of recent Indian feminist theorizations of sexuality, in order to unpack the fraught relation between the study of sexuality and the study of gender in a South Asian context, and the implications of such a relation for studying sexuality in the diaspora. I consider how a film like *Fire* travels across multiple national sites and accrues multiple audiences and meanings in the process of such travel. Although slight reference was made to Chughtai's story during the *Fire* controversy, I would like to restore "The Quilt" as an important intertext to *Fire*. In so doing, I resituate Mehta's film in relation to alternative models of female homoerotic desire that contest Eurocentric structures of visibility and sexual subjectivity on the one hand, and hegemonic structures of authentic communal and national identity on the other. Both *Fire* and "The Quilt" make apparent the way in which, by placing queer female desire squarely at its center, the space of home is reworked and transformed from within.

Situating Sexuality: Genealogies of Indian Feminism

Feminist work on South Asia is crucial to a project on queer diasporas since it allows us to identify the legacies of gender and sexual ideologies that were first consolidated within the bourgeois anticolonial nationalist movement in India in the late nineteenth and early twentieth centuries. These constructions of gender and sexuality have taken on new forms and meanings in the contemporary moment within state and religious nationalisms in South Asia, as well as within South Asian immigrant communities in the diaspora. Clearly, as Ratna Kapur argues, the debates on sexual morality that have surrounded contemporary cultural texts such as *Fire* must be situated in relation to an older history of Hindu nationalist formulations of sexuality and the home.[8] However, as I will discuss, much of this feminist scholarship also stops short at critical instances, in that it fails to address the production of normative and deviant sexualities as central to both the colonial and nationalist projects.

Feminist critics working on South Asia have provided some of the most sophisticated thinking on the centrality of gender ideologies to colonial, nationalist, and contemporary religious discourses and have further extended these arguments to theorizing the concomitant role of sexual ideologies within such discourses. In the introduction to their groundbreaking collection of feminist historiography, for instance, Kumkum Sangari and Sudesh Vaid follow Partha Chatterjee in arguing that the early Indian nationalism of the *bhadralok*, or Bengali middle class, in the late nineteenth century is predicated on "a series of oppositions between male vs. female, inner vs. outer, public vs. private, material vs. spiritual."[9] The newly created private space of the *bhadralok* home, the authors point out, is one that defines itself in opposition to working-class women and depends on the reconstitution of patriarchal familial ideologies through the figure of the "ideal woman" as the carrier of "tradition."[10] Sangari and Vaid argue that from its inception, elite Indian nationalism is predicated on the regulation and surveillance of women's sexuality and the construction of a "respectable" middle-class sexual morality that both vilifies and excludes those women who are "either relatively independent and literate . . . or [those] from the lower strata, courtesans and prostitutes, i.e. women who have hitherto had greater access to a 'public' sphere of street, marketplace, fair and festival."[11]

Attention to the construction of a private, middle-class, "respectable" sexuality in the formation of bourgeois nationalist subjectivities, as articulated by Sangari and Vaid, has been taken up in more recent work by South Asian feminist scholars analyzing contemporary religious nationalisms in South Asia. Amrita Chhacchi notes that Hindu and Muslim communal identity in contemporary India is predicated on the control of women's sexuality as legislated through both Hindu and Muslim "personal law." Such laws, Chhacchi argues, have historically "laid out the boundaries of the community and established a particular family structure—patriarchal, patrilineal, monogamous—as the norm."[12] In tracing the continuities between discourses of anticolonial nationalism and those of contemporary religious nationalism/communalism, Chhachhi (citing Tanika Sarkar) notes that both rely on the figure of "an inviolate, chaste, pure female body,"[13] in whose defense nationalist/communal identity is mobilized. Paola Baccheta further explicates the deployment of sexuality in religious nationalist discourse by demonstrating the ways in which the Rashtriya Swayamsevak Sangh (RSS), a right-wing Hindu nationalist organization in India, projects a perverse and excessive sexuality onto its Muslim "Others": within RSS rhetoric, "the counterpart to the chaste Hindu male is the Muslim male polygamist or rapist, and to the chaste, motherly Hindu woman is the Muslim woman as prostitute or potential wife."[14] In other words, female sexuality becomes the ground on which the borders between (male supremacist) religious and national collectivities are drawn. Ritu Menon's and Kamla Bhasin's research on the post–Partition Indian government's "recovery operation" of Hindu Indian women who were abducted to Pakistan during the Partition makes clear the ways in which women's bodies are quite literally exchanged between nations as a violent means by which to produce religious/ national solidarity.[15] As these various critics amply demonstrate, anticolonial nationalism in colonial India and religious nationalism in contemporary South Asia intersect in their deployment of sexual and gender ideologies that harness women's sexuality (their sexual conduct and reproductive capacity in particular) to the propagation of the community/group/nation.

The postcolonial feminist scholarship on South Asia that I have briefly outlined above has been profoundly instructive in tracing the gendered and sexualized nature of colonial, anticolonial nationalist, and contemporary nationalist discourses. Yet despite its powerful critique of "woman" as emblematic of the concept of home as nation, as feminized domestic space, and as a site of chaste and unsullied spirituality,[16] such work is marked by a curious lack of attention to the production of heterosexuality and homosexuality within these discourses.[17] A recent instance of this particular blind spot in postcolonial South Asian feminist theorizations of nationalism and sexuality is apparent in Kumari Jayawardena's and Malathi de Alwis's anthology *Embodied Violence: Communalising Women's Sexuality in South Asia*. The collection is especially strong in exploring the various means by which women's sexuality has historically been disciplined and controlled under nationalist movements. However, the contributors fail to adequately articulate how one of the most powerful methods of disciplining and controlling female sexuality within such movements has been the prescription of state-sanctioned heterosexuality as the structure within which female nationalist subjects are housed. This particular collection, as well as the works by the other critics cited above, recognizes that sexuality historically secures the grounds for the production of gendered colonial, bourgeois nationalist, and religious nationalist subjects. It is therefore all the more surprising that even such attempts to specifically consider the imbrication of discourses of nationalism and women's sexuality still presume the heterosexuality of the female subject. Women's sexual autonomy, as imagined by these critics, never extends beyond the boundaries of heterosexuality; the possibility that there may exist other forms of non-heteronormative subjectivities that challenge the logic of such nationalisms is never addressed. By failing to examine the existence and workings of alternative sexualities within dominant nationalisms, such analyses leave intact the very structures of gender and sexual subordination that they seek to critique and dismantle.

If much of the feminist scholarship on South Asia stops short of analyzing the interconnections between the production of "respectable" and "perverse" sexualities and the production of bourgeois nationalism in India, it does provide a powerful critical frame within which to begin such an inquiry. Mrinalini Sinha's essay on the formation of a "respectable" Indian sexuality in colonial India works within the critical frame provided by South Asian feminist scholarship while beginning to articulate heterosexuality and nationalism as overlapping and mutually constitutive structures of domination.[18] Sinha's analysis focuses on the late-nineteenth- and early-twentieth-century debates among colonial officials and elite bourgeois nationalists on the restructuring of heterosexual family norms in colonial India, through legislation such as the Age of Consent Act (1891) and the Child Marriage Restraint Act (1929). Sinha notes that the Acts, far from transforming unequal gender, class, and caste relations, instead served to accommodate preexisting social hierarchies within new social arrangements conducive to the formation of nationalist subjectivities and the political community of the "modern" nation state.[19]

The 1929 Child Marriage Restraint Act, which raised the age of marriage for women, was passed after the 1927 publication of the American writer Katherine Mayo's incendiary *Mother India*, a so-called exposé of the plight of Hindu girls and women at the hands of "barbaric" Hindu men. Mayo's book, as Sinha states, linked Indian nationalism to the excessive sexuality and sexual pathology of Hindu society.[20] The reformist nationalist response to Mayo's book reversed the charge of sexual pathology by arguing that the East was marked by a heightened sense of spirituality lacking in the materialist West. Such nationalist responses make apparent how the notion of Eastern sexual propriety, as defined against Western sexual degeneracy, was used as a means by which to shore up a newly created Indian nationalist subjectivity. Homosexuality in particular, and "sexual deviance" and "sexual perversion" in general, were deployed within the counter-rhetoric of Indian nationalists as markers of Western decadence.[21] For instance, Sinha cites a book written in Hindi by an Indian woman, Chandravati Lakhanpal, entitled *The Reply to Mother India*. Lakhanpal's text, Sinha notes, "dwelt on homosexual practices, to which elite British males were exposed in English public schools, and quoted at length from Havelock Ellis and other famous authorities on sex to argue that 'sexual perversion' was more common in Britain than in India."[22] Similarly, in another response to Mayo's book, the Indian feminist Muthulakshmi Reddi countered the charge of sodomy and pederasty that Mayo charged was endemic to Hindu society by claiming no knowledge of "such immoral and unnatural practices" in India. Reddi goes on to reverse the charge of indecency onto the West by referring to "the famous Leadbeater case," in which Charles Leadbeater, a priest at the Theosophical Society in Madras in the 1920s, was accused of sodomizing young Indian boys.[23] Thus imperial feminists like Mayo, as well as anticolonial nationalist feminists like Lakhanpal and Reddi, evoked the specter of homosexuality as a marker of abject otherness and foreignness, and as a means by which to claim their respective locations as modern and civilized. Sinha argues that such a deployment of sexuality, which pitted Western sexual and moral codes against indigenous ones, "reflected the coming of age of a new nationalist perspective on Indian domestic and sexual norms . . . [one that] allowed the reformist nationalist elite . . . to 'indigenize' and domesticate the norms of bourgeois domesticity in a manner that would enable the nationalist elite to address the West or Britain as 'Indian.' "[24]

I rehearse Sinha's argument in some detail here because it allows us to crucially extend the feminist scholarship on "respectable" Indian sexuality by Vaid, Sangari, Sarkar, and others, by bringing to the fore the critique of state-sanctioned heterosexuality implicit in their work. Sinha's essay also suggests the necessity of a critical examination of a discourse of homosexuality and "sexual perversion" in anticolonial and contemporary nationalist politics in India and provides a useful point of departure in tracing the linkages between these various discourses. Sinha herself acknowledges that "the contemporary implications of a discourse of same-sex relations—whether or not self-consciously gay—for the politics of Indian nationalism today" remain beyond the scope of her essay.[25] In a significant attempt to pick up where Sinha's essay leaves off, the anthology *A Question of Silence? The Sexual Economies of Modern India* addresses more explicitly the deployment of discourses of "perverse" and "respectable" sexualities within colonial and postcolonial India.[26] In the introduction to their important collection, the editors, Mary John and Janaki Nair, note that Indian feminism has situated questions of women's sexuality predominantly within a framework of victimization: "the Indian women's movement, to the extent that it specifically foregrounds sexuality, has usually concentrated on the question of enforcing laws that would act as a restraint on male privileges over the bodies of women."[27] The editors instead argue for a recognition of the centrality of discourses of sexual morality to both colonial and nationalist formulations of modernity and citizenship: "It was not . . . the confessional couch or the hystericized woman that generated knowledge and anxieties about sexuality in modern India so much as, on the one hand, the administrative urgency of the colonial power to make sense of and thereby govern a baffling array of 'types and classes' . . . and on the other, the nationalist need to define the dutiful place of the citizen/subjects of the incipient nation."[28] Yet while John and Nair recognize that "the dominant and exclusionary structures of heterosexuality . . . have rarely been a focus of explicit critique" within Indian feminist scholarship,[29] the full implications and meanings of a thorough engagement with the question of alternative sexualities still seem to elude them. Alternative sexualities demand theorization not only because such work denaturalizes and points to "the taken-for-granted aspects of our sexual economies,"[30] as the editors suggest. Rather if, as Indian feminist scholars have demonstrated over the past two decades, the hallmark of modernity within nationalist ideologies is the virtuous, domestic, asexual woman, then it is perhaps within those spaces that are deemed outside the modern, and appear as primitive, irrational, and perverse within nationalist framings, that we can look for alternative formulations of community and nation.

Mapping *Fire*

An analysis of *Fire*'s reception both within and outside India underscores the inadequacy of feminist analyses that seek to destabilize heterosexuality without adequately grappling with the significance of alternative sexualities in the constitution of communal and nationalist collectivities. The film and the controversy it engendered demand that we explore more fully the ways in which challenges to state-sanctioned sexual subjectivities are managed within hegemonic articulations of community and nation, and how they simultaneously threaten to interrupt the coherence of such entities. The violent hostility of religious nationalists in India toward a diasporic film like *Fire* highlights the urgent need for feminist scholarship both in India and in the diaspora to extend its scope of analysis in two directions: first, to view heterosexuality and contemporary nationalisms as overlapping structures of domination; and second, to move beyond the nation-state in order to account for the transnational circuits that both prop up *and* challenge contemporary nationalisms.

Fire is but the most obvious example of the increasing visibility of films dealing with alternative sexualities that are produced by Asian diasporic filmmakers and that have an increasingly global circulation. For instance, Ang Lee's 1993 film, *The Wedding Banquet* (which has as its protagonist a gay Taiwanese businessman living in New York), gained huge audiences in Taiwan, the United States, and other international markets. In his reading of *The Wedding Banquet*, Mark Chiang argues that the film "cannot be read solely from within the frameworks of national culture, either Chinese or American, but must be read across them in a transnational analysis that attends to the local and global."[31] Similarly, the politics of *Fire*'s reception in India, the United States, and Canada raises questions of how queerness, as represented and circulated through diasporic cultural forms, becomes legible within a variety of competing and contradictory discourses: first, within developmental narratives of gay and lesbian identity in Euro-American contexts; second, within a discourse of religious nationalism in India, which is reproduced in the diaspora; and third, within liberal humanist discourses within both India and the diaspora. The necessity of utilizing a queer diasporic framework becomes particularly apparent when tracing the ways in which the film's representation of female homoerotic desire signifies very differently within these various discourses.

Fire both adheres to and challenges a developmental narrative of gay and lesbian identity, which underlies dominant Euro-American discourses on non-Western sexualities. The film opens with a scene of the adult protagonist Radha's memory / fantasy of herself as a young girl, sitting beside her parents in an open field of yellow flowers. Her mother urges the young Radha to "see the ocean" lying just beyond the landlocked field: "What you can't see you can see, you just have to see without looking." This scene, with its exhortation to "see" without looking, to "see" differently, recurs and resonates throughout the film and suggests an analogy with the ways in which *Fire* interrogates the notion that the proper location of lesbianism is within a politics of visibility in the public sphere. However, the film's counterhegemonic representation of queer female desire is undercut and complicated by its own history of production, distribution, reception, and consumption. Funded largely with Canadian money, *Fire* had circulated from 1996 to 1998 mostly at international film festivals in India, Europe, and North America and had a lengthy art house release in major U.S. cities. Thus, prior to its general release in India in November 1998, it was available to a limited audience in India but gained a significant South Asian diasporic viewership as well as a mainstream lesbian and gay audience in the United States and Canada. Given the trajectory of the film's reception, it is worth asking how the film has become available and legible to its diasporic and international audiences.

Fire takes place in the middle-class neighborhood of Lajpat Nagar, in New Delhi, and tells the story of the burgeoning love and desire that emerges between Radha (Shabana Azmi) and her new sister-in-law Sita (Nandita Das), in a joint-family household. Mehta quickly establishes the familiar familial violences and compulsions that inhabit the household: the women do most of the labor for the family business while their husbands ignore or abuse them. Radha's husband, Ashok, is tender and attentive not to Radha but to his guru, with whom he spends all his free time and who preaches sexual abstinence, while Sita's husband, Jatin, is too preoccupied with his Westernized Chinese girlfriend to attend to Sita. The two women eventually turn to each other for sex and emotional sustenance. Mehta rather conventionally frames the dilemma of her heroines as one in which "modernity," with its promise of individual freedom and self-expression, pulls inevitably against "tradition," which demands that the women adhere to the roles prescribed for them as good Hindu wives and remain chaste, demure, and self-sacrificing. Indeed, their very names bespeak these roles. In Hindu mythology, Radha is the consort of the god Krishna, who is famous for his womanizing; together Radha and Krishna symbolize an idealized, transcendent heterosexual union. Sita, the heroine of the Hindu epic *Ramayana*, proves her chastity to her husband, Ram, by immersing herself in fire, and thus represents the ideal of wifely devotion and virtue. The image of Sita emerging unscathed from her *agni pariksha*, or trial by fire, is the inescapable motif around which the women's lives revolve throughout the film: for instance, the background noise in their daily lives is the popular serialization of the *Ramayana*, which plays incessantly on the television. Das's Sita, however, refuses to inhabit the overdetermined role of her legendary namesake: with her penchant for donning her husband's jeans instead of her heavy silk saris, and her willingness to pursue her attraction to Radha, she becomes the emblem of a "new India" and its promise of feminist self-fulfillment. Conversely, the stultifying effects of "tradition" are embodied in the character of Biji, the mute, paralytic grandmother who keeps a disapproving eye on the activities of her daughters-in-law.

The dichotomies through which the film is structured—between Biji and Sita, saris and jeans, silence and speech, self-denial and self-fulfillment, abstinence and desire, tradition and modernity—implicate it in a familiar teleological narrative of progress toward the individual freedom offered by the West, against which "the non-West" can only be read as premodern. In fact, a number of U.S. critics have used the film as an occasion to replay colonial constructions of India as a site of regressive gender oppression, against which the West stands for enlightened egalitarianism.[32] Within the dominant discursive production of India as anterior to the West, lesbian or gay identity is explicitly articulated as the marker of full-fledged modernity. After Ashok spies the two women in bed together, Sita comments to Radha, "There is no word in our language to describe what we are to each other," to which Radha responds, "You're right; perhaps seeing is less complicated." Film critics in the United States, most notably Roger Ebert, have taken this exchange (as well as Mehta's own pronouncement in the press notes that "Indians don't talk about sex") as proof of the West's cultural superiority and advanced politicization: "Lesbianism is so outside the experience of these Hindus that their language even lacks a word for it."[33] Indeed, almost all mainstream U.S. reviewers stress the failure of "these Hindus" to articulate lesbianism intelligibly, which in turn signifies the failure of the non-West to progress toward the organization of sexuality and gender prevalent in the West.[34] To these critics, ironically, lesbian or gay identity becomes intelligible and indeed desirable when and where it can be incorporated into this developmental narrative of modernity.

Because *Fire* gains legibility within such narratives for at least some North American, non–South Asian viewers (both straight and gay), it is helpful to resituate it within other discourses of non-heteronormative sexuality that are available to South Asian and South Asian diasporic audiences. Just as Mira Nair's *Monsoon Wedding* can be productively read as a diasporic translation of *Hum Aapke Hain Koun . . . !,* so too can *Fire* be read as a diasporic appropriation and transformation of Ismat Chughtai's "The Quilt." Reading the film through the story provides an alternative to the tradition-modernity axis by foregrounding the complex model of queer female desire suggested by the film but foreclosed by its mainstream U.S. reception. The mirrored relation between *Fire* and "The Quilt" underscores the film's critique of neocolonial constructions in which non-Western sexualities are premodern and in need of Western political development, and challenges dominant Indian nationalist narratives that consolidate the nation in terms of sexual and gender normativity.

Tracing the convergences and incommensurabilities between *Fire* and "The Quilt" reveals the ways in which an apparently geographically and culturally "rooted" national text ("The Quilt") is translated into a mobile, diasporic text

(*Fire*) that is in turn consumed within the national space (India). This is not to create a false binary between the apparent fixity of national forms and the mobility of diasporic forms. Chughtai herself was a major figure (and one of the few women) in the influential, Marxist-oriented Progressive Writers Association in the 1930s and 1940s in Lucknow, North India, a group that included Krishan Chander, Sadat Hasan Manto, Rashid Jahan, and other leading figures of Urdu literature. The group was launched in 1935 in London by Urdu writers strongly influenced by the recent formation of the International Association of Writers for the Defence of Culture, the antifascist organization begun in Paris by European modernists such as André Malraux and André Gide.[35] Chughtai's short stories, novels, and essays bear the marks of these transnational influences, while they simultaneously challenge Marxist orthodoxy in their focus on the complex interrelation of class with gender and sexuality in middle-class Muslim households in late-colonial India.[36]

Chughtai's nuanced engagement in "The Quilt" with the "home" as national, psychic, and domestic space is evident in all of her subsequent work, particularly her semiautobiographical 1944 novel *The Crooked Line* (*Terhi Lakir*), for which "The Quilt" provided a blueprint of sorts.[37] The novel radically departs from canonical novels of nation formation by narrating the birth of the Indian nation through its female Muslim protagonist. Revisiting the terrain of "The Quilt" and drawing explicitly on Chughtai's own experiences as a headmistress of a girls' school in Aligarh, North India, the novel explores the intense intergenerational, cross-class erotic relations between women and girls that mark female homosocial spaces such as the Muslim middle-class home or the girls' boarding school. Chughtai saw much of her family traumatically leave India for Pakistan after the Partition of 1947; her wry, humorous stories detailing the psychic and domestic interiors of elite Muslim families are shadowed by questions of homelessness and the cataclysmic uprootings caused by Partition and communal violence.[38] In an essay entitled "From Here to There," Chughtai recalls her trip to Karachi, Pakistan, in 1975 to visit relatives she had not seen since they left India during the Partition nearly thirty years earlier. She writes,

> Pictures of relatives and friends and heaps of gifts added to the weight of my luggage. So many people came to see me off at the airport. Bombay was calling out to me, Karachi was holding me back. It seems as if I'm leaving one world to go to another. The journey is an hour and a half long . . . How long the road that stretches from here to there! How great the distance![39]

Chughtai's suspension between these two points of belonging, between here and there, Karachi and Bombay, maps out an alternative geography of affect that cannot abide by the logic of the bounded, discrete nation-state and that lays bare the arbitrariness of national borders. Chughtai's own movements within and between these geographic, national, and psychic spaces speak to the ways in which the "nation" itself is marked by fissures, ruptures, and movements within its very borders. These multiple movements compel us to rethink the conventional distinction between "diaspora" and "nation": the nation is marked by diasporic movement just as the diaspora becomes a part of the nation. As such, Chughtai's work can be understood as belonging not so much to the nation—whether India or Pakistan—but rather to what Avtar Brah terms "diaspora space," which she defines as follows:

> diaspora space as a conceptual category is "inhabited," not only by those who have migrated and their descendants, but equally by those who are constructed and represented as indigenous. In other words, the concept of diaspora space (as opposed to that of diaspora) includes the entanglement, the intertwining of the genealogies of dispersion with those of "staying put." The diaspora space is the site where the native is as much a diasporian as the diasporian is the native.[40]

For Brah, the concept of diaspora space is useful in that it troubles ethnocentric notions of Englishness that are defined over and against the foreignness and alienness of nonwhite British populations. While the notion of diaspora space usefully recasts claims to nativism within the former imperial power, it can also productively be applied to the postcolonial nation in order to disrupt overly fixed notions of national homogeneity and boundedness. Understanding Chughtai as inhabiting diaspora space means that we must read her work not as representative of an apparently pure, "authentic" national culture but rather as a product of multiple displacements and exiles that cross-cut the "home" as domestic and national space. Chughtai's work thus importantly prefigures the genre of queer diasporic literature that I engage with in chapter 6.

Beyond Visibility: Ismat Chughtai's "The Quilt"

"The Quilt" puts forth a particular conceptualization of female homoerotic pleasure that challenges colonial constructions of "oppressed Indian women,"[41] and exceeds and escapes existing theorizations of "lesbian" subjectivity. As such, it converges with the moments of queer incursion in the absence of "lesbians" that are apparent in Bollywood cinema. "The Quilt" must be understood not as a representative "lesbian" narrative but through the very structures set up by the story itself; these demand that female homoeroticism be located as simply one form of desire within a web of multiple, competing desires that are in turn embedded in different economies of work and pleasure. In particular, Chughtai's respacialization of female homoerotic desire through tropes of concealment and visibility, secrecy and disclosure, challenges dominant (and often universalizing) paradigms of same-sex desire. To cite just one out of many instances of this universalizing tendency within queer theory, Eve Sedgwick, in her paradigm-shifting *Epistemology of the Closet*, claims the closet as "the defining structure for gay oppression in this century," thereby disregarding other possible epistemic categories or tropes of spacialization that may exist outside, or indeed within, a Euro-American context.[42] Conversely, Chughtai's work demands a consideration of those bodies and spaces that fall outside the rigid narrative configurations constructed by such sweeping theoretical gestures, and instead opens up a potentially generative site of alternative narratives and significations of female homoerotic desire.

"The Quilt" is set within the confines of the household of a wealthy landowner (the Nawab) and his wife (the Begum, or lady of the house) and is narrated by an adult who tells the story through the eyes of her childhood self. As a young girl, she has been "deposited" in the Begum's home by her mother in the hopes that this sojourn with her aunt will initiate her into proper feminine behavior, given that she has a penchant for fighting with the boys rather than "collecting admirers" as her older sisters do.[43] The adult narrator frames the story as a remembered childhood instance of both fear and fascination, where the Begum's quilt—"imprinted on [her] memory like a blacksmith's brand"[44]—embodies the scene of her own ambivalent sexual awakening and desire for the Begum. Memory in the text works not to evoke a narrative of nostalgia, one that imagines home as a site of subjective wholeness or originary, heterosexual identity; rather, the narrator remembers the domestic arena experienced by her childhood self as an apparent site for the inculcation of gender-normative behavior as well as of complicated, non-normative arrangements of pleasures and desires. This anti-nostalgic narrative radically destabilizes conceptions of the domestic as a site of compulsory heterosexuality, while the partial knowledge afforded by the child's gaze (one that is unable to fully grasp the meanings of the scenes that it witnesses) allows Chughtai to simultaneously resist articulating these arrangements of desires within pre-scribed frameworks as "lesbian" or "homosexual."

It quickly becomes evident that the question of space, territoriality, and access is critical to the narrative framing of the story, as well as to the articula-tion of the desiring subject, whether male or female. The Nawab, we are told, has a curious "hobby" of "keep[ing] an open house for students; young, fair and slim-waisted boys, whose expenses were borne entirely by him," and whose "slim waists, fair ankles and gossamer shirts" torture the Begum as she glimpses them through "the chinks in the drawing-room doors."[45] The Begum witnesses this scene of pleasure, commerce, and desire but she is absolutely shut out of its circuits of exchange—predicated as they are on the consumption and circulation of food, money, and labor—and is thus rendered valueless within its terms: "Who knows when Begum Jan started living? Did her life begin . . . from the time she realised that the household revolved around the boy-students, and that all the delicacies produced in the kitchen were meant solely for their palates?"[46] The introduction of the female servant Rabbo into the narrative, however, shifts the spacial focus of the story away from the Nawab's drawing room and this partially glimpsed scene of an eroticized (male) homosociality, to one that centers on the *zenana* and, in particular, the space beneath the Begum's quilt.

It is Rabbo's entrance into her life that allows the Begum to finally "start liv-ing," in that it marks her entry into an alternative homosocial economy of de-sire that functions parallel to the dominant desiring economy of the household within which the Nawab and the boys operate. The money-food-pleasure nexus that frames the scene of male-male desire also marks the relation be-tween the two women, but it signifies somewhat differently within the context of an eroticized female homosociality. Denied access to the "real," material resources of the household, the Begum and Rabbo generate their own, draw-ing sustenance and nourishment from the work that their bodies do in the production of pleasure. Indeed, their erotic pleasure is insistently figured in the text in terms of food and the satiation of hunger: "Rabbo came to [the Begum's] rescue just as she was starting to go under. Suddenly her emaciated body began to fill out. Her cheeks became rosy; beauty, as it were, glowed through every pore! It was a special oil massage that brought about the change in Begum Jan."[47] Here and elsewhere, the text reveals an intense preoccupation with touch, smell, and the enumeration of various body parts (lips, eyes, skin, waist, thighs, hands, ankles) as each becomes libidinally invested through Rabbo's relentless massaging of the Begum's body; as such, the narrative refuses to conceptualize the desired and desiring body as a highly localized and conscribed site of eroticism. Instead, the story configures female desire and pleasure as an infinitely productive and transformative activity that generates and is generated by the literal and metaphoric production and consumption of food. The child narrator, for instance, describes the activity under the quilt in the terms available to her as "the sounds of a cat slobbering in the saucer."[48] She later comments: "Smack, gush, slobber—someone was enjoying a feast. Suddenly I understood what was going on! Begum Jan had not eaten a thing all day and Rabbo, the witch, was a known glutton. They were polishing off some goodies under the quilt for sure."[49] Rabbo's touch becomes for the Begum "the fulfillment of life's essential need—in a way, more important than the basic necessities required to stay alive."[50] Female homoerotic desire, then, is predicated on a survival economy of work and pleasure as intermingled.

While it would be tempting to read the representation of female same-sex eroticism within the text as a paradigm of "lesbian" desire, such a categorization shuts down precisely what is most useful about Chughtai's story. The text resists positing the scene of desire between women as a privileged or purely enabling site outside the hegemonic workings of the household and militates against an easy recuperation of any such space of undiluted resistance or subversion. For instance, as references to the "gluttony" of Rabbo and the Begum make clear, Chughtai evokes female homoerotic desire not only through images of satiation but through those of insatiability, greed, and excess as well. The space beneath the quilt, functioning as it does as a site of nonreproductive pleasure—one that has no use-value within a heterosexual economy of desire—can only be figured in terms of overindulgence and waste. Furthermore, the narrator locates the scene of female homoerotic sexuality within a conflicted relation of pleasure, desire, and disgust, where she finds herself simultaneously attracted to and repulsed by the physicality she witnesses between Rabbo and the Begum. The narrator's ambivalence to such physicality is underscored by her repeated evocations of decay and nausea,[51] and it is most apparent in her reaction to the Begum's advances: Tahira Naqvi's translation has the narrator "nauseated" by the Begum's touch,[52] while Susie Tharu's and K. Lalitha's reading of the same line describes the narrator as "driven to distraction" by

"the warmth of [the Begum's] body."[53] While the text in these instances references dominant configurations of female sexuality,[54] its representation of female homoerotic desire is not reducible to nor fully contained by such framings. Instead Chughtai posits an eroticized female homosociality that functions
within multiple discourses, and that contains numerous, often contradictory
significations. The erotic circuits within which Rabbo, the Begum, and the
girl narrator circulate are marked by radically uneven positions of power,
both generational and economic. There are similarly uneven eroticized male
homosocial economies in the text; indeed, in the narrative's mapping out of
intersecting trajectories of erotic pleasures between men and boys, women and
women, women and girls, masters and servants, desiring relations are always
infused and cross-cut by other economies of power. Calling to mind the
uneven erotic relations between women in *Razia Sultan* or *Khalnayak*, women
as desiring subjects in Chughtai's story constantly shift in and out of multiply
and hierarchically coded gendered, generational, and class positions, so that the
text refuses to allow particular configurations of homoerotic desire to settle
into stable structures of sexual identity.[55]

The servant Rabbo figures the text's resistance to conflating sexual practices
with identity, for it is through her that Chughtai is able to rework the category
of female subalternity in terms of space, gendered agency, masculinity, and
desire. Chughtai complicates the notion of domestic labor, desire, and servitude in her refusal to delineate unambiguous relations of exploitation and
domination within the household. The figure of the female servant occupies a
privileged space of indeterminacy within the gendered and class-marked economy of the household—a location that allows subalternity to be conceptualized
beyond mere functionality or instrumentality. Whereas the Begum occupies
spaces that are more and more limited as the narrative progresses—from the
"prison" of the house at large, to the "closed doors" of her "sanctum," to the
territory beneath the quilt—Rabbo is granted tremendous mobility and access
to the various classed and gendered spaces of the house. In addition, her ability
to leave the confines of the house—as she does when she visits her errant son—
contrasts sharply with the Begum's increasingly constricted spacial existence.
Indeed, with her ability to transgress spacial boundaries, Rabbo becomes the
purveyor of both bodily and psychical knowledge, effecting miraculous transformations on the Begum's body, as well as relieving her of periodic "fits"
of hysteria.

Rabbo's spacial, social, and sexual mobility makes her an object of both envy and anxiety within the household: she is repeatedly referred to as a "witch," as possessing unsettling powers that are beyond the understanding of the girl narrator and the other members of the household.[56] Indeed, if "possession" implies both the ownership of property as well as the taking over or inhabiting of another body, Rabbo—in a reversal of the typical mistress-servant relation— can be seen as "possessing" the Begum. This reversal is most evident in the Begum's monstrous metamorphosis as she advances on the narrator, where the Begum appears "possessed."[57] The "claustrophobic blackness" of the room, the darkening of her "upper lip" and "deep eyes" bring to mind earlier descriptions of Rabbo as "black . . . like burnt iron ore."[58] The startling conflation of the "white" body of the Begum with Rabbo's "black" one within this scene of female homoerotic desire can be read not so much as a reinscription of dominant models of "lesbian" sexuality as predicated on narcissistic identification (where, as Valerie Traub has pointed out, "identification with" is conflated with "desire for").[59] Rather, it reads as a textual imperative toward an adequate theorization of female homerotic desire as functioning within a visually coded economy of class difference.

Significantly, this scene also underscores the ways in which the text militates against reading Rabbo as the "real lesbian" in the story, despite familiar dominant discursive productions that locate the "truth" of sexual, class, and gender difference and transgression on particular, designated bodies.[60] For example, the masculinity that characterizes Rabbo and signifies her obvious transgression of a classed and gendered ambit of femininity is not solely locatable on her dark, "solidly packed" body but marks the various scenes of women as desiring subjects. Chughtai masculinizes her female characters when and where they desire or are desired: the Begum's overt masculinity in this scene, as she turns her "arduous heat" on the child narrator, echoes earlier passages where the narrator describes the Begum's face—with its downy upper lip and "temples covered with long hair"—as transformed under her own "adoring gaze" into "that of a young boy."[61] Chughtai thus resists reading female homoerotic desire only on certain bodies and in certain instances; instead, desiring subjects within the story occupy multiple locations within a structure of visuality that renders desire visible through specific markers of class and gender. At the same time, the inscription of such markers on the bodies of the Begum and Rabbo speaks to Chughtai's investment, in this instance, in a hegemonic logic of visibility that demands that bodily surfaces be intelligible in particular ways. That female desiring agency can only signify and be signified through exterior bodily transformations that work within a visual register of class and gender difference undercuts, to a certain extent, the destabilizing effects of the text's representation of desire as always mutable, unfixed, and mobile.

Just as the text refuses to locate desire solely on particular bodies—and hence avoids reifying desires into identity structures—it also refuses to privilege particular sites as the proper locations of the practice of such desire. Shifting critical scrutiny away from the space beneath the quilt to the quilt itself suggests the possibility of a reterritorialized desire that exceeds the master narrative of the closet as a way of theorizing alternative sexuality. The quilt can be read not so much as a concealing device beneath which the "truth" or visual "proof" of sex and desire lie, as much as a kind of mediating and constantly shifting surface that negotiates and marks the border between different economies and organizations of erotic pleasure. The quilt—as a surface area that is suspended between that which is hidden and that which is visible—calls these categories into question and suggests the impossibility of viewing the spaces they connote as discrete territories. Instead, a much more complicated relation between inside and outside, secrecy and disclosure, visibility and invisibility is suggested by the discursive function of the quilt in the narrative. The text on one level seems to privilege what D. A. Miller terms the "will-to-see,"[62] in the girl narrator's insistent attempts to (quite literally) bring to light the curious goings-on beneath the quilt. Indeed, the narrative is propelled by this scopic drive, this desire for "proof" and the promise of eventual revelation of the "truth" beneath the quilt. The story's final scene, where the narrator does catch a glimpse of what lies beneath the quilt, causes the abrupt shutting down of the narrative:

> Once again the quilt started billowing. I tried to lie still, but it was now assuming such weird shapes that I could not contain myself . . . In the dark I groped for the switch. The elephant somersaulted beneath the quilt and dug in. During the somersault, its corner was lifted one foot above the bed. Allah! I dove headlong into my sheets! What I saw when the quilt was lifted, I will never tell anyone, not even if they give me a lakh of rupees.[63]

This sudden blankness, effected by the narrator's refusal (and inability) to disclose what she sees, defers and thwarts the will-to-know that the narrative produces, and the scopic satisfaction that it promises but fails to deliver. The ultimate refusal to enunciate with which the story ends may initially appear as a capitulation to the "prohibition on a certain naming" and the denial of entry of "lesbian" sexuality into the realm of representation—an apparent consignment to unspeakability of female homoerotic sex and desire.[64] I would argue, however, that the failure to name the activity under the quilt speaks, rather, to the impossibility of containing the erotic configurations within the text through a strategy of "naming," of making "sayable" that which must first be produced as visible. Instead of marking "lesbian" sexuality as spectral or unspeakable, the girl's silence encapsulates the text's refusal to grant this space beneath the quilt privileged status as the paradigmatic site of "lesbian" sexuality; the very notion that the "truth" of sex can be revealed or spoken is evoked, only to be overturned. As such, "The Quilt" foreshadows the framing of female homoeroticism evident in Bollywood song and dance sequences such as "*Choli ke peeche kya hai*" (What is beneath your blouse) that I discussed in the previous chapter. Female homoerotic pleasure within Chughtai's text quite simply exceeds the enclosed space beneath the quilt, just as it does the structures of visibility and visuality that the text references. Rather, it saturates all points of the text, eluding location within the ocular field through its manifestation as oral and aural, in the sensations, sounds, and smells with which the narrative is infused. The sight beheld by the narrator, as well as her subsequent failure to disclose, then, become merely incidental; there is no secret that can possibly be revealed, spoken, or withheld given the continuous eruptions of multiple desires that permeate the text. The text's refusal to say, name, and speak the "truth" of sex is precisely what allowed it to bypass the charges of obscenity leveled against it. In the 1983 *Manushi* interview, Chughtai recalls successfully winning the court case:

> The obscenity law prohibited the use of four letter words. *Lihaf* does not contain any such words. In those days the word "lesbianism" was not in use. I did not know exactly what it was. The story is a child's description of something which she cannot fully understand. I knew no more at that time than the child knew. My lawyer argued that the story could be understood only by those who already had some knowledge. I won the case.[65]

Chughtai's repeated insistence on "not knowing" must be read as a strategy of disarticulation allowing female homoerotic desire to elude a colonial legal apparatus that functions squarely within the logic of categorization, visibility, and enumeration.

The quilt, then, represents a textured and layered form of sexuality that resists solidifying into structures of identity. Same-sex desires and practices in the text produce quilted effects, rather than identity effects, as Chughtai maps out multiple, uneven erotic relations that are simultaneously stitched into and undermine dominant circuits of pleasure and commerce. Chughtai's refusal to privilege either the sight or the site of same-sex desire means that the text resists being rendered intelligible within dominant narratives of "lesbian" sexuality. Indeed, reading the text through such dominant configurations of pleasure, identity, and visibility only obscures Chughtai's contestation of precisely those hegemonic formulations.

Sex in the Postcolonial House

If the diasporic feminist translations of the Bollywood genre that I discussed in the previous chapter fix queerness onto particular bodies and efface queerness on others, how does *Fire* translate the homoerotics of "The Quilt" into a diasporic text, fifty years after its publication in India? What is lost or gained in this particular process of translation? *Fire* to a certain extent flattens out the uneven and hierarchical erotic relations in "The Quilt" by translating the mistress/servant relation to an egalitarian one between two middle-class women. The film most radically departs from the script of Chughtai's story in its depiction of the male servant Mundu, who shares the domestic space with the two women. In "The Quilt," the voyeuristic gaze of the young girl/narrator sets in motion homoerotic cross-generational and cross-class relays of power and desire; in *Fire*, the voyeuristic gaze is held instead by Mundu, who functions in the narrative not so much as a worker but rather as both spy and witness to the women's desire. It is he, for instance, who silently watches the growing attraction between the two women and finally, in the film's climactic ending, reveals what he sees to Radha's husband, Ashok. Thus while the figure of Rabbo allows Chughtai to rearticulate female subalternity as a space of possible agency amid oppressive gender and class formations, Mehta's characterization of Mundu simply reiterates familiar formulations of domestic servitude. Unlike Chughtai's nuanced treatment of class and gendered subalternity in the context of middle-class domesticity, in *Fire* the figure of Mundu functions instrumentally, in that he provides the necessary narrative impetus for the women to finally leave the confines of the home at the film's ending.

Yet *Fire* also echoes Chughtai's depiction of queer female desire emerging at the interstices of rigidly heterosexual structures, detailing the ways in which desire is routed and rooted within the space of the middle-class home. In the film, as in Chughtai's text, the men in the family are able to access pleasure and fantasy through unofficially sanctioned sites that function as "escape hatches" from the strictures of conjugal heterosexual domesticity. Ashok, for instance, immerses himself within the homosociality of religious discipleship, Jatin trades in porn videos and escapes into sex with his exotically "other" Chinese girl-friend, while Mundu (who nurses an unrequited love for Radha) has a habit of masturbating to porn videos stolen from Jatin in front of the old grandmother, Biji. Thus, for the men, desire may be blocked within the officially sanctioned gender and class arrangements of the home but it nevertheless emerges within these other locations. Radha and Sita, however, like Chughtai's Begum before Rabbo's arrival, are absolutely shut out of these economies of desire within which the men circulate; they are in effect like Biji, mutely witnessing men's access to pleasure, fantasy, and desire while being denied their own.

For Radha and Sita then, like the women in Chughtai's story, queer desire becomes the means by which they are able to extricate themselves from the terms of patriarchal heteronormativity by creating their own circuits of plea-sure, desire, and fantasy. While some critics have suggested that *Fire*'s depiction of lesbian sexuality capitulates to the familiar notion of lesbianism as merely a reaction to failed heterosexual marriages,[66] I would argue that, at least in the middle-class urban Indian context that Mehta details, it is precisely within the cracks and fissures of rigidly heteronormative arrangements that queer female desire can emerge. As in Chughtai's text, where queer female desire is routed through and against heterosexuality, the attraction between Radha and Sita is enabled by those spaces of sanctioned female homosociality legislated by nor-mative sexual and gender arrangements. In one scene, for instance, the two sisters-in-law massage each other's feet at a family picnic, transforming a daily female homosocial activity into an intensely homoerotic one while the other family members unwittingly look on. Here the slide from female homo-sociality to female homoeroticism serves to locate female same-sex desire and pleasure firmly within the confines of the home and "the domestic," rather than a safe "elsewhere." In this scene, as well as in another where Radha rubs oil into Sita's hair, the women exploit the permeable relation and slippages be-tween female homosociality and female homoeroticism.

Furthermore, the erotic interplay between Radha and Sita references the specific modality of South Asian femininity in the popular Indian films like *Utsav* or *Razia Sultan*, where the performance of hyperbolic femininity encodes female same-sex eroticism within sites of extreme heteronormativity. The trope of dressing and undressing that threads through popular Indian cinematic depictions of female homoeroticism marks *Fire* as well: in the absence of their husbands, the two women indulge in not only dressing each other but dressing for each other, donning heavy silk saris, makeup, and gold jewelry. Their eroticizing of a particular aesthetic of Indian femininity brings to mind the problematic sketched out by Kaushalya Bannerji in the South Asian lesbian and gay anthology *Lotus of Another Color.*[67] Bannerji remarks on her alienation from a white lesbian aesthetic of androgyny, given her "fondness for bright colors, long hair, jewelry"—bodily signs that have multiple meanings for her as an Indian Canadian woman but read simply as markers of a transparent femme identity within a white lesbian context. Bannerji's presentation of a South Asian femininity elicits fetishistic responses from white lesbians, whereas for her, this particular aesthetic is a means of negotiating and reconciling categories of both racial and sexual identity. Similarly, the two protagonists in *Fire* derive pleasure from a particular, middle-class version of South Asian (and specifically North Indian) femininity that sometimes slips into an equally class-marked articulation of female homoerotic desire.[68] If "The Quilt" detaches masculinity from male bodies and instead uses it as a mobile signifier of female homoerotic desire, *Fire* follows in the tradition of the "femme films" of the Bollywood genre (to use Patricia White's phrase) and detaches femininity from its naturalized relation to heterosexuality.[69] Working against a logic that makes queer female desire visible only when it leaves the ambit of normative, middle-class femininity, *Fire* defamiliarizes the markers of conventional femininity by making them signify not the women's availability to heterosexuality but rather their desire for each other.

While *Fire* references Bollywood film through the production of a queer hyperbolic femininity, it also points in even more explicit ways to the uses of the particular gender and sexual codes of popular cinema in articulating queer desire. In one scene, for instance, Sita (dressed in a suit with her hair slicked back) and Radha (as a Bollywood film heroine) engage in a playful lip-synching duet that both inhabits and ironizes the genre of Bollywood songs. Whereas Radha's fantasy space is that of the field that gives way to the ocean, this evocation of popular Indian cinema becomes Sita's fantasied site of erotic and gender play. This scene of cross-gender identification stands apart from an earlier scene of playful cross-dressing, where Sita discards her sari and dons her husband's jeans and smokes his cigarettes as a way of temporarily laying claim to masculine authority, freedom, and privilege. In the later scene, cross-dressing is not a means by which to claim male privilege but rather functions as an articulation of same-sex desire; thus the film suggests that if one mode by which to make lust between women intelligible is through the representation of hyperbolic femininity, another is through the appropriation of popular culture and its particular gender dynamics.

Clearly, then, the "mythic mannish lesbian" (to use Esther Newton's term) that haunts Euro-American discourses of twentieth-century lesbian sexuality is not the dominant modality through which female same-sex desire can be read here.[70] Rather, within the context of the middle-class Indian home in the film, it is Radha and Sita's performance of queer femininity that emerges as the dominant mode or aesthetic through which female same-sex desire is rendered intelligible. The film suggests an alternative trajectory of representing female homoeroticism in a South Asian context, one at odds with conventional Euro-American "lesbian" histories that chart a developmental narrative from a nineteenth-century model of asexual "romantic friendship" between bourgeois women in privatized, domestic, gender-segregated spaces, to a modern, autonomous, "lesbian" identity, sexuality, and community.[71] The film's depiction of the ways in which this privatized, seemingly sanitized "domestic" space can simultaneously function as a site of intense female homoerotic pleasure and practices calls into question a narrative of "lesbian" sexuality as needing to emerge from a private, domestic sphere into a public, visible, "lesbian" subjectivity.[72]

Thus Fire, like "The Quilt," refuses to subscribe to the notion that the proper manifestation of same-sex eroticism is within a politics of visibility and identity. Rather, it suggests that in a South Asian context, what constitutes "lesbian" desire may both look and function differently than it does within Euro-American social and historical formations, and that it may draw from alternative modes of masculinity and femininity. In other words, the film makes explicit the ways in which not all female same-sex desire culminates in an autonomous "lesbianism," and not all "lesbianism" is at odds with domestic marital arrangements. One critic's assessment that Fire's depiction of lesbian sexuality is "extremely tame by Western standards" must therefore be read as an articulation of precisely the teleological narrative of sexual subjectivity that the film both reiterates and revises.[73] However, in *Fire*'s "modernized" version of "The Quilt," the two women eventually do leave the confines of the household rather than continue to exist within it as do Chughtai's characters. Thus *Fire*, coming fifty years after the publication of "The Quilt," is available for recuperation within (and bears the marks of) the narrative of sexual emancipation and public visibility circulated by contemporary international lesbian and gay politics, even while it provides a critique of this very narrative.

Fire Storms: Hindu Nationalist and Liberal Responses

In its representation of the complicated desiring relations between women in the seemingly traditional space of the home, "The Quilt" directly confronts notions of proper Indian womanhood on which anticolonial nationalist ideologies depend. As Geeta Patel argues, in locating female homoeroticism within the confines of the *zenana* and not as that which occurs "elsewhere," Chughtai both "queries and queers the arena of 'the domestic,'" while challenging the symbolic function of women as bearers of inviolate tradition within nationalist narratives.[74] Chughtai's configuration of female desiring subjects also troubles dominant representations of Muslim women as generic, chaste, and oppressed, as immured in the home and lost to the living. Female interactions within the *zenana* of "The Quilt" instead produce a particular relation between female homosociality and female homoerotic practices, one that, as Geeta Patel phrases it, "denaturalize[s] the apparently necessary slide from marriage into heterosexuality."[75] Similarly, *Fire*'s representation of female homoerotic desire within the home challenges contemporary Hindu nationalist ideologies that rely on Hindu women's sexual purity and sanctity as a means of ensuring group solidarity and vilifying Muslim minorities. Queer desire in the film functions as a modality through which the women resist complicity with the project of Hindu nationalism and its attendant gender and sexual hierarchies. Within the logic of the film, escaping heterosexuality is synonymous with escaping the violences of dominant Hindu nationalism: the few moments where the two women are seen together outside the space of the house take place within explicitly non-Hindu spaces such as mosques and tombs. Indeed, the film ends with a shot of the two women at Nizamuddin Dargar, a Sufi shrine, having finally left the household behind.

It is precisely *Fire*'s implicit critique of Hindu nationalism that prompted Shiv Sena activists to ransack theaters showing the film in December 1998; as one Shiv Sena member said of the film's depiction of the two women having sex, "this scene is a direct attack on our Hindu culture and civilization."[76] Interestingly, Indian liberals within India as well as in the diaspora were quick to counter the charge of perversion and obscenity leveled at the film from the Hindu right by seizing on the film's strategy of disarticulation and nonspecification (where it refuses to label the women under the fixed sign of "lesbian"). This liberal humanist defense argues that the film is not about lesbianism at all, given that it refuses to name its heroines as lesbians; rather, this argument holds, lesbian desire in the film functions allegorically and merely stands in for larger, more important issues such as women's emancipation as a whole.[77] The problematic nature of this liberal humanist defense of *Fire* was particularly evident in the filmmakers' own pronouncements about the film. At one event, for instance, the producer, David Hamilton, suggested that the film had raised the ire of Hindu nationalists because of the way it addressed issues of "artistic freedom, choice, and women's equality."[78] The question of sexuality was conspicuously absent from his interpretation of the controversy. Hamilton was at least in part taking his cue from the filmmaker, Deepa Mehta, herself, who repeatedly defended the film by using the rhetoric of women's emancipation and personal choice: "the lesbian relationship in the film is merely a symbol of an extreme choice my heroines make . . . it is not a lesbian film . . . rather, I think of it as humanistic."[79] Such a statement prefigures and replicates the incommensurability of queerness and feminism that characterizes her later film, *Bollywood/Hollywood*, as well as the other diasporic feminist films discussed in chapter 4.

These are curious evaluations of the outburst against *Fire* given that the Shiv Sena directed their outrage very specifically at the lesbian relationship between the two women, and worse still, at the fact that the film locates this lesbian relationship within the confines of Hindu familial domesticity. As Shiv Sena leader Bal Thackeray complained, "Why is it that lesbianism is shown in a Hindu family? Why are the names of the heroines Radha and Sita and not Shabana or Saira?"[80] In the same vein, a senior government official in Maharashtra argued, as justification for the banning of the film, "if women's physical needs get fulfilled through lesbian acts, the institution of marriage will collapse, and the reproduction of human beings will stop."[81] As both these comments amply demonstrate, the extreme anxiety that the film provokes among the Hindu right stems from the threat that its representation of queer desire in the home poses to the Hindu nationalist project. It is precisely this threat posed by queer representation that liberal humanist arguments—in their recasting of the film's queer content in terms of a feminist desire for self-determination—fail to recognize. The liberal critique of right-wing attacks on *Fire* converges with particular instances of Indian feminist scholarship on sexuality, to the extent that both are marked by the subsumption of queerness into feminism, and the subsequent elision of queerness altogether.

Queer Diasporic Activism

The reactions to *Fire* within and outside India force us to consider the function of cultural representation as a site of both "promise and peril,"[82] a site of both the subversion of nationalist ideologies and the reiteration of homophobic sentiments. *Fire* gains multiple and contradictory meanings as it circulates within India, within the South Asian diaspora, and within film festival circuits and theaters in Europe and North America. As the film circulates within India, it may pose a potent challenge to right-wing Hindu nationalism, yet it is simultaneously available for recuperation within a liberal humanist framework that subsumes sexuality under a civil rights rubric. Similarly, as it travels outside India, the film both resists and plays into dominant developmental narratives of modernity. I have focused on *Fire* in particular since it is emblematic of the ways in which South Asian diasporic texts travel along increasingly complex trajectories of production and reception. In a Euro-American context, the film's strategy of disarticulation—where it refuses to collapse female homoerotic acts, desires, and practices into static identities—challenges dominant conceptions of what lesbian and gay identity looks like in the West; yet in an Indian context, this very strategy simultaneously allows for the elision of queer desire and the challenge it poses to dominant conceptions of community, home, and nation. The violent debates that have surrounded *Fire* demand that we develop frames of analysis supple enough to account for these transnational movements and the various discourses of gender and sexuality to which they give rise.

The diasporic political mobilization that took place around the *Fire* controversy between South Asian queer activist groups in the United States and lesbian groups in India offers one such frame of analysis. The activist links

forged between the New York–based South Asian Lesbian and Gay Association (SALGA) and the New Delhi–based Campaign for Lesbian Rights (CA-
LERI), for instance, create a potent counterdiscourse that intervenes into multiple discourses. CALERI was formed in December 1998 as a response to the
attacks on *Fire* and comprises a coalition of lesbian, feminist, and progressive
organizations whose "stated goal is one of gaining and promoting [lesbian]
visibility."[83] CALERI spearheaded protests against the Shiv Sena during the *Fire*
controversy and has also campaigned for the repeal of Section 377 of the Indian
Penal Code that criminalizes homosexuality. The organization is clearly working within the register of visibility, naming, and identity that, as I have argued,
Fire and "The Quilt" avoid. CALERI found that the only way to counter the
elision of sexuality within progressive defenses of the film was to enact a reverse
discourse, responding to the film's strategy of disarticulation with one of explicit articulation and naming.[84]

The transnational activist flows between CALERI and SALGA challenge the
violent nationalist rhetoric of the Hindu right, the liberal/feminist subsumption of non-heteronormative sexualities, and conventional gay and lesbian
discourse that situates non-Western sexualities in a developmental relation to
metropolitan sexualities. These interventions are enacted through a complicated negotiation of conservative claims to modernity and national authenticity. As I have suggested, lesbian and gay organizations in the West tend to see
the naming of alternative sexualities under the rubric of "gay" or "lesbian" as
the marker of modernity, and the adoption of such identities as indicators of
the relative evolution of non-Western locations. Conversely, Hindu nationalist
ideologies within India—which are subsequently reproduced by conservative
immigrant organizations in the diaspora—constitute the modernity of the
Hindu nation through the production of a pure, heterosexual past and the violent excision of alternative sexualities from the national imaginary. If, within
Hindu nationalist discourse, the diaspora can only signify as the inauthentic
Other of the nation, within dominant models of gay and lesbian organizing,
the diaspora is the origin of liberating sexual discourses. The transnational
organizing strategies adopted by CALERI and SALGA challenge the neocolonial
ideologies implicit in mainstream gay and lesbian organizing, as well as the
consolidation of an essential "Indianness" as imagined by the Hindu right.
They also simultaneously critique the effacement of sexuality within a progressive liberal-humanist agenda. In their press releases immediately following the

attacks against *Fire*, SALGA activists pointedly drew lines of connection between the rights of sexual minorities and the advocacy of artistic freedom and
anticommunalism: "Supporting lesbian rights in India is the only option for
our government if it is committed to putting an end to communalism, anti-
secularism, and the forms of fundamentalism that threaten the lives of our
constitutionally protected minorities."[85] In so doing, queer activists in the
diaspora were expressly taking their lead from queer activists in India, rather
than simply imposing diasporic agendas and models of organizing on Indian
activists. Indeed, SALGA members were explicitly cognizant of the need to
guard against, as they put it, "the imperialist tendencies of international work
that get disguised under the rubric of international solidarity work" in their
dealings with CALERI.[86] By consistently reinserting sexuality back into the
arguments in defense of the film, queer activists both in India and the United
States demanded that sexuality be seen as central to issues such as anticensor-
ship and anticommunalism that have long concerned leftist organizers in India.
Given that significant funding for Hindu nationalist organizations in India
comes from immigrant communities in the United States, Canada, and elsewhere,[87] such queer diasporic alliances speak to the ways in which transnational circuits of commerce and culture are also being mobilized in the
service of alternative visions of community, home, and nation.

6

NOSTALGIA, DESIRE, DIASPORA

Funny Boy and *Cereus Blooms at Night*

In the early 1990s, newspapers catering to Trinidad's East Indian population were awash with heated arguments about the increasing popularity of chutney, a form of popular music and dance initially performed by Indo-Trinidadian women in the context of women-only, prewedding celebrations.[1] The furor surrounding chutney was fueled by the fact that, by the late 1980s, more and more Indian women were performing the songs and dances in public spaces rather than in the confines of their homes. This move from the private to the public prompted culturally conservative Hindu organizations in Trinidad to denounce chutney and its offspring, chutney soca, as "vulgar, degrading and obscene."[2] Echoing the controversies generated by Deepa Mehta's *Fire* and Ismat Chughtai's "The Quilt," the debates surrounding chutney music expose the imbrication of discourses of female sexuality, diasporic identity, and the "home" as domestic, communal, and national space. The chutney controversy in Trinidad, like the battle over SALGA's inclusion in the India Day parade in New York City, is yet another instance of how the space of public culture in the diaspora emerges as a contested terrain where heteronormative notions of female sexuality are both enacted and challenged. In the cases of both the chutney and India Day parade disputes, a diasporic male elite attempted to counter nationalist framings of the diaspora as the inauthentic Other to the nation by positioning women's bodies as the site of an imagined communal purity and authenticity. Indeed, what particularly galled chutney's detractors was that the dancing was performed not only in public space but primarily by middle-aged Indian women. These women were seen, as one speaker from a Hindu cultural group put it, as "the once flower of the race, the personification of virtue and chastity, the epitome of humility and uprightness."[3] Such a statement makes glaringly apparent how colonial constructions of respectable female sexuality and proper womanhood as enshrined within the home, initially consolidated during the period of Indian indentureship in Trinidad, continue to resonate in the public culture of the postcolonial present. These constructions powerfully maintain the boundaries of communal identity in the diaspora.

The "chutney polemic," as the ethnomusicologist Peter Manuel terms it,[4] has received a fair amount of attention from scholars and critics interested in gender, nationalism, and popular culture. In her essay "Left to the Imagination: Indian Nationalisms and Female Sexuality in Trinidad," for instance, Tejaswini Niranjana carefully contextualizes the chutney phenomenon within histories of both Trinidadian and Indian nationalisms. Indian nationalist discourse in the early twentieth century, she argues, imagined the indentured Indian woman in Trinidad as licentious and immoral, so as to produce a female nationalist subject in India that was at once modern yet virtuous and chaste.[5] While Niranjana's analysis convincingly demonstrates the centrality of discourses of women's sexuality to nationalist definitions of "Indianness" in both India and Trinidad, it is unable to imagine the ways in which women's sexuality may exceed the heterosexual parameters put in place by these nationalist discourses. This blind spot becomes particularly apparent in Niranjana's understanding of chutney, which she frames as a representation of Indian women's sexual autonomy in the face of opposition from a Hindu male elite. Niranjana argues that for this elite, chutney raised the fearful specter of miscegenation between Indian women and Afro-Trinidadian men, given that it exposed Indian women's bodies to a public (male) gaze. As Niranjana states, "the disapproval of 'vulgarity' can be read . . . as an anxiety regarding miscegenation, the new form chutney becoming a metonym for the supposed increase in the relationships between Indian women and African men."[6] Indian women's bodies served as the terrain on which Indo- and Afro-Trinidadian men competed over the right to represent the nation. Certainly, as Niranjana suggests, the controversy crystallized the ways in which diasporic nationalism is predicated on the notion of women's bodies as communal property. However, what remains unmarked in Niranjana's otherwise useful analysis is an acknowledgment of alternative forms of desire that may emerge within the women-only spaces where chutney music was originally performed. By presuming that Indo-Caribbean women's sexuality is always and everywhere heterosexual, Niranjana's analysis takes as a given what is in actuality discursively produced by successive waves of colonial and nationalist ideologies.

Similarly, Peter Manuel, in one of the only book-length accounts of Indo-Caribbean music and the "chutney polemic" in particular, betrays a simultaneous recognition and disavowal of the homoerotics of the dance space that chutney produces. Manuel writes that chutney dancing, like the sexually suggestive "wining" of Afro-Caribbean women at Carnival,[7] was "misinterpreted" by "outraged critics" as "lesbianism, but it is better seen as a celebration of autosexuality or female sexuality per se in a way that is not dependent on the presence of men . . . Accordingly, chutney's defenders have celebrated it as a form of women's liberation."[8] Manuel in effect evacuates the possibility of female homoeroticism by couching the pleasure that women derive from dancing with and among each other as evidence solely of (heterosexual) "women's liberation." As in Niranjana's analysis, the possibility that queer female desire (whether or not it is articulated as "lesbian") may in fact be an important component of the pleasures afforded by chutney dancing is abruptly foreclosed.

Interestingly, Manuel's history of the development of contemporary chutney soca traces a lineage back to the 1950s in Guyana, where "during wedding festivities, men would also dance in chutney style with one another or with male transvestite dancers."[9] Manuel contains and neutralizes this rather remarkable mention of histories of queer public cultural space by stressing that the Trinidadian men who today perform chutney may appear "effeminate" to the untrained eye but that "male partners should not be assumed to be gay lovers."[10] He later concedes, however, that "although male dance partners need not be assumed to be homosexual, the Trinidad chutney scene has opened space for a small but flamboyant gay subculture, which includes a popular semiprofessional transvestite film-style dancer. As has been the case to some extent in the United States, gay liberation in Trinidad has followed in the wake of women's liberation."[11] What is particularly striking in these statements is Manuel's attempt to reestablish the chutney scene as a predominantly heterosexual space of "liberation" for straight women and, to a lesser extent, a queer space of "liberation" for gay men. Both Niranjana and Manuel, then, inadvertently replicate the nationalist framings of gender and sexuality that they set out to critique. They do so by enacting the familiar discursive move of equating queerness with men and femaleness with heterosexuality that I have traced throughout this book. Within this schema, queer *female* desire, pleasure, and subjectivity is indeed rendered impossible, and the queer public cultural space that the performance of chutney may produce and make available is effaced.

I open this chapter with an evocation of the chutney controversy in Trinidad, and the implicit heteronormativity of some of the scholarship that documents it, as it is yet another instance that reveals the necessity of an analysis of diasporic public cultures that is at once both feminist *and* queer. Without such an analysis, we remain unable to fully grasp the deep investment of diasporic and state nationalisms in disciplining female sexuality and legislating heteronormativity. As is evident from Niranjana's essay, a feminist reading of a diasporic cultural practice like chutney makes apparent how home as household, community, and nation is consolidated through the containment of unruly female bodies. A *queer* feminist reading, however, identifies the ways in which those bodies, desires, and subjects deemed impossible within dominant diasporic logic intervene into the public culture of the diaspora. These queer incursions into diasporic public culture reterritorialize the home by transforming it into a site where non-heteronormative desires and practices are articulated and performed.

The "chutney polemic" thus provides an unexpectedly useful point of entry into a discussion of a growing body of work that can be seen to constitute a genre of queer South Asian diasporic literature. This literary genre suggests an alternative formulation of home in the diaspora that powerfully challenges the hegemonic constructions of diasporic identity that were so in evidence during the chutney debates. A consideration of queer diasporic literature also makes evident the inadequacy and dangers of feminist theorizing of diasporic public culture that ignores its queer valences. Ismat Chughtai's "The Quilt," with its beautifully nuanced re-inscription of home through queer female desire, serves as an important precursor to this emergent genre, which must be situated in a skewed relation to the genres of "exile literature" and "immigrant literature."[12] If exile literature is marked by the trauma of forced separation from a homeland and a yearning for return, and the "immigrant genre" as defined by Rosemary

George alternately revels in "a detached and unsentimental reading of the experience of 'homelessness,' "[13] queer South Asian diasporic literature is necessarily characterized by yet another relation to home. While queer diasporic literature eschews claims to immutable origins and unsullied pasts on which dominant articulations of both the nation and diaspora depend, the specter of home—as household, community, and nation—continues to haunt it. Rather than simply doing away with home and its fictions of (sexual, racial, communal) purity and belonging, queer diasporic literature instead engages in a radical reworking of multiple home spaces. The queer diasporic body is the medium through which home is remapped and its various narratives are displaced, uprooted, and infused with alternative forms of desire.

In *Funny Boy*,[14] Shyam Selvadurai's 1994 novel in six stories, the upper-middle-class Sri Lankan Tamil narrator traces the seven years of his childhood and adolescence in Colombo that preceded the Tamil-Sinhalese riots in 1983, and his family's subsequent migration as refugees to Canada. This experience of migration forms the ground on which the narrative unfolds; the novel is structured in terms of remembrance, with the narrator Arjie recalling a "remembered innocence of childhood . . . now colored in the hues of a twilight sky."[15] Such a phrase, coming early on in the novel, seems to signal that the text can be comfortably contained within the genre of exile literature, one that evokes from the vantage point of exile an idyllic, coherent, pre-exilic past shattered by war and dislocation. Similarly, the novel's parallel narrative of Arjie's sexual awakening initially locates the text within an established genre of coming out stories, where the protagonist grows into an awareness of his "true" homosexual identity that places him outside the purview of home and family.

This narrative of migration and sexual exile with which *Funny Boy* begins is also referenced in Shani Mootoo's 1996 novel, *Cereus Blooms at Night*,[16] which opens in a small town in a fictionalized pre-Independence Trinidad. Early in the novel, we are privy to the growing attraction between the Indo-Trinidadian Sarah and the white daughter of the local reverend, as it emerges within the house in which Sarah lives with her husband and two daughters. Quite abruptly, however, the two women exit both the house and the narrative as a whole as they set sail for the "north," apparently unable to reconcile queer desire within the exigencies of the home. The sudden disappearance of the two women from the narrative may initially appear to be Mootoo's capitulation to the familiar notion of a "lesbian" subject having to leave a Third World home of gender and sexual oppression in order to come out into the more liberated West.

A closer look at both novels, however, reveals a far more complicated relation between travel, sexual subjectivity, and the space of home as household, community, and nation. While *Funny Boy* references the familiar narratives of exile and coming out, it reworks the conventions of these genres and also rearticulates the very notions of exile and sexual subjectivity. Similarly, Mootoo's novel traces the various forms of travel and motion undertaken by sexual subjects both within the home and away from it. The disruption and remaking of home space through queer desire that marks all the queer diasporic texts I have engaged with throughout the book resonates particularly powerfully in these novels. While "home" in both texts is on one hand a seemingly static place that the various characters escape from and return to, it also produces and is marked by its own particular forms of travel and transitivity. As is the case with Chughtai's work, both novels map out Avtar Brah's notion of "diaspora space," which "includes the entanglement of genealogies of dispersion with those of 'staying put.'"[17] *Funny Boy* and *Cereus Blooms at Night* allow for an understanding of diaspora as produced both in the process of travel and "at home"; by importing home into the diaspora, the novels enact a similar reversal of the nation-diaspora hierarchy that, as I argued in chapter 2, is effected by transnational cultural practices such as Bhangra music.

South Asian Diasporic Texts in the House of Asian America

While queer diasporic literature reworks the formulation of home found in exilic and immigrant literatures, this genre also allows for a reconsideration of the place of South Asian American cultural texts within the frameworks of South Asian studies and Asian American studies. South Asian American cultural production has thus far rested somewhat uneasily between these two frames of reference that are often imagined in opposition to one another.[18] Yet in an essay written in 1991, Sucheta Mazumdar argues this apparent split between area studies and ethnic studies upholds a false binary that masks the explicitly transnational and internationalist thrust of an ethnic studies project at its very inception. As Mazumdar states, "The need is to define a new paradigm which contextualizes the history of Asian Americans within the twentieth-century global history of imperialism, of colonialism, of capitalism. To isolate Asian American history from its internationalist underpinnings, to abstract it from the global context of capital and labor migration, is to distort this history."[19] Mazumdar's call for establishing and acknowledging the connections between area studies and ethnic studies has been taken up in much of the subsequent work on South Asian American and South Asian diasporic cultural politics.[20] The last few years have seen an explosion of work by South Asian scholars in the United States and Canada who situate the politics of South Asian diasporic cultures within the context of North American racialization on the one hand, and histories of colonialism, nationalism, and communalism in South Asia on the other. Such work marks an important intervention into both Asian American studies and South Asian studies: it links the current category of "South Asian American" to prior histories of anticolonial struggle in South Asia, as well as to the labor migrations precipitated by British colonialism in Europe, North America, East and South Africa, and the Caribbean.

Vijay Prashad's *The Karma of Brown Folk* can be seen to have inaugurated this new body of scholarship, in that it intervenes into both South Asian and Asian American studies by drawing the lines of connection between discourses of U.S. Orientalism and right-wing Hindu nationalism in the United States and South Asia. Prashad is careful to point out that the conservative discourses of community and culture in South Asia and the diaspora that he critiques are consolidated through particular gender ideologies that place an excess of meaning on South Asian women's bodies. Yet what remains to be further articulated is an analysis of how these conservative notions of "family," "kinship," "tradition," and "culture" in South Asia and the diaspora rely on the maintenance of heteronormativity.[21] Without such an analysis, the modes of activism and cultural production undertaken by queer and feminist subjects in the diaspora invariably appear secondary to "real" politics, such as that of the labor struggles of New York City's taxicab drivers that Prashad details.[22] I mention Prashad's book here because it is indicative of the crucial contributions made by a new body of South Asian American scholarship, while it also gestures to the particular points within such scholarship that await further elaboration. The novels of Selvadurai and Mootoo in turn constitute an important intervention into this body of work. While the imaginative landscapes of these novels similarly trouble fixed notions of the proper objects of Asian American studies or South Asian studies, queer South Asian diasporic literature builds on the analyses of Prashad and others inasmuch as they offer a more fully realized theory of how heteronormative notions of gender and sexuality are central to the maintenance of colonial, racist, and ethnic absolutist structures of domination. Such systems of logic, these novels suggest, are most fruitfully destabilized through alternative formulations of gendered and sexual subjectivity.

Other recent scholarship in South Asian American cultural studies more explicitly attempts to reconcile South Asian American cultural production with Asian American studies. Such work has often revolved around the questions of the inclusion, recognition, and acknowledgment of South Asian communities and cultures within the boundaries of Asian America. In the 1998 anthology *A Part Yet Apart: South Asians in Asian America,* for instance, Rajiv Shankar characterizes this relation between South Asians and the category of "Asian American" as follows:

> South Asians want their unique attributes to be recognized and their particular issues discussed; and some of them want this to occur within the Asian American paradigm, for they think that they must surely belong there. Yet they find themselves so unnoticed as an entity that they feel as if they are merely a crypto-group, often included but easily marginalized within the house of Asian America.[23]

It seems more useful to replace this preoccupation with belonging, visibility, recognition, and incorporation with the question of how a serious engagement with South Asian diasporic cultural production would force a radical reframing of Asian American studies as it was originally conceived. Rather than reiterating a plaintive call for inclusion, I want to suggest that this position of marginality or "ex-centricity" to a dominant Asian American paradigm is a potentially generative and fruitful one for South Asian diasporic cultural critics. It provides a space not from which to call for "belonging" within the "house of Asian America" but from which to rethink the very notions of house, home, community, belonging, and authenticity. The novels I discuss in this chapter mobilize three conceptual categories—"queer," "diaspora," and "South Asian"—that have until recently been ex-centric to the dominant model of Asian American studies, and that challenge and extend its scope in critical ways. A queer South Asian diasporic project is aligned with an increasing number of feminist and queer critics who, over the past decade, have taken exception to an early model of Asian American cultural nationalism, one that implicitly viewed the prototypical Asian American subject as male, heterosexual, working class, U.S. born, and English speaking.[24] Such static notions of Asian American identity have necessarily given way to new models that take into account the shifting demographics of Asian American communities in the United States as well as the ever-increasing mobility of people, capital, and culture throughout the world.

Reconceptualizing Asian American subjectivity through the framework of a queer South Asian diaspora, then, disrupts the notion of the Asian American subject as essentially masculinist and heterosexual, as well as the belief that Asian American subjectivity is comprehensible exclusively within the boundaries of the U.S. nation-state. By placing South Asian cultural practices in productive relation to an Asian American studies paradigm, I am not making an argument for the incorporation and visibility of a heretofore orphaned and invisible group within the "house of Asian America." Indeed, arguments for inclusion do nothing to dismantle the very structures of inclusion and exclusion on which communities and identities are based. Rather, I am interested in how foregrounding queer South Asian diasporic cultural practices creates a different paradigm of Asian American studies, one that demands that we place analyses of sexual subjectivity and racialization within the United States and Canada in relation to older histories of U.S. and British colonialism in Asia and the Caribbean. The framework of a queer South Asian diaspora thus demands a remapping of Asian America, so that its borders extend north to Canada and south to Latin America and the Caribbean.

The reformulation of home through queer desire and subjectivity in queer South Asian diasporic literature situates it in contradistinction to the work that has become representative of South Asian American writing in North America, such as the fiction of more established writers like Bharati Mukherjee and Chitra Banerjee Divakaruni. The same developmental narrative that marks a film like Deepa Mehta's *Fire* structures Mukherjee's and Divakaruni's fiction as well: their female protagonists travel from an India that functions as the symbolic space of gender oppression and "old world dutifulness" (to use Mukherjee's phrase), to an America that fulfills its promises of progress, individual freedom, and feminist self-enlightenment.[25] Furthermore, in the writings of both Mukherjee and Divakaruni, this teleological progress narrative is coterminous with a narrative of heterosexual romance, within which the female protagonists are firmly situated. The familiar binarisms of East and West, tradition and modernity, home and away, diaspora and nation that structure these examples of diasporic fiction are exploded by the queer diasporic novels of Selvadurai and Mootoo. Both texts exemplify an alternative mapping of Asian America: they are written by first-generation South Asian Canadians and negotiate the various legacies of colonialism and nationalist movements in the home spaces from which they came (Sri Lanka on one hand and Trinidad on the other) through the production of queer desire and affiliation. While both novels are only slowly making their way onto Asian American studies syllabi, it is precisely in the queer and diasporic dimensions of these texts that the most powerful and indispensable critiques of dominant formulations of national, racial, sexual, and gender identity are taking place.

Pigs Can't Fly: Shyam Selvadurai's *Funny Boy*

"Pigs Can't Fly," the first story in *Funny Boy*, lays out the complex system of prohibition, punishment, and compulsion that governs and structures gender differentiation. The story tells of the childhood game that Arjie and his girl cousins play in the house of their grandparents, which entails an elaborate performance of a wedding ceremony. The pleasure Arjie takes in playing the part of the bride causes intense embarrassment and consternation for the adults, who decree that henceforth Arjie is to play with the boys. Arjie's eventual, traumatic banishment from the world of the girls and his forced entry into proper gender identification is figured in terms of geography and spacialization, of leaving one carefully inscribed space of gender play and entering one of gender conformity: Arjie is compelled to leave the inner section of the compound inhabited by the girls and enter the outer area where the boys congregate. Similarly, Arjie is barred from watching his mother dress in her room, which throughout his childhood has been the site of his most intense spectatorial pleasure. The gendered spacialization of the domestic sphere in the story mirrors and reiterates nationalist framings of space that posit the "inner" as an atavistic space of spirituality and tradition, embodied by the figure of the woman, as opposed to the "outer" male sphere of progress, politics, materiality, and modernity.[26] But by portraying the inner sphere not simply as a space of gender conformity but also of gender play and fantasy, the story refigures the gendered spacialization of the nation by revealing how non-heteronormative embodiments, desires, and pleasures surface within even the most heteronormative of spaces. As we have seen in the various texts I have engaged with throughout the book, this reterritorialization of domestic and national space takes place through a queering of public culture. For Arjie, dressing up as the bride—complete with shimmering white sari, flowers, and jewelry—is a way of accessing a particular mode of hyperbolic femininity embodied not only by his mother but by the popular Sri Lankan female film stars of the day.

Throughout *Funny Boy*, Selvadurai deftly makes apparent the ways in which institutionalized heterosexuality, in the form of marriage, undergirds ethnic and state nationalisms. Thus Arjie's queer reconfiguration of the wedding has implications far beyond the domestic sphere, in that it suggests other ways of imagining kinship and affiliation that extend further than the horizon of nationalist framings of community. The game itself, brilliantly titled "Bride-Bride," offers a reconfiguration of the contractual obligations of heterosexuality and gender conformity. Arjie installs himself in the most coveted role— that of bride—and makes it abundantly clear that the part of groom occupies the lowest rung of the game's hierarchy. Indeed, the game is predicated on the apparent non-performativity of masculinity, as opposed to the excessive feminine performance of Arjie as bride.[27] The game's title, then—"Bride-*Bride*," rather than "Bride-Groom" or simply "Bride"—references both the unimportance of the groom and the hyperbolic femininity embodied by the figure of the bride, as well as the potentiality of a female same-sex eroticism that dispenses with the groom altogether. In other words, the game not only speaks to a particular mode of queer male femininity and cross-gender identificatory pleasure but also suggests the possibility of a female homoeroticism located within the home that works through the absence and irrelevance of the groom. Indeed, we can read Deepa Mehta's *Fire* as (quite literally) staging the game of "Bride-Bride" within a female homosocial context.

Arjie thus sutures himself into the scene of marriage, radically displacing it from the matrix of heterosexuality and calling into question the very logic and authority of heteronormativity. "Pigs Can't Fly" encodes gender differentiation within multiple narratives, not all of which are necessarily pathologizing: while Arjie's father reads Arjie's cross-gender identification as unnatural and perverse, his mother is unable to come up with a viable explanation for the logic of gender conformity. When pushed by Arjie to explain why he can no longer play with the girls or watch her dress, she resorts to a childhood nursery rhyme, retorting in exasperation, "Because the sky is so high and pigs can't fly, that's why."[28] Her answer attempts to grant to the fixity of gender roles the status of universally recognized natural law and to root it in common sense; however, such an explanation fails to satisfy Arjie, and his mother seems equally unconvinced by it but is unable to imagine an alternative order of things. Thus the varied, multiple discourses around gender that mark the domestic sphere militate against an overly reductive reading of "home" space as merely oppressive. Instead, gender conformity and nonconformity are narrativized through competing discourses in the story, where the rhetoric of nonconformity as perversion is undercut by the antinormative performance of gender in "Bride-Bride," as well as by Arjie's mother making apparent the nonsensical nature of gender codification.

The story ends with Arjie's dawning realization that he is doomed to being "caught between the boys' and the girls' worlds, not belonging or wanted in either."[29] This exile from the space of gender fantasy shadows the other, various exiles that Arjie experiences in each of the subsequent chapters. These follow a similar narrative arc as "Pigs Can't Fly," in that they end with Arjie's coming into consciousness of the gender, sexual, ethnic, and class constraints that limit his life and the lives of those around him, and that move him further and further away from the brief, idealized moment of gender fantasy and freedom of his childhood. For instance, Arjie's sexual encounters with his Sinhalese classmate Shehan, and his realization that such homoerotic sex has pushed him outside the purview of family as he has known it, produce a form of exile that is layered onto the previous ones and that prefigures the ones to come. Significantly, the initial sexual encounter between the two boys takes place not in the house itself but in the garage at the edges of the family compound. The literal and figurative remove of queer sexuality from the family scene is forcefully brought home to Arjie as he and Shehan rejoin his parents for lunch after their encounter in the garage. As he looks around the table at the faces of his parents, he realizes with horror that the act in the garage has opened up an unbridgeable distance between him and the rest of his family and has "moved [him] beyond his [father's] hand."[30] Arjie's sexual awakening and his realization that queer desire can only exist at the margins of home can initially be situated within the narrative tradition of the coming out story. Such narratives are often characterized as journeys toward an essential wholeness, toward the discovery of a true gay identity through a teleological process of individuation that is granted representative status. Indeed, the novel's title, *Funny Boy*, can be read as a reference to Edmund White's 1982 narrative of gay coming of age in the fifties, *A Boy's Own Story*.[31] However, unlike White's text, where sexuality is privileged as the singular site of radical difference and the narrator's sole claim to alterity, sexuality in *Funny Boy* is but one of many discourses—such as those of ethnic identity and forced migration—all of which speak to multiple displacements and exiles. For instance, gender inversion in "Pigs Can't Fly" is not so much a primary marker of Arjie's latent homosexuality, a childhood signifier of adult homosexuality as charted along a linear narrative of sexual development that ends with a fully realized "gay" subject. Rather, cross-gender identification in the story takes on numerous, complex valences given the novel's engagement with questions of loss and memory in the context of diasporic displacement.

It is from the vantage point of "a new home . . . in Canada" that the narrator remembers the intense pleasure derived from the ritual of becoming "like the goddesses of the Sinhalese and Tamil cinema, larger than life" and of watching his mother dress.[32] Thus the narrator's evocation of these remembered instances of cross-gender identificatory practices and pleasures becomes a means by which to negotiate the loss of home as a fantasied site of geographic rootedness, belonging, and gender and erotic play. Indeed, if "home," as Dorinne Kondo states, is for "peoples in diaspora" that which "we cannot not want,"[33] home for a queer diasporic subject becomes not only that which "we cannot not want" but also that which we cannot and could never have. Home in the queer fantasy of the past is the space of violent (familial and national) disowning: if queer desire and gender inversion exile Arjie from the space of the family and the domestic sphere, his Tamilness exiles him from the home space of the nation. Cross-gender identification—through the game of Bride-Bride and in his mother's dressing room—allows Arjie to momentarily lay claim to domestic space and its gendered arrangements. The remembrance of such moments mediates the multiple alienations of the queer diasporic subject from "home" as familial, domestic, and national space. "Pigs Can't Fly" speaks to the centrality of South Asian popular cinema in producing a queer diasporic imaginary and reveals the ways in which queer subjects reaccess home through an engagement with, and intervention into, public culture. Evoking the uses of popular film for queer diasporic audiences that I discussed in chapter 4, for Arjie it is the icons of Sri Lankan cinema—images of "the Malini Fonsekas and the Geeta Kumarasinghes"—that act as the vehicle through which "home" is conjured into being, mourned, and reimagined. Furthermore the specificity of the Tamil and Sinhala screen goddesses who fuel Arjie's fantasy life decenters Bollywood as the hegemonic cinematic force in South Asia and instead makes visible other, local points of cultural reference that are drawn on to produce queer diasporic public cultures.

The relation between cross-dressing and "home" spaces that the novel maps out echoes the anthropologist Martin Manalansan's depiction of the uses of drag within contemporary gay Filipino communities in New York City. Manalansan finds that for diasporic Filipino gay men, drag is inextricably intertwined with nostalgia, evoking "the image and memory of the Filipino homeland while at the same time acknowledging being settled in a 'new home' here in the U.S."[34] Similarly, the narrator's memory of cross-dressing in *Funny Boy* negotiates multiple cultural and geographic sites, while suggesting the uses of nostalgia for queer diasporic subjects. Arjie's performance of queer femininity radically reconfigures hegemonic nationalist and diasporic logic, which depends on the figure of the woman as a stable signifier of "tradition." Within a queer diasporic imaginary, the lost homeland is represented not by the pure and self-sacrificing wife and mother but rather by a queer boy in a sari. This project of reterritorializing national space, and the uses of drag in such a project, are explicitly articulated within South Asian queer activism and popular culture in various diasporic sites. In an example of the ways in which queer public culture reconfigures the nation, a SALGA flier for a party celebrating the publication of Selvadurai's novel depicts a sari-clad figure exclaiming, "Shyam was right! I look better in Mummy ki sari!" On the one hand, the flier makes apparent the ways in which the popular cultural practices (parties and drag performances) and literary texts like *Funny Boy* inform and produce each other and thus call into existence a space of queer diasporic public culture. The flier also replaces the woman-in-sari that typically stands in for India with a gay male/transgendered performance of queer femininity that references and remembers nonheteronormative childhoods in other national sites.[35]

The novel as a whole tracks various desiring relations, both hetero- and homosexual, such as those between the Tamil Radha and the Sinhalese Anil, between Arjie's mother and her Dutch-descended Burgher lover, and between Arjie and Shehan. None of these forms of desire fit within the logic of ethnic or state nationalisms, and they are disciplined and regulated by increasingly brutal means as the novel progresses. While "Pigs Can't Fly" concludes with

Arjie's traumatic awareness of the hegemonic power of dominant gender ideologies, the following chapter, "Radha Aunty," traces his growing awareness of dominant ethnic and nationalist ideologies, and their particular investment in gender and sexual normativity. Arjie's young aunt Radha has the misfortune of falling in love with a Sinhalese man, Anil, on the eve of a period of heightened violence against Tamils. This violence climaxes, at the end of the novel, with Arjie's family being expelled from Sri Lanka and seeking refugee status in Canada. Radha initially acts as a co-conspirator in Arjie's gender play; she takes delight in the pleasure that he derives from imagining in great detail her own future wedding ceremony and in dressing in her make-up and jewelry. After being violently attacked during a riot, however, Radha turns away from Anil and agrees to marry a more suitable Tamil businessman approved of by her family. The story makes clear how women's bodies become the literal and figurative battleground on which ethnic nationalist ideologies play out. By the story's end, the bohemian Radha is transformed into a "real" bride, with the heavy mask-like make-up, gold jewelry, flowers, and silk saris of Arjie's fantasy life. However, here the hyperbolic femininity of the bride is sutured firmly to heterosexuality and is annexed to the project of maintaining the inviolability of ethnic boundaries. In sharp contrast to the queerness of the wedding scene as performed by Arjie in "Pigs Can't Fly," the wedding in "Radha Aunty" serves to discipline bodies and desires that do not conform to ethnic absolutist notions of community. Here femininity signifies not gender play, fantasy, and pleasure but rather Radha's acquiescence to this logic of ethnic absolutism. The pathologizing of Arjie as a feminine boy, then, is revealed to be but one component in the same structure of domination that renders Radha's heterosexual, female body symbolic of communal purity and tradition.

The centrality of gender and sexual normativity in the consolidation of ethnic and state nationalisms, and the costs this consolidation exacts on queer and female bodies, are made further apparent in the novel's penultimate chapter, "The Best School of All." The story details the ways in which Arjie's school, where his father has sent him to become a "real man," functions as a site for the indoctrination of normative gender and sexual identity as well as ethnic affiliation. For instance, the boys must call their classmates by their surnames, which marks each student as irreducibly Tamil or Sinhalese. As the intimacy between Arjie and Shehan grows, they shift from calling each other by their ethnically marked surnames (Selvaratnam and Soyza) to their more neutral given names. Echoing the ways in which queer female desire provides a space for the critique of communal politics in *Fire*, in *Funny Boy* queer male desire similarly interrupts the normative gender, sexual, and ethnic nationalist logic of the school space that stands in for Sri Lanka as a whole. Yet while queer desire here, as in Kureishi's *My Beautiful Laundrette*, undercuts the logic of ethnic / racial purity and authenticity, it does not transcend it: after his house is burnt down during the riots, it occurs to Arjie for the first time that Shehan is Sinhalese and he is not; this realization becomes "a thin translucent screen" through which Arjie now comes to view Shehan.[36] Thus other vectors of power, difference, and privilege are woven into the very fabric of queer desire and are inextricable from it.

The novel's final section, "Riot Journal," makes all the more evident the ways in which the home is reconfigured in queer diasporic memory. The novel's episodic structure is abandoned here and the book shifts to present tense and first person as Arjie, in terse journal entries, documents the horrors of the 1983 massacre of Tamils by Sinhalese. This splintered, fragmented format brusquely interrupts the more conventional structure of the previous chapters and marks the fact that queer diasporic histories cannot be contained within a teleological, developmental narrative. In the midst of the carnage, Arjie has sex with Shehan for the last time before traumatically leaving with his family for Canada: "I have just returned from seeing Shehan. I can still smell his particular odour on my body, which always lingers on me after we make love . . . I am reluctant even to change my clothes for fear that I will lose this final memento."[37] The smell of Shehan's body lingering on Arjie's clothes becomes "a final memento" not only of a remembered scene of homoerotic desire but of Sri Lanka, of home itself. The text thus queers the space of Sri Lanka as home by disrupting the logic of nationalism that consolidates the nation through normative hierarchical sexual and gender arrangements; these arrangements coalesce around the privatized, bourgeois domestic space of home as a site of sanitized heterosexuality.

The mapping of homoeroticism onto the national space of Sri Lanka also challenges the implicit imperialist assumptions underlying conventional coming out narratives that locate the Third World as a site of sexual oppression that must be left behind in order to realize a liberated gay subjectivity. The moment in the narrative where Arjie remembers home through the smell of his lover's body encapsulates the text's deployment of what I would call a generative or enabling nostalgia and homesickness. Here the home that is evoked signifies multiply: as both national space and domestic space, it is the site of homoerotic desire and cross-gender identification and pleasure, of intense gender conformity and horrific violence, as well as of multiple leave-takings and exiles. The text thus also complicates the axes of a conventional exilic novel with fixed points of origin and departure. Instead, Selvadurai's stories detail the layered crises and multiple losses, the leave-takings and exiles that occur within the site of home itself.

Home Work: Shani Mootoo's *Cereus Blooms at Night*

As in Selvadurai's *Funny Boy* and Ian Rashid's *Surviving Sabu*, in *Cereus Blooms at Night* non-heteronormative sexualities travel within and away from the space of home and transform the very meanings of home in the process. Mootoo's novel allows for a conceptualization of sexuality in motion: in the context of diasporic movement and migration as well as in relation to those movements that occur within and across bodies that seemingly remain geographically rooted with the home. Unlike both *Funny Boy* and *Surviving Sabu*, however, Mootoo's novel provides a sustained articulation of a queer diasporic project that revolves around a complex model of female diasporic subjectivity, and allows us to consider what a queer diasporic project would look like with a female subject at its center. As such, it extends and brings into fruition the brief glimpse of a queered femininity suggested by Mina's performance in *East Is East*, as discussed in chapter 3. Like *Surviving Sabu*, *Cereus* responds to and revises the tropes of masculinity and unhousing that are so central to V. S. Naipaul's *A House for Mr. Biswas*. Mootoo's radical reworking of homes and houses in *Cereus* provides a necessary counterpoint to Naipaul's melancholic vision of masculine failure as well as to Rashid's alternative yet still limited vision of a queer male genealogy.

A House for Mr. Biswas, published at the very moment of Trinidad's independence, fits quite comfortably into the mold of "national allegory" as articulated by Fredric Jameson in his oft-cited (and much debated) essay "Third World Literature in the Era of Multinational Capitalism."[38] Jameson's claim that in "all third-world texts . . . the story of the private individual destiny is always an allegory of the embattled situation of the public third-world culture and society" has been strongly criticized by many postcolonial critics.[39] Aijaz

Ahmad, for instance, takes to task Jameson's sweeping generalizations about "all Third World literatures," and his overly tidy oppositions between First and Third World literatures and readers.[40] Yet Naipaul's novel—following as it does Biswas's chronic failure to create "an adequate house in which to install an adequate self," as Rosemary George phrases it—easily allows itself to be read along the lines of Jameson's premise.[41] Conversely, *Cereus Blooms at Night*, which can be read as an important intertext to Naipaul's novel, does not resolve itself so easily into national allegory. Rather Mootoo's novel is primarily concerned with those subjectivities, desires, and modes of collectivity that escape nationalist narratives and that fall outside their teleological structures. While questions of housing remain central for Mootoo, her novel maps the violences that undergird the home as it is prescribed within the logic of colonialism. If Naipaul's novel is unable to imagine a way of "being at home" outside patriarchal colonial logic, Mootoo's text suggests alternative forms of kinship, affiliation, and genealogy that resist the logic of blood, patrilineality, and patriarchal authority on which Naipaul's vision of housing ultimately rests.

Mootoo's novel traces the physical and psychic costs of colonialism as they play out over variously gendered, sexualized, and racialized bodies. In contrast to the realist mode of Naipaul's novel, *Cereus Blooms at Night* is situated in a semi-fictionalized (post)colonial location: England is transposed within Mootoo's literary landscape into the forbidding-sounding "Shivering Northern Wetlands" while Trinidad is translated into a tropical Caribbean island called "Lantanacamara." The narrative unravels the life of Mala Ramachandin, who at the novel's opening is seen as a mute old woman in a Lantanacamara nursing home, and who has been befriended and cared for by the novel's narrator, an effeminate gay male nurse named Tyler. By means of shifts across time and narrative voice, we learn that when Mala was a young girl, her Indian mother Sarah fell in love and absconded with Lavinia, the white daughter of the local "Wetlandish" missionary family. Mala and her sister Asha are left to the mercy of their father Chandin, who as a young boy had been adopted by the white missionary family in their attempt to convert other poor Indian plantation workers to Christianity. After Sarah leaves him for Lavinia, Chandin turns abusive, raping Mala and Asha for years until Asha escapes and leaves the island; Chandin is eventually killed in a final violent encounter with Mala.

This synopsis does not do justice to the complexity of the text as it raises questions around the production and disavowal of queer bodies and desires in the context of home as household, community, and nation. The novel's contestation of hegemonic colonial, national, and diasporic framings of sexuality and home spaces must be read against the sexual, racial, and gendered repercussions of indentureship in Trinidad. Clearly there is a risk in using a specific historical frame to situate a novel as self-consciously antirealist as Mootoo's. Nevertheless, the novel's framing of questions of home, sexuality, and movement is informed by the particularities of indentureship in Trinidad. Indeed the novel can be read as both a response to and repudiation of its various legacies, and it forces a consideration of indentureship as central to processes of racial, gender, and sexual subjectification in the Caribbean. Precipitated by Britain's continued need for cheap labor in the aftermath of slavery in the British colonies, half a million workers were brought from India to work on British Caribbean sugar plantations between 1838 and 1917 through a strategy of what Madhavi Kale calls "imperial labor reallocation."[42] Yet as Indira Karamcheti asserts, Indian indenture is often an erased narrative in Caribbean historiography and fails to signify against what she calls "the overwhelming, dominating presence of another people's displacement."[43] While a number of historians and cultural critics have pointed out the complex relations between slavery and indentureship in the Caribbean in terms of the maintenance of racial hierarchies and continued labor exploitation, there remains a need to fully articulate the effects of indentureship on colonial and postcolonial subject constitution in the Caribbean.

Feminist historians including Madhavi Kale, Rhoda Reddock, Patricia Mohammed, and others have begun this task in their work on Indian women and indentureship. Reddock's work, for instance, details the discursive production of the category of the Indian immigrant, and the Indian woman immigrant in particular, within a juridical framework of countless criminal and labor laws that sought to govern immigrant existence.[44] Indentureship was marked from its inception by a discourse of sexual morality, one which sought to curb the "erotic autonomy" (to use Jacqui Alexander's phrase) of Indian immigrant women.[45] Both the British colonial state and immigrant Indian men labeled single Indian women (who were the majority of those women who migrated) as outcasts, immoral, and prostitutes. Reddock and Mohammed argue that a variety of competing discourses and interests intersected in the need to control and legislate Indian female sexuality. First, Indian immigrant masculinity attempted to reconstitute itself through the control of "unruly" Indian female sexuality. Second, Indian immigrant women were instrumental within the gendered discourse of anticolonial nationalism in India, where arguments against indentureship were articulated as safeguarding the purity and sanctity of Indian womanhood. Finally a Victorian discourse around domesticity and ideal womanhood sought to "domesticate" Indian women immigrants by transforming them from wage laborers to dependent housewives.[46]

This last strategy, of framing Indian women as housewives rather than wage earners, is important to elaborate as it has tremendous consequences for the creation of gender hierarchies and the regulation of Indian women's bodies during the post-indentureship period and beyond. Reddock points out that between 1870 and 1900, new legal mechanisms were put in place to keep Indians on the estates as a stable, self-reproducing work force. Earlier ordinances that sought to regulate the movement of workers—such as the 1847 Ticket to Leave Law that prohibited workers from leaving the confines of the estate—were compounded by new land laws. These laws facilitated the creation of Indian peasant proprietorship by giving male "heads of household" land instead of a return passage back to India. Simultaneously, under a systematic process of what Reddock calls "housewifization," women workers were increasingly removed from public wage labor to perform unpaid, privatized labor on family property. The colonial state thus legislated hierarchized, patriarchal, heterosexual nuclear family units as necessary for peasant farming. Significantly, this period saw a tremendous increase in violence perpetuated by Indian men against Indian women, often in the form of murder. Madhavi Kale argues that violence was used as a major method of control against Indian women who sought to assert their sexual autonomy in the face of increasing legislation that would keep them firmly within the confines of conjugal domesticity.[47] According to Prabhu Mohapatra, colonial authorities sought to prevent these "wife murders" in late-nineteenth-century British Guyana by strengthening marriage legislation and consolidating the male-dominated nuclear Indian family.[48] Thus the colonial state, in conjunction with Indian immigrant male interests, sought to legislate and naturalize hierarchical nuclear family arrangements within this newly constructed space of the Indian immigrant home. As Kale writes, "Indentured labor was peculiarly suited to imperial, post-emancipation conditions because it recognized and implicitly capitalized on a racial differentiation—indeed racial hierarchy—within the empire by contributing to naturalizing [and] universalizing a bourgeois-imperial sexual division of labor that was not only predicated on, but also reproduced, women's banishment to the domestic: to domestic space, labor, identity."[49] In other words, heteronormativity and the consolidation of the domestic space were used as disciplinary mechanisms of the colonial state, both producing and keeping intact the racial, gender, and sexual hierarchies necessary for the continuance of a cheap and stable workforce.

As I suggested in my discussion of chutney music, recent critical attempts to unravel contemporary discourses of female sexuality in Trinidad stop short of fully exploring the linkages between the legislation of heteronormativity, the disciplining of female sexuality, and the consolidation of colonial systems of labor. The effacement of queer female desire and agency by contemporary scholars is particularly significant in the context of how rhetoric around Indian women's sexuality was mobilized by the British colonial state and Indian nationalists during the indentureship period. Madhavi Kale notes that the "sexualization of [Indian] women and the labor they performed was [central] to emergent bourgeois-capitalist notions of free labor, freedom and nation."[50] British proponents of the indentureship system were particularly concerned with couching indentured labor as "free" rather than coerced or slave labor, and this category of "free labor" became crucial to post-emancipation definitions of Britain as an imperial power. It also kept racial hierarchies in the colonies intact: Kale convincingly argues that "free" Indian labor was used as a means of disciplining and devaluing the newly emancipated black laboring population.[51] Indian women, however, were excluded from this category of "free labor" as they were seen as unfit for field labor and wage earning and were consigned to the space of the domestic. Indeed, as Kale asserts, "the model, ideal laborer was almost always male. The idea of free women laborers represented a contradiction in terms."[52] The process of "housewifization" had the effect of curtailing both the laboring and sexual agency of Indian women, in that it harnessed their sexuality and labor power to the maintenance of the heterosexual, conjugal family unit. Thus, by eliding queer female desiring agency in their analyses of contemporary discourses of Indian women's sexuality, cultural critics and scholars collude with the particular brand of heteronormativity initially put in place to legitimize continued labor exploitation under indentureship.

Cereus Blooms at Night opens up the space within which the normalizing discourses surrounding Indo-Caribbean women's sexuality can begin to be unpacked. It is precisely the construction of home under indentureship as a site of the violent establishment of sexual and gender normativity that Mootoo's novel contests. The novel suggests that if heteronormativity—and more specifically heterosexuality—is a means by which to discipline subjects under colonialism, then one of the means by which to escape the sexual and gendered logic of colonialism is by escaping heterosexuality. Given the complex valences of home under indentureship, it is not surprising that Mootoo's novel is intensely preoccupied with evoking various home spaces: the white missionary home, the "native" home that Chandin's Indian plantation worker parents inhabit, and finally Chandin's own home, which his daughter Mala reterritorializes after killing Chandin. There are also those other shadowy home spaces that exist outside the island—Canada, Australia, the Wetlands—that characters disappear to and return from, and that place the island and its inhabitants within a larger framework of diasporic travel and movement. The white missionary home in the novel is figured as the quintessential English home in the colony, that space of "public domesticity" where the workings of "the empire are replicated on a domestic scale."[53] As Rosemary George has pointed out in her work on gender, domesticity, and empire, the setting up of home in the empire was seen as crucial to the consolidation of imperial rule. George states, "The management of empire [in colonial discourse] is represented as essentially home-management on a larger scale: there are doors to be locked, corners to be dusted, rooms to be fumigated and made free of pests, children (i.e. "natives") to be . . . educated . . . and disciplined, boundaries to be drawn and fences mended."[54] Similarly, the home of the missionary family into which Chandin the native / child is granted entrance is marked by order, thrift, and cleanliness, the attention to decorum and neatness that are the hallmarks of colonialism's "civilizing" project. George also points out that it is against a construction of the "native" home as lack or excess that the colonial home is able to invent itself. Indeed, Chandin—like Naipaul's Mr. Biswas—is as in thrall to the image of colonial domesticity and nuclear familial bliss as he is disgusted by the memory of his own parents' mud house, the odor from the latrine mingling with the smells of incense, spices, and coal. This attention to smell, as I will discuss, becomes crucial to the novel's framing of home.

The home that Chandin sets up after leaving the missionary household and marrying Sarah is a failed attempt at replicating the domestic idyll of the missionary home; it is also an attempt to reproduce the patriarchal nuclear family as it took shape under indentureship. Chandin, in a replication of Mr. Biswas's ordeals, tries and fails to build his dream house "of stone and mortar . . . with special rooms for this and that—a library, a pantry, a guest room."[55] The emergence of queer interracial desire between Sarah and her white lover within this home space, however, radically destabilizes the terms of colonial domesticity, unharnessing Indian women's sexuality from the propagation of the heterosexual, national family unit. As in Chughtai's "The Quilt" and Mehta's *Fire*, female homoerotic desire in Mootoo's novel emerges from within the patriarchal confines of the home, within the cracks and fissures of heterosexuality, and is inextricable from the violences of colonialism and misogyny. Queer desire enables Sarah to quite literally remove herself from the sexual, racial, and gendered logic consolidated under indentureship. Chandin's response to both Sarah's refusal to abide by this logic and his own subsequent loss of patriarchal authority is to habitually rape and abuse both Mala and her sister Asha. The horror of incest in the novel functions to make visible the trauma of indentureship and its repressed histories of gendered and sexualized violence; Mala's bruised and violated body becomes an archive of these histories.[56] Thus incest in the text has multiple valences: it represents the implosion of the heterosexual nuclear family as legislated under the colonial regime of indentureship. It also echoes earlier histories of gendered violence on which the heterosexual family unit under colonialism is predicated. This "other" home space, then, shadows the sanitized missionary home and lays bare all that colonialism both produces and seeks to disavow.

Chandin's death and Mala's subsequent remaking of her house mark the creation of an alternative space of "not-home," one that explodes the gendered and racialized terms of the domestic as set forth under indentureship. Ironically inhabiting the colonial construction of the native home as excess, Mala allows the house to become overrun with wild birds, insects, snails, and reptiles and lives not inside the house but on the verandah, surrounded by their sounds and smells. If the colonial missionary home is marked by economy, order, and sanitization—a distinct lack of smell—the alternative, antidomestic home space that Mala creates is marked by an excess of smell: the stench of decomposition and foulness intermingles with the heady, intoxicating aroma of cereus blossoms. Mala revises ideologies of "housewifization" set in place during indentureship, as well as the colonial injunction that urges good housekeeping as the gendered labor of empire: her housekeeping consists of carefully drying and burying the corpses of snails and insects, of stacking furniture into impenetrable walls that serve not to protect the house from intruders but rather to carve out a home space outside the domestic.

For Mala as for Sarah, escaping the violences of the patriarchal colonial home is inextricable from escaping the violences of heteronormativity. The novel thus allows us to rearticulate queerness in the shadow of colonialism. Mootoo's text, echoing Mina's performance of queer femininity in *East Is East* and Chughtai's formulation of queer desire within the home, imagines queerness as residing not solely in particular bodies that are specifically marked as "lesbian." Mala, for instance, is explicitly named as queer in the novel in the sense that she extricates herself from the terms of heterosexual domesticity. Queerness in *Cereus* thus extends to all those bodies disavowed by colonial and national constructions of home: bodies marked by rape and incest; biologically male bodies that are improperly feminine, such as that of Tyler, the nurse who works in the old age home to which Mala is forcibly removed after her own home is burnt down; and biologically "female" bodies that are improperly masculine, such as that of Otoh, Tyler's lover.

Indeed, the character Otoh embodies the ways in which travel and movement occur within the space of home itself, within bodies that are in motion without leaving home. Otoh, we are told, is born biologically female but transformed himself so flawlessly into a boy over the years that no one in Lantanacamara, not even his parents, seems to remember that he was once a girl. The seamlessness of Otoh's transgender transition opens Mootoo to the charge that she has positioned Otoh as the quintessential transitional subject, a figure that acts as a metaphor for other forms of crossing and travel in the novel while denying the specificity of transgender subjectivity. However, I would argue that Otoh's seamless transformation—like Mala's radical antidomesticity—instead speaks to an antirealist system of logic the text sets forth. We can call this alternative logical system one of productive contradiction: indeed, Otoh's very name is an acronym of "on the one hand, on the other hand," his favorite phrase that betrays his propensity for seeing both sides of a situation but not committing to either. Rather than naming a disinvested sexual and gender fluidity, Otoh—like Mala, who lives in the inside/outside space of the verandah—can be seen as making inhabitable those liminal spaces deemed impossible within heteronormative logic: he is outside femininity yet within a nominally female body; he is situated within masculinity yet attracted to Tyler's queer femininity. The logic of "on the one hand" embodied by Mootoo's characters is ultimately a refusal to adhere to the fixities of place, race, gender, and sexuality legislated by the colonial regimes of both slavery and indentureship. The gender and sexual ideologies of indentureship quite literally fix bodies in place; the various forms of transitivity and motion undertaken by Mootoo's characters both within and away from the space of home, then, must be read as working against this colonial injunction to fixity. If legislated heterosexuality, in the context of patriarchal family arrangements, is one of the primary means by which the colonial state keeps bodies fixed in place, then the novel suggests that queer bodies and queer desires become the means by which to escape the totalizing logic of colonial order. Clearly, however, this is not to suggest that movement or queerness in the novel can be conceptualized in terms of a celebration of an easy fluidity. Rather than leveling out the differences between the various forms of raced, gendered, and sexual movements that it traces, Mootoo's novel suggests the impossibility of viewing one particular trajectory to the exclusion of others. As in Selvadurai's novel, current movements and transitivities are always shadowed by prior displacements, and Mootoo maps the forced, traumatic, and painful movements precipitated by slavery, indentureship, and colonialism onto the very bodies of her characters. In other words, Mootoo grounds the movements of her characters within the continuing legacies of colonialism, while suggesting the strategies by which those subjects positioned outside the terms of communal belonging reimagine their relation to multiple home spaces.

At the end of Naipaul's novel, Mr. Biswas finally moves into his own house only to discover that it merely has the façade of the pristine domestic space he so longs for: the foundations are rotting, the roof leaks, the doors refuse to shut. Mr. Biswas dies in this space of failed colonial domesticity, unable to imagine another kind of home. At the end of Mootoo's novel, on the other hand, the various characters who have struggled against *and* inhabited the space of the home—Otoh, Tyler, and Mala—are united in the nursing home where Mala lives and Tyler works. The nursing home is another space of public domesticity marked by the strict enforcement of rules and regulations. Yet in this seemingly incongruous setting, violence finally gives way to desire as Tyler and Otoh find love and Mala renews her relationship, long dormant, with Otoh's father. It is, once again, Mala's "housekeeping" that allows this unlikely space—one that is opened by violence and maintained through queer alliance—to become the location of a new form of collectivity. Signaling her refusal of the institutional strictures of the nursing home, Mala builds and rebuilds a wall in her room with its sparse furniture. What looks like the mind-numbing behavior of senility is of course a continuation of her life's work: the invention of new architectures of being and the erection of a counterdomestic space in the very heart of the home and nation.

In the novels of Mootoo and Selvadurai, desire must be conceptualized in motion, traveling as it does both diasporically and "in place." The characters in both novels, as in the other texts discussed throughout the book, infuse the space of home with multiple forms of queer desire, and thus lay bare the fiction of sanitized heterosexuality on which home as household / community / nation depends. Nostalgia as deployed by queer diasporic subjects is a means by which to imagine oneself within those spaces from which one is perpetually excluded or denied existence. If the nation is "the modern Janus," a figure which at once gazes at a primordial, ideal past while facing a modern future,[57] a queer diaspora instead recognizes the past as a site of intense violence as well as pleasure; it acknowledges the spaces of impossibility within the nation and their translation within the diaspora into new logics of affiliation. The logic of "pigs can't fly" becomes transformed, within diasporic public culture, into the alternative queer logic that allows for two brides in bed together, a marriage without a groom, pigs with wings. In other words, a queer diasporic logic displaces heteronormativity from the realm of natural law and instead launches its critique of hegemonic constructions of both nation and diaspora from the vantage point of an "impossible" subject.

7

EPILOGUE

Queer Homes in Diaspora

Throughout this book, I have gestured toward the ways in which the home as both nation and diaspora is refigured within a queer diasporic imaginary. The queer public culture I have sought to document here forcefully challenges conventional diasporic and nationalist discourses that forget, excise, and criminalize queer bodies, pleasures, desires, histories, and lives. In so doing, queer diasporic cultural forms suggest alternative forms of collectivity and communal belonging that redefine home outside of a logic of blood, purity, authenticity, and patrilineal descent. Queerness names a mode of reading, of rendering intelligible that which is unintelligible and indeed impossible within dominant diasporic and nationalist logic. The necessity of such a reading practice was quite literally brought home to me as I was nearing the completion of this book and found myself having the vertiginous experience of sitting with my mother in a gleaming new multiplex theater in Chennai (Madras), South India, watching *Kal Ho Naa Ho* (Whether or Not There Is a Tomorrow, dir. Nikhil Advani, 2003), a recent Bollywood, Hindi-language blockbuster set in New York City. The Tamil-speaking audience cheered and applauded excitedly as various images of a post-9/11 Manhattan skyline flashed on the screen. In the midst of the requisite shots of tourist New York— South Street Seaport, the Statue of Liberty, the Chrysler and Empire State buildings—my mother and I were startled to catch a glimpse of the apartment complex in which I had grown up and where she had spent twenty-five years of her life. Indeed, much of the action in the film takes place in and around our old neighborhood, in the stubbornly unfashionable area around East 25th Street, although it also shifts to Queens, New Jersey, and Staten Island, tracing the rather unglamorous trajectory of South Asian settlement in the New York area. The PATH train and the Staten Island ferry, which link Manhattan to suburban South Asian enclaves in New Jersey and Staten Island, feature prominently in the film. *Kal Ho Naa Ho* refracted through a Bollywood gaze an urban landscape of New York City that is deeply familiar to me and that I have come to identify as home. Watching the film in Chennai—a city to which my mother has ostensibly returned home but where she remains irreducibly foreign after thirty years in the diaspora—crystallized many of the questions I have tried to grapple with in this book. This viewing experience made viscerally apparent to me how the home as national and diasporic space is continuously created and consumed within the realm of transnational public culture, and underscored the necessity of producing reading practices that can grasp the ever-increasing slippages and overlaps between nation and diaspora that characterize this realm.

The film itself follows the romantic exploits and familial relations of an Indian diasporic family in New Jersey and was a major hit both in India and in the South Asian diaspora, where it was strenuously marketed. *Kal Ho Naa Ho* is but the latest in a series of films produced in Bollywood that are set in the diaspora—or more specifically, in the global cities of the North, such as New York or London; these films provide diasporic audiences with a nationalist mirror image of themselves that they in turn incorporate and consume. As such this genre of Bollywood films reverses the forms of cinematic translation I traced in chapter 4: if feminist filmmakers like Mira Nair and Deepa Mehta reimagine the home of the nation from the vantage point of the diaspora, a new genre of Bollywood films reimagines the diaspora from the vantage point of the nation. Purnima Mankekar's analysis of one such film, *Dilwale Dulhaniya Le Jayenge* (Men with Heart Take the Bride, dir. Aditya Chopra, 1995), contextualizes the changing representations of the diaspora on the Bollywood screen within India's embrace of globalization and economic liberalization in the 1990s. During this period, she argues, the diasporic (male) subject in popular Indian cinema shifted from being seen as a disloyal, errant native son to a "knight in shining armor" able to rescue the "damsel in distress," that is, the Indian nation, with an influx of capital investment.[1] This nationalist framing of diaspora claims the Indianness of the diasporic subject (figured as male) as long as he embodies the mobility of transnational capital.[2] Mankekar is quick to point out the gendered logic of this current reclamation of the diaspora: Indianness is maintained in the diaspora only by predictably positioning diasporic women as the placeholders for communal identity and tradition.[3] Clearly this new framing of diaspora's relation to the nation is figured not only through a narrative of normative gender relations, as Mankekar argues, but through one that naturalizes heterosexuality as well.

The reconfiguration of the relation between diaspora and nation through a consolidation of heteronormativity is particularly evident in *Kal Ho Naa Ho*. Like *Dilwale Dulhaniya . . .* , *Kal Ho Naa Ho* is similarly invested in asserting the essential Indianness of its diasporic characters, despite their apparently seamless entry into mainstream American society. Here, however, the "knight in shining armor" is not the diasporic male who returns to the nation, but rather Aman, the male nationalist subject (in the form of Bollywood hearthrob Shah Rukh Khan) who magically arrives from India just in time to teach the film's hapless diasporic characters about life, love, and pride in their Indian heritage. Significantly, the diasporic family is initially constituted as a female-headed household: the father is conspicuously absent, leaving the mother to manage the debt-ridden family business, a diner in New Jersey. Indeed, the film opens with the mother desperately staving off creditors who threaten to close down the business. Aman's fortuitous appearance reinstitutes a nationalist, patriarchal authority into the diasporic family scene. At his suggestion, the mother of the family is able to save the diner from losing out to the Chinese, family-run restaurant across the street by changing its name from the "New York City Café" to the "New Delhi Café," jettisoning the doughnuts for samosas, and replacing the American flag with the Indian tri-color. The female-headed, diasporic Indian family is only able to fully partake of the "American Dream" that has eluded them when Aman, as patriarchal purveyor of a newly globalized India, repackages their Indianness as a valuable commodity that can be "modernized" into a sure-fire recipe for success and upward mobility in capitalist America.[4] Thus the film envisions a new global imaginary, where India and its diaspora—both structured along patriarchal lines—are able to smoothly function together in the interests of transnational capital.

In this respect, *Kal Ho Naa Ho* is similar to *Dilwale Dulhaniya . . . , Hum Aapke Hain Koun . . . !* and the other neoconservative romances (to use Thomas Waugh's phrase)[5] produced by Bollywood in the 1990s that reassure their transnational viewership both in India and the diaspora that globalization and "traditional" Indian values go hand in hand. However, what is startling in *Kal Ho Naa Ho* and sets it apart from these other neoconservative romances is the way in which representations of (male) homosexuality are folded into, and indeed buttress, this triumphalist narrative of Indian cultural superiority, patriarchal authority, and transnational mobility. Even as *Kal Ho Naa Ho* fits squarely within the genre of the neoconservative romance, it also bears traces of an earlier genre, that of the prototypical Bollywood buddy movie and its particular mapping of gender and sexual arrangements.[6] Typically within this genre, a triangulated, homosocial relation between the two male stars and the heroine serves to both contain and enable male homoeroticism. Thomas Waugh argues that in Bollywood films in the 1990s there was a "growing ambiguity and complexity, playfulness and boldness, of this traditional homosocial formula," as it became increasingly self-conscious and self-referential, partly in response to the emergence of a visible and vocal gay movement in India.[7] In a move that echoes *Monsoon Wedding*'s translation of the queer codes of Bollywood cinema into a Hollywood idiom, *Kal Ho Naa Ho* similarly "outs" the generic conventions of the Bollywood buddy movie by explicitly and parodically referencing male homosexuality. At various moments throughout the film, for instance, Aman and his male buddy are taken for gay lovers by a disapproving housekeeper, an apparent misrecognition that is predictably played for laughs. Similarly, in the midst of a song and dance sequence celebrating the joys of *pyar* (love) in all its forms, the camera briefly focuses on two white gay men embracing on a park bench, before it goes on to present an array of heterosexual couples holding hands on New York City streets. Ultimately, however, the film predictably reasserts the dominance of heteronormative familial and romantic arrangements: Aman conveniently dies of a tragic heart condition, exiting the homosocial triangle and paving the way for marriage and childbearing as his male buddy declares his love for the film's female love interest.

I point to these anxious citations of male homosexuality in *Kal Ho Naa Ho* as they mark the most recent strategy through which Bollywood as a national cinema manages queerness in the context of globalization. These moments, I would argue, function to simultaneously acknowledge, contain, and disavow the threat that queer male desire—definitively annexed to the diaspora—poses to a nationalist framing of home. By locating queer male desire firmly within the diaspora rather than in India, the film keeps intact the heteronormativity of the home space of the nation. Significantly, these citations of male homosexuality, comfortably contained as they are within diasporic space, do not disrupt the seamlessness of the new global imaginary of the film but in fact appear as coterminous with it. Just as the film's diasporic characters learn to modernize Indian tradition so that it falls in line with an entrepreneurial, capitalist American ethos, the film itself references male homosexuality in increasingly explicit terms as a way of marking the increasing modernity and cosmopolitanism of Bollywood cinema itself, as it comes to more fully approximate some of the strategies of gender and sexual representation evident in mainstream Hollywood cinema. In this sense, the turn within Bollywood cinema toward mainstream Hollywood conventions parallels the ways in which the feminist diasporic filmmakers I discussed in chapter 4 "modernize" Bollywood form and content for a non–South Asian, international viewership. The "modernization" of Bollywood form and content in *Kal Ho Naa Ho*, however, interpellates a specifically South Asian, transnational viewership through its fantasy of immigrant success, upward mobility, and the reconstitution of the patriarchal family. *Kal Ho Naa Ho*'s representation of male homosexuality is hardly at odds with the new relation between diaspora and nation that the film maps out—it is in fact deeply implicated within it.

However, if male homosexuality is not only imaginable but even desirable within this new global landscape, queer female desire or subjectivity exists, crucially, outside the frame of the possible. Once again, as I have argued throughout this book, the coordinates of the female figure remain inevitably fixed as wife, mother, and daughter. This continued impossibility and unimaginability of queer female desire and subjectivity—even as queer male desire ascends to ever greater visibility—speaks to the radically asymmetrical ways in which queer male and female bodies are constructed and disciplined within diasporic and nationalist discourses as they take shape on the terrain of transnational public culture. A film like *Kal Ho Naa Ho* reveals how conventional discourses of diaspora and nation, as they are reconstituted in and through globalization, are able to absorb and neutralize the challenge posed by queer male desire by rendering it visible only to recruit it back into a patriarchal logic. In this context, queer female pleasures, bodies, and subjectivities may act as the recalcitrant material that stands outside of this logic. This is not to suggest that lesbian desire is somehow naturally resistant to the forces of global capital or hegemonic nationalism. Nevertheless it is significant that the modernity of the nation is figured through queer male desire and the simultaneous unthinkability of queer female desire. Queer female desire is utterly unintelligible within the film precisely because, to return to José Rabasa's formulation of "lo imposible," it "calls for the demise" of hegemonic constructions of nation and diaspora on which patriarchal logic rests.[8]

If the consignment of queer male desire to diasporic space serves only to solidify the heteronormativity of the home space of the nation, I would like to end with a final evocation of how this conflation of queerness and diaspora is both embraced and reworked within a queer *female* diasporic imaginary. The work of the British Asian photographer Parminder Sekhon rescues queer female desire from a logic of impossibility by installing it at the very heart of the home as both national and diasporic space. In so doing, queer feminist work such as Sekhon's fulfills the radical potential of the notion of a queer diaspora, a potential that is foreclosed by the availability of gay male desire to recuperation within patriarchal narratives of home, diaspora, and nation in a globalized landscape. Sekhon is well known in the Black British arts scene from her work in the 1990s where she created a series of public service posters on HIV/AIDS targeted to South Asian communities in the UK. Similar to the interventionist graphics of WHAM (Women's Health Action Mobilization) and other activist arts collectives in the United States in the early 1990s, many of Sekhon's images used the idiom of glossy Benetton or Gap ads to insert into public space those lives and bodies—queer, brown, HIV positive—studiously effaced within a dominant nationalist and diasporic imaginary. The collapse of public and private that characterizes her work is particularly apparent in her documentation of queer South Asian life in London: her photographs are populated by glamorous South Asian butch-femme couples, the drag queens of Club Kali (London's queer South Asian night club), and drag kings who nostalgically evoke the masculinity of Bollywood film stars of the 1940s and 1950s. These images do the crucial work of providing a rich, material archive of queer South Asian public culture and attest to the unceasingly imaginative ways in which queer diasporic communities carve out literal and symbolic spaces of collectivity in inhospitable and hostile landscapes.

In one of her most compelling series of photographs, entitled "Urban Lives," Sekhon uses the streets of predominantly South Asian neighborhoods in London as a backdrop for portraits of paired figures, one nude and one clothed.

Parminder Sekhon, "Southall Market," 2003.
Photo courtesy of the artist.

The images are named for the streets and neighborhoods in which the figures are situated—Tooting, Bethnal Green, Whitechapel, Southall—and provide a litany of geographic locales that evoke a history of working-class, South Asian settlement in London. In a particularly striking and moving photograph Sekhon pairs her own nude, pierced body with that of her elderly mother, in a *salwar kameez* and woolen sweater, as they stand in front of a market in Southall, the South Asian neighborhood where Sekhon grew up and her mother still lives. The mother grips the handle of a battered shopping cart as she, like Sekhon, gazes directly into the camera. Behind them is the detritus of the market, empty stalls, discarded cardboard boxes, and packing crates. The light is indeterminate, it could be early morning or twilight, the low clouds and uniform grayness of the sky reflected in the rain-slicked pavement on which they stand. As is the case with many of the texts I have engaged with in this book, a conventional queer or feminist reading would render this image intelligible by situating it within a familiar binary structure that equates queerness with modernity, visibility, sexual liberation, and revelation (embodied by Sekhon), over and against the tropes of "tradition," concealment, secrecy, and modesty (embodied by her mother). A queer diasporic reading, in contrast, works against this neocolonial logic and allows us to identify the ways in which Sekhon evokes this series of binary oppositions—tradition/modernity, secrecy/disclosure, invisibility/visibility, queer/straight, first generation/second generation—only to overturn and disrupt them. In an interview with queer art critic Cherry Smyth, Sekhon explains her choice of Southall Market as the setting for her photographs:

> I grew up in Southall and my mother tried to persuade me to go to Southall Market every Saturday morning. I hated it and I tried to avoid the inevitable standoff each week. Those mothers lagging behind Stepford Daughters, dragging trolleys all over Southall on the way to and from the market, I couldn't bear it. In the end she did stop asking but it was hard 'cause I couldn't do the simplest of normal things that was required of me . . . When you go there [to Southall], it's completely you and you're part of it, but all at once you're so invisible too, not being married and not straight.[9]

Both Sekhon's statement and the image allow for a more complicated formulation of the relation of queer female diasporic subjects to home space than one that is characterized merely by alienation and repression. While Sekhon clearly articulates the ambivalent relation of undutiful queer daughters to immigrant mothers who seek to inculcate heteronormative domesticity, the image both calls to mind and revises Ian Rashid's *Surviving Sabu* in its complex relay of desire and identification between the bodies of mother and daughter. Sekhon's queerness is formed in and through her relation to home space, even as it radically disrupts and reterritorializes this space. Her nude body—like Mina's performance in *East Is East*—places queer female subjectivity at the center of diasporic public cultural space. Through Sekhon's lens, we glimpse an alternative construction of diaspora organized around queer lives, desires, bodies, cultures, and collectivities, which remains utterly unintelligible and unimaginable within dominant state and diasporic nationalist frameworks. Sekhon's work, as well as the other queer diasporic texts and cultural practices I have engaged with in these pages, allows us to identify the ways in which those who occupy impossible spaces transform them into vibrant, livable spaces of possibility.

NOTES

1 Impossible Desires

1. For an analysis of the racist ideology espoused by the British politician Enoch Powell in the 1960s, see Anna Marie Smith, *New Right Discourse on Race and Sexuality*.

2. See Ian Iqbal Rashid, "Passage to England," for a discussion of *My Beautiful Laundrette*'s reception by the "cultural left" in the UK in the 1980s.

3. In its most general sense, the term "communal" is used here and throughout the book to reference notions of community and collectivity; more specifically, my use of "communal" is meant to evoke the term "communalism," which in the South Asian context names a politics of religious nationalism and the persecution of religious minorities, particularly on the part of the Hindu right.

4. The category of "South Asian" encompasses populations that originated from Bangladesh, Bhutan, India, Nepal, Pakistan, and Sri Lanka. Annanya Bhattacharjee provides a useful gloss on the term, which gained increasing currency in the 1980s and 1990s within progressive communities in the United States in order to signal a broad politics of coalition that rejected the narrow nationalisms of mainstream South Asian diasporic organizations. Bhattacharjee notes that despite its progressive valence, "South Asian" as an identity marker remains a deeply problematic term, given its origins in area studies and cold war rhetoric, as well as its capacity to evade questions of Indian regional hegemony. See "The Public/Private Mirage," 309–10. Despite these limitations, I find the category "South Asian" invaluable in tracing the lines of commonality and difference between various experiences of racialization of diasporic communities within

different national locations. Clearly the history of racialization of immigrants from the Indian subcontinent is vastly different depending on religion, class, and nation of origin in each of these national sites. Nevertheless the term continues to be useful as it produces strategic transnational identifications that allow for a critique of dominant notions of community in both South Asia and the diaspora.

5. Stuart Hall, "Cultural Identity and Diaspora," 245.

6. Ibid.

7. Joseph Roach, *Cities of the Dead*, 2.

8. Ibid., 20.

9. Ibid., 6.

10. Hall, "Cultural Identity and Diaspora," 245.

11. Frantz Fanon, *Black Skin, White Masks*, 151–53.

12. Stefan Helmreich, "Kinship, Nation and Paul Gilroy's Concept of Diaspora," 245.

13. Braziel and Mannur, "Nation, Migration, Globalization," 7.

14. Hall, "Cultural Identity and Diaspora," 244.

15. For an elaboration of how diasporic cultural forms reverse the diaspora-nation hierarchy, see Gayatri Gopinath, "Bombay, U.K., Yuba City."

16. Hall, "Cultural Identity and Diaspora," 244.

17. For instance, as Anupam Chander documents, the right-wing Hindu nationalist government of the Bharatiya Janata Party (BJP) issued "Resurgent India Bonds" following the international sanctions imposed on India after its nuclear tests in 1998. The BJP promoted the bonds by appealing to the diasporic nationalism of NRIs in an attempt to encourage them to invest in the "homeland." See Chander, "Diaspora Bonds." See also Vijay Prashad, *The Karma of Brown Folk*, 21, for a discussion of the Indian government's production of the category of "NRI" as an attempt to garner foreign exchange.

18. Another stark illustration of the double-sided character of diaspora was apparent during the savage state-sponsored violence against Muslims in Gujarat, India, in February 2002. The Hindu nationalist state government in Gujarat received the support of NRIs even while other anticommunalist NRI organizations in New York and San Francisco mobilized against the violence and the government's complicity in the killing and displacement of thousands of Indian Muslims.

19. Sunaina Maira, for instance, documents the ways in which second-generation Indian American youth in the United States are drawn to Hindu religious nationalist ideology as a way of fulfilling a desire to be "truly Indian." Maira, *Desis in the House*, 137.

20. I understand "globalization" and "transnationalism" as a range of processes that, following Arjun Appadurai's formulation, includes the global movements of labor, technology, capital, media, and ideologies. See Appadurai, "Disjuncture and Difference

in the Global Cultural Economy." While transnationalism is the result of the exigencies of late capitalism, I also concur with Lisa Lowe and David Lloyd's assessment that understanding transnationalism as the homogenization of global culture "radically reduces possibilities for the creation of alternatives"; "Introduction," in *The Politics of Culture in the Shadow of Capital*, 1. This book is therefore concerned with the particular cultural forms and practices that arise out of, and in contestation to, transnational capitalism.

21. Visweswaran, "Diaspora By Design," 5–29.

22. Vijay Mishra, *Bollywood Cinema*, 235.

23. Prashad, *The Karma of Brown Folk*, 74.

24. Jenny Sharpe, "Cartographies of Globalisation, Technologies of Gendered Subjectivities," forthcoming. I thank the author for permission to discuss her unpublished manuscript.

25. Some of the most influential works in the broad field of gender and nationalism in South Asia include the following: Kumkum Sangari and Sudesh Vaid, eds., *Recasting Women*; Zoya Hassan, ed., *Forging Identities*; Lata Mani, *Contentious Traditions*; Ritu Menon and Kamala Bhasin, eds., *Borders and Boundaries*.

26. Key exceptions include Ruth Vanita, ed. *Queering India*; Giti Thadani, *Sakhiyani*; Shohini Ghosh, "*Hum Aapke Hain Koun . . . !*"; Paola Baccheta, "When the (Hindu) Nation Exiles its Queers."

27. See Purnima Mankekar, "Brides Who Travel," for an examination of representations of diasporic women's sexuality in Hindi cinema.

28. Tejaswini Niranjana, "Left to the Imagination." See also Madhavi Kale, *Fragments of Empire*, for a discussion of Indian women's sexuality in the British Caribbean and discourses of both Indian and British nationalism.

29. See, for instance, Lisa Lowe's analysis of Asian immigrant women's labor in "Work, Immigration, Gender."

30. For collections that begin to map out this terrain, see Arnaldo Cruz Malavé and Martin Manalansan, eds., *Queer Globalizations*; Elizabeth Povinelli and George Chauncey, eds., *Thinking Sexuality Transnationally*.

31. Following from George Mosse's groundbreaking analysis of sexuality in Nazi Germany in *Nationalism and Sexuality*, an important body of work has emerged over the past decade that has unraveled the complex interrelation between discourses of sexuality and those of the nation. For a few key examples of this increasingly large and complex field, see Andrew Parker, ed., *Nationalisms and Sexualities*; M. Jacqui Alexander, "Erotic Autonomy as a Politics of Decolonization"; Anne McClintock, *Imperial Leather*; and more recently Licia Fiol Matta, *A Queer Mother for the Nation*.

32. Some exemplary instances of this growing body of literature in U.S. ethnic

studies include the following: Martin Manalansan, *Global Divas*; José Muñoz, *Disidentifications*; Juana María Rodríguez, *Queer Latinidad*; Robert Reid Pharr, *Black Gay Man*; Philip Brian Harper, *Are We Not Men?*; David L. Eng, *Racial Castration*; Roderick Ferguson, *Aberrations in Black*; Nayan Shah, *Contagious Divides.*

33. See Martin Manalansan, "In the Shadow of Stonewall," for an important interrogation of contemporary gay transnational politics.

34. Lowe and Lloyd, *The Politics of Culture in the Shadow of Capital*, 1.

35. The imbrication of narratives of "progress," "modernity," and "visibility" is made obvious in what Alexander terms "prevalent metropolitan impulses that explain the absence of visible lesbian and gay movements [in non-Western locations] as a defect in political conciousness and maturity, using evidence of publicly organized lesbian and gay movements in the U.S. . . . as evidence of their orginary status (in the West) and superior political maturity." Alexander, "Erotic Autonomy as a Politics of Decolonization," 69.

36. Tejaswini Niranjana, *Siting Translation*, 3.

37. I thank Alys Weinbaum for her thoughtful feedback on the question of translation.

38. Antoinette Burton, *Dwelling in the Archive.*

39. Partha Chatterjee, *The Nation and Its Fragments*, 133.

40. Biddy Martin and Chandra Talpade Mohanty, "Feminist Politics."

41. For an elaboration of the notion of "staying" for queer subjects, see Anne Marie Fortier, "Coming Home."

42. Burton, *Dwelling in the Archive*, 29.

43. As such, I trace the genealogy of this project back to the rich body of radical women of color scholarship of the late 1970s and 1980s that insistently situated lesbian sexuality within a feminist, antiracist, and anticolonial framework. Such work includes Audre Lorde's *Zami*; Cherrie Moraga, *Loving in the War Years*; Cherrie Moraga and Gloria Anzaldúa, eds., *This Bridge Called My Back*; Gloria Anzaldúa, *Borderlands/La Frontera*; Barbara Smith, ed., *Home Girls.*

44. Queer Euro-American scholarship has done the crucial work of revealing the heteronormativity of dominant U.S. nationalism. Such work includes Gayle Rubin's groundbreaking essay "Thinking Sex"; Michael Warner, *The Trouble with Normal*; Lisa Duggan, *Sapphic Slashers* and *The Twilight of Equality?*

45. Paola Baccheta, "When the (Hindu) Nation Exiles its Queers."

46. For a discussion of how the "Indian immigrant bourgeoisie" constructs itself as unnamed and universal, see Annanya Bhattacharjee, "The Habit of Ex-Nomination."

47. Bhattacharjee, "The Public/Private Mirage."

48. Maira, *Desis in the House*, 49.

49. I thank Chandan Reddy for asking me to elaborate on the specificity of different modes of domination.

50. José Rabasa, "Of Zapatismo."

51. Ibid., 421.

52. Paul Gilroy, *Small Acts*.

53. See Appadurai and Breckenridge, "Public Modernity in India," for an explication of the term "public culture" in relation to South Asia. The authors use "public culture" in contradistinction to Habermas's notion of the "public sphere" as a depoliticized zone dominated by the mass media. Instead, the term "public culture" captures the sense of resistance, co-optation, critique, and agency with which subaltern groups interact with popular culture.

54. José Muñoz theorizes the ephemeral nature of queer cultural production in "Gesture, Ephemera, Queer Feeling," 433. For an extended discussion of queer archives and public cultures, see Ann Cvetkovich, 1–14.

55. Dipesh Chakravarty, *Provincializing Europe*, 66.

56. M. Jacqui Alexander, "Erotic Autonomy as a Politics of Decolonization," 86.

57. Monica Ali, *Brick Lane*.

58. Ismat Chughtai's recently translated and reprinted work includes *The Quilt and Other Stories*, *The Heart Breaks Free*, and *The Crooked Line*.

59. Shyam Selvadurai, *Funny Boy*.

60. Shani Mootoo, *Cereus Blooms at Night*.

61. See, for instance, the following: Nice Rodriguez, *Throw It to the River*; Ginu Kamani, *Junglee Girl*; Lorde, *Zami*; R. Zamora Linmark, *Rolling the R's*; *My Mother's House* (dir. Richard Fung, 1993); Achy Obejas, *Memory Mambo*.

2 Communities of Sound

1. I borrow this apt phrase from Josh Kun. For a trenchant critique of Madonna's penchant for cultural theft and tourism, see his article "Sayuri Ciccone."

2. Muñoz, *Disidentifications*, 12.

3. Muñoz understands "queer and Latino counterpublics" as "spheres that stand in opposition to the racism and homophobia of the dominant public sphere." *Disidentifications*, 143.

4. "Bombay, U.K., Yuba City."

5. Paul Gilroy, *The Black Atlantic*, 16.

6. I elaborate on this relation between diaspora and nation that is effected by Bhangra music in "Bombay, U.K., Yuba City," 316–17.

7. While the Bhangra industry in the UK was, and continues to be, largely male-

dominated, there were important exceptions during the Bhangra boom of the 1980s. I ended my 1995 article by referencing the example of the 1991 song "Soho Road" by the popular Bhangra group Apna Sangeet. "Soho Road" is a duet between a male and a female vocalist that narrates diasporic movement through the travels of a female diasporic subject. As such, it works against the standard preoccupation with racialized masculinity or lost homelands that characterizes the lyrics of many Bhangra songs. See "Bombay, U.K., Yuba City," 317–18. My thanks to Rekha Malhotra for bringing this track to my attention. Virinder Kalra also cites the female Bhangra vocalist Mohinder K. Bhamra as one of the "founders of modern Bhangra." See Kalra's analysis of Bhangra lyrics from the 1970s to the 1990s in his article "*Vilayeti* Rhythms: Beyond Bhangra's Emblematic Status to a Translation of Lyrical Texts."

8. Recent work on South Asian American racial formation, for instance, shows how diasporic links to South Asia, both affective and financial, among South Asian American communities are used to support right-wing Hindu fundamentalist organizations in South Asia and in the diaspora. At the same time, organizations such as the New York–based Youth Solidarity Summer program are attempting to instill in South Asian American youth different visions of South Asian diasporic identity that are explicitly anticommunalist and progressive. See Vijay Prashad, *Karma of Brown Folk*, and Sunaina Maira, *Desis in the House*, for a historicization of South Asian American diasporic formations.

9. As Virinder Kalra notes, "it is the fact of dispersal, a sense of loss, a yearning for home and other themes concerned with migration which emerge from an analysis of Bhangra songs" of the 1970s and 1980s. The lyrics of many of the songs from this period betray a nostalgic evocation of rural Punjab, while also pointedly critiquing the racism that awaits Asian male migrants to the U.K. "*Vilayeti* Rhythms," 85–86.

10. Stuart Hall, "Cultural Identity and Diaspora," 245. The sheer pleasure and exuberance of this new articulation of racial and national identity effected through Bhangra music is the 1980s is wonderfully captured in Gurinder Chadha's 1989 documentary *I'm British but . . .* (BFI, 1989).

11. See Anna Marie Smith, *New Right Discourse on Race and Sexuality*, for an excellent analysis of the simultaneous demonization of the "homosexual" and the "black immigrant" under Thatcherism.

12. Kalra, "*Vilayeti* Rhythms," 87.

13. Ibid.

14. Kalra provides the following translation for some of the lyrics of Kalapreet's track "Us Pardes": "In this land your dignity lies torn to shreds./Even with your pockets full/You still wander the streets like a beggar/You are riding about on a horse/With no direction./And you came to England my friend/Abandoning your home, Punjab./

People here value you/By the color of your skin./All day long you toil with your hands . . . Your brothers were hung in the fight for freedom/Today you humbly ask/For slavery!" "*Vilayeti* Rhythms," 88.

15. See Gopinath, "Bombay, U.K., Yuba City," 314–15, for a gender critique of Apache Indian's concert performance in New Delhi in 1993.

16. Ibid., 306.

17. See Maira, *Desis in the House*, for a valuable ethnography of South Asian club culture in New York City. See also Ashley Dawson, "Desi Remix."

18. See Dawson, "Desi Remix" (section 20) for an analysis of Mutiny's production of a transatlantic, antiracist, and progressive South Asian political movement.

19. See Claire Alexander's insightful ethnography of working-class Bangladeshi young men in London in *The Asian Gang*, 243.

20. Ibid., 229.

21. As ADF puts it on their 1998 track "Hypocrite": "Beware, this is the digital underclass/Coming from places you've only seen from your car/Accountant, lawyer, financial advisor/PR consultant, journalist, advertiser/We know your game and you think we're playing it/When the bill comes through the door you're going to be paying it!" Asian Dub Foundation, "Hypocrite," *Rafi's Revenge*, London Records, 1998.

22. The problematic mainstreaming of British Asian music in the 1990s is more fully explored in New York–based director and deejay Vivek Renjen Bald's riveting documentary *Mutiny* (2003). Bald clearly shows how the brief moment of media attention did not lead to any lasting opportunities for most British Asian musicians. I regret that because I only had the chance to view Bald's film after the writing of this chapter, I was not able to more fully engage with it here.

23. Koushik Banerjea, "Sounds of Whose Underground?," 65.

24. Ibid.

25. Ibid., 67.

26. See Prashad, *Karma of Brown Folk*.

27. John Hutnyk and Sanjay Sharma, "Music and Politics," 59.

28. John Hutnyk, *Critique of Exotica*, 51.

29. Lisa Lowe and David Lloyd, "Introduction," 15.

30. Prashad, *Karma of Brown Folk*, 38.

31. George Lipsitz, *Dangerous Crossroads*, 72.

32. Ibid., 75.

33. It is significant that Cornershop's single "Brimful of Asha" only shot to the top of the charts after it was remixed by Norman Cook, a collaborator with Fatboy Slim. This illustrates the circuitous routes that South Asian diasporic popular culture must travel in order to be audible to the mainstream.

34. Rupa Huq, "Asian Kool?," 79.

35. Ian McCann, "Bhangramuffin," 18.

36. Hutnyk, *Critique of Exotica*, 134.

37. See Gopinath, "Bombay, U.K., Yuba City."

38. It is important to note here that ADF's linking of antiracist politics and anti-colonial nationalist histories is not unique to this particular moment in British Asian music. Indeed, as Virinder Kalra has documented, a central thematic feature of early British Bhangra bands in the 1970s and 1980s was the evocation of anticolonial nationalist heroes such as Singh in order to critique contemporary anti-Asian racism in Britain. See "*Vilayeti* Rhythms," 89–93.

39. Seminar on Feminist Interventions in South Asia, UC Santa Cruz, May 2–3, 2002. I thank the participants for their useful comments and suggestions regarding an earlier version of this chapter.

40. Josh Kun, "Rock's *Reconquista*," 259.

41. Asian Dub Foundation, "Black White," *Rafi's Revenge*, London Records 1998.

42. See Hutnyk, *Critique of Exotica*, 87–113, for an extended critique of the "souveniring of sound and culture" effected by white bands such as Kula Shaker who pepper their music and self-presentation with decontextualized South Asian cultural markers.

43. Asian Dub Foundation, "Jericho," *Facts and Fictions*, Nation Records, 1995.

44. See "Bombay, U.K., Yuba City" for a discussion of how Bhangra musicians in the 1970s and early 1980s saw Bhangra as a solution to feeling "lost" within a racial landscape organized around black and white.

45. Ashley Dawson, "Dub Mentality."

46. K. Anthony Appiah usefully summarizes Sassen's notion of global cities in the following terms: "They are not, like the cities of the past, at the hearts of geographically bounded regions whose economies they center: rather, then connect remote points of production, consumption and finance . . . The global city can become increasingly isolated from—indeed actively antagonistic to—a regional culture or economy." "Foreword," in Saskia Sassen, *Globalization and Its Discontents*, xii.

47. Dawson, "Dub Mentality," 14.

48. As Swasti Mitter defines it, an "enterprise zone" in the "First World" is similar to the export processing zones of the "Third World" and is set up with similar incentives to attract capital, offering investors exemption from property taxes as well as "considerable freedom from health, safety and environmental regulations." *Common Fate Common Bond*, 81. Chrissie Stansfield's 1987 documentary *Bringing It All Back Home* details the beginning of this transformation of the Docklands from a depressed working-class enclave into a state-subsidized zone of high-end businesses, shops, and renovated loft spaces. Importantly, the documentary makes critical linkages between the increasing

mobility of British capital as it engages in offshore production, and the growth of "enterprise zones" within the UK itself. The documentary also points to the increasing use in the early 1980s of a casualized female work force in the UK predominantly made up of Asian immigrant women.

49. Dawson, "Dub Mentality," 13.

50. See Swasti Mitter, "The Capital Comes Home," for a detailed discussion of Asian immigrant women in homeworking and sweatshop industries in the UK in the 1970s and 1980s.

51. Naila Kabeer, *The Power to Choose*, 4.

52. Ibid., 14.

53. Ibid., 216.

54. Mitter, *Common Fate Common Bond*, 130–31.

55. Zuberi, *Sounds English*, 220.

56. Hutnyk, *Critique of Exotica*, 68.

57. Ibid., 7–8.

58. Zuberi, *Sounds English*, 212.

59. David Hesmondhalgh, "International Times," 286.

60. Clara Connelly and Pragna Patel, "Women Who Walk on Water."

61. Sassen, *Globalization and its Discontents*, xxi.

62. Ibid., xxv.

63. Mark Anthony Neal, *Soul Babies*, 6.

64. The perils of this masculinist rendering of diaspora are also apparent in recent attempts to document the history of the Asian Underground music scene. For instance, in his important documentary film *Mutiny* (2003), Vivek Renjen Bald carefully traces the political and historical context of antiracist organizing in British Asian communities from the 1960s to the 1990s, out of which many of the Asian Underground artists emerged. Yet the contribution of women as well as queers (both men and women) to the creation of this scene as well as to the history of antiracist struggle in the UK remains somewhat muted in the film.

65. See, for instance, Kalra, "*Vilayeti* Rhythms"; K. Banerjea and P. Banerjea, "Psyche and Soul"; Claire Alexander, *The Asian Gang*, 240–41.

66. Kalra, "*Vilayeti* Rhythms," 96.

67. Ibid., 93–96.

68. This is Kalra's own translation of the Punjabi lyrics. "*Vilayeti* Rhythms," 94–95.

69. Ibid., 95.

70. Ibid., 94.

71. Lisa Lowe, *Immigrant Acts*, 158.

72. Ibid., 164.

73. Mitter, *Common Fate Common Bond*, 123.

74. Aiwha Ong describes Taylorism or "scientific management" as "the essence of Fordist production." "The Gender and Labor Politics of Postmodernity," 71.

75. Kalra, "*Vilayeti* Rhythms," 95.

76. Mitter, *Common Fate Common Bond*, 123. Mitter defines the "ethnic sweatshop economy" as sweatshops run by (invariably male) racialized immigrant entrepreneurs that employ racialized immigrant women from their own community.

77. Ibid., 122.

78. Lowe, *Immigrant Acts*, 156.

79. Ibid.

80. Aiwha Ong, "The Gender and Labor Politics of Postmodernity," 86.

81. Dipesh Chakravarty, *Provincializing Europe*, 66.

82. Ibid., 67.

83. Ibid.

84. Chakravarty, *Provincializing Europe*, 64.

85. Mitter defines "homeworkers" as individuals (predominantly immigrant women) who supply contractors with very low-wage, machining work that is classified as "unskilled." These contractors in turn supply manufacturers and ultimately retailers. Mitter's research documents the shift in the 1980s as low-wage garment industry jobs in East London and the West Midlands were increasingly transferred from factories and sweatshops to homeworkers. Homeworkers provide manufacturers "access to a captive and disposable workforce [which] becomes an essential strategy for reducing unnecessary overhead costs." "Industrial Restructuring and Manufacturing Homework," 47.

86. *Bringing It All Back Home* (dir. Chrissie Stansfield, 1987).

87. Chakravarty, *Provincializing Europe*, 64.

88. Monica Ali, *Brick Lane*.

89. Kabeer, *The Power to Choose*, 8.

90. Falu Bakrania, "Roomful of Asha."

91. Falu Bakrania, e-mail communication, March 31, 2004. I thank Falu Bakrania for sharing her thoughts with me, and for her feedback on this chapter. See Bakrania, "Re-Fusing Identities."

92. José Muñoz, "Gesture, Ephemera, Queer Feeling," 433.

93. Ibid., 431.

94. For an analysis of a male homoerotic tradition in Sufi spiritualism, poetry, and music, see Saleem Kidwai, "Introduction."

95. Michael Warner, "Publics and Counterpublics." Warner distinguishes "publics" from "audiences" or "groups" through the following five characteristics. A public is (1) self-organized, (2) a relation among strangers, (3) addressed both personally and imper-

sonally, (4) constituted through mere attention on the part of the member of the public, (5) the social space created by the circulation of discourse. I thank Chandan Reddy for bringing this article to my attention.

96. Warner, "Publics and Counterpublics," 51.

97. See, for instance, the review of Parveen's music by Munmun Ghosh, "Abida Parveen," where he describes her voice as "rich, manly and wholesome."

98. See José Muñoz, for an explication of what he terms "queer counterpublics" in *Disidentifications*, 146.

99. José Quiroga, *Tropics of Desire*, 151.

100. Sassen, *Globalization and its Discontents*, xx–xxi.

3 Surviving Naipaul

1. Claire Alexander, "(Dis)Entangling the 'Asian Gang': Ethnicity, Identity and Masculinity," 128. Hanif Kureishi's *My Son the Fanatic* (dir. Udayan Prasad, 1997) interestingly reverses this standard narrative of "traditional" parents and assimilated offspring by positing the father as a secular first-generation Pakistani immigrant who is baffled by his British-born son's turn toward radical orthodox Islam.

2. I am grateful to Rosemary George for alerting me to the reference to *Pakeezah* in this scene.

3. Ayub Khan-Din, *East is East: A Screenplay*. My thanks to Beheroze Shroff for alerting me to this text.

4. I borrow this phrase from Lisa Lowe, *Immigrant Acts*, 158.

5. Rosemary George, *The Politics of Home*, 91–93.

6. Frantz Fanon, *Black Skin, White Masks*, 152–53.

7. Laura Mulvey, "Visual Pleasure and Narrative Cinema."

8. Fanon, *Black Skin, White Masks*, 151–52.

9. See Robert Reid-Pharr, *Black Gay Man*, 70–72, for an analysis of Fanon's scathing critique of Martinican woman writer Mayotte Capecia in *Black Skin, White Masks*.

10. Ella Shohat/Robert Stam, *Unthinking Eurocentrism*, 11.

11. José Muñoz, *Disidentifications*, 11.

12. Vijay Mishra, "The Diasporic Imaginary," 445.

13. For an analysis of Naipaul's reception in the so-called First and Third Worlds, see Rob Nixon, *London Calling*. See also Michael Gorra, *After Empire*; and Bruce King, *V. S. Naipaul*.

14. Michael Powell, *A Life in Movies*, quoted in Arthur Pais, "Sabu's Daughter Scripts the Second Coming of 'The Thief of Baghad.' "

15. My thanks to James Kyung Lee for initially suggesting the uses of the notion of a

"Brown Atlantic." For a critique of Gilroy's Black Atlantic framework in relation to South Asian diasporic cultural production, see Gayatri Gopinath, "Bombay, U.K., Yuba City."

16. Vijay Prashad, *The Karma of Brown Folk*, 28–30.

17. Naipaul, *A House for Mr. Biswas*, 210. See Rosemary George's discussion of masculine failure in the novels of Naipaul and Joseph Conrad in *The Politics of Home*, 91–93.

18. George, *The Politics of Home*, 93.

19. Naipaul, *A House for Mr. Biswas*, 218.

20. Ibid., 275.

21. Ibid., 134.

22. Ibid., 120.

23. Ibid., 92.

24. Salman Rushdie, *Midnight's Children*.

25. See Mrinalini Sinha, *Colonial Masculinity*.

26. George, *The Politics of Home*, 93.

27. V. S. Naipaul, *The Mimic Men*.

28. I borrow this phrase from E. Ann Kaplan, *Looking for the Other*, 222.

29. Eng, "Heterosexuality in the Face of Whiteness," 358.

30. Muñoz, *Disidentifications*, 11.

31. See Homi Bhabha, *The Location of Culture*, 37.

32. Eng, "Heterosexuality in the Face of Whiteness," 363 n. 25.

33. Kobena Mercer, *Welcome to the Jungle*; Reid-Pharr, *Black Gay Man*; Philip Brian Harper, *Are We Not Men?*; David Eng, *Racial Castration*; Nayan Shah, *Contagious Divides*.

34. Reid-Pharr, *Black Gay Man*, 81.

35. Eng, *Racial Castration*, 223–24. See also Mark Chiang, "Coming Out into a Global System," 374–95, for an excellent reading of *The Wedding Banquet*.

36. Eng and Hom, *Q&A*, 1.

37. Eng, *Racial Castration*, 205.

38. Ibid., 16.

39. As Claire Alexander writes in her study of "Asian gangs" in the UK, "This 'between two cultures' identity crisis among Asian youth constitutes the dominant discourse" around Asian youth culture in mainstream media in the UK. "(Dis)Entangling the 'Asian Gang,'" 128.

40. Homi Bhabha, "Are You a Man or a Mouse?" 57–68.

41. Ibid., 58.

42. Anna Marie Smith, *New Right Discourse on Race and Sexuality*, 181.

43. Ibid., 23.

44. Harper, *Are We Not Men?*, x.

45. Bhabha, "Are You a Man or a Mouse?" 58.

46. Ibid., 63.

47. I am most grateful to Jody Greene for suggesting the connection between *East Is East* and *Mary Poppins*, and for pointing me toward Jon Simons's article.

48. Sumita Chakravarty, *National Identity and Indian Popular Cinema 1947–1987*, 270.

49. Ibid., 293.

50. Rachel Dwyer comments, "Many films, notably those of Meena Kumari and the courtesan genre, have been read as camp, and provide inspiration for drag performers, from Bombay's gay parties to London's Club Kali Chutney Queens." In *All You Want is Money, All You Need Is Love*, 52.

51. See Patricia Uberoi, "Dharma and Desire, Freedom and Destiny," 145–71, for an account of "podoerotics" in Hindi cinema.

52. As Sumita Chakravarty writes, "As an image of female oppression, of class oppression, and of psychic and moral ambivalence, the haunting figure of the prostitute can be a searing indictment of social hypocrisy and exploitation." *National Identity and Indian Popular Cinema*, 304.

53. See Jackie Stacey, *Star Gazing*, 80–125.

54. Stacey provides a sophisticated analysis of escapism that Hollywood movies represent for female viewers by situating it within the specific historical context of 1940s Britain. See *Star Gazing*, 80–125.

55. A. Sivanandan, *A Different Hunger*, 131–32.

56. Stuart Hall, "Racism and Reaction," 25. Quoted in Smith, *New Right Discourse on Race and Sexuality*, 132.

57. Jon Simons, "Spectre over London," 1.

58. Ibid., 4.

59. Smith, *New Right Discourse on Race and Sexuality*, 130.

60. This enactment of the reliance of metropole on periphery is also evident on a formal level: Mina's performance slyly reverses the presumed lines of influence that exist between First and Third world popular cultural forms. Rather than the Bollywood musical (*Pakeezah*) being seen as derivative or imitative of the Hollywood musical *(Mary Poppins)*, we can read the latter to be dependent on the form and structure of the former. In a film such as the much-applauded musical *Moulin Rouge* (dir. Baz Luhrmann, 2001), for instance, Bollywood is explicitly referenced as the template of the Hollywood musical. Mina's performance thereby makes apparent the various effacements engendered by contemporary discourses of race, gender, and class in Britain.

61. *Tongues Untied* (dir. Marlon Riggs, 1989).

62. Anne Marie Fortier makes a similar and related argument in "Coming Home" when she critiques the construction of queer subjects as urban subjects within contemporary queer studies. Such a construction, she argues, elides the ways in which some queer subjects choose to be simultaneously "out" while "staying put," often in small towns and rural areas.

4 Bollywood/Hollywood

1. Ziauddin Sardar, "Dilip Kumar Made Me Do It," 21.

2. For a discussion of the reception of popular Indian cinema among non–South Asian international audiences in North Africa, the Middle East, China, and Eastern Europe, see Ravi Vasudevan, "Addressing the Spectator of a 'Third World' National Cinema."

3. My discussion of popular Indian cinema is limited to "Bollywood" cinema—that is, Hindi-language films emerging from the Bombay film industry—which constitutes the largest and most influential sector of Indian commercial cinema. The immense complexity of the different regional and linguistic cinemas that make up Indian commercial cinema more broadly is beyond the scope of this discussion.

4. Key exceptions include Brian Larkin, "Indian Films and Nigerian Lovers"; Mark Liechty, "Media, Markets and Modernization"; Minou Fuglesang, *Veils and Videos*.

5. Vijay Mishra, "The Diasporic Imaginary," 446.

6. Vijay Mishra, *Bollywood Cinema*, 237.

7. Janet Staiger, *Perverse Spectators*, 2.

8. Ibid., 37.

9. Valerie Traub, "The Ambiguities of 'Lesbian' Viewing Pleasure," 309.

10. Judith Mayne, "Paradoxes of Spectatorship"; Chris Straayer, *Deviant Eyes, Deviant Bodies*; Patricia White, *unInvited*; Jackie Stacey, *Star Gazing*; Jacqueline Bobo, *Black Women as Cultural Readers*.

11. Mayne, "Paradoxes of Spectatorship," 159.

12. Straayer, *Deviant Eyes, Deviant Bodies*, 53.

13. Traub, "The Ambiguities of 'Lesbian' Viewing Pleasure," 322.

14. White, *unInvited*, 32.

15. Ibid., 43.

16. Mayne, "Paradoxes of Spectatorship," 158.

17. White, *unInvited*, 197.

18. For recent influential studies of Indian popular cinema, see Ravi Vasudevan, ed., *Making Meaning in Indian Cinema*; Sumita Chakravarty, *National Identity and Indian Popular Cinema, 1947–1987*; Madhava Prasad, *Ideology of the Hindi Film*; Ashish Nandy, ed., *The Secret Politics of Our Desires*.

19. Lalitha Gopalan's *Cinema of Interruptions* signals a welcome and necessary shift within Indian film studies to a serious consideration of female spectatorship; her work takes to task conventional models of film studies that fail to "anticipat[e] audiences that also endow Indian popular cinema with meaning that exceeds its own intended horizon of address," 8.

20. Prasad, *Ideology of the Hindi Film*, 5 n. 14.

21. Ibid., 5 n. 5.

22. Ibid., 43.

23. Vasudevan, "Introduction," 10.

24. Ibid., 14.

25. Moinak Biswas, "The Couple and Their Spaces," 133.

26. Prasad, *Ideology of the Hindi Film*, 95.

27. Quoted in White, *unInvited*, 47.

28. White, *unInvited*, 47.

29. Prasad identifies the "feudal family romance" as "the dominant textual form of the popular Hindi cinema"; this form includes "a version of the romance narrative, an average of six songs per film, as well as a range of familiar character types"; *Ideology of the Hindi Film*, 30–31. Rachel Dwyer further elaborates on the song/dance sequence in Hindi movies: "A Hindi movie has a song every twenty minutes or so, with a total of between six and eight in a film. Songs are sung usually by the hero and heroine, possibly the vamp, but never by the villain. Songs fulfill several important functions, including advancing the narrative . . . They also allow things to be said which cannot be said elsewhere, often to admit love to the beloved, to reveal inner feelings, to make the hero/heroine realize that he/she is in love." In Dwyer, *All You Want Is Money, All You Need Is Love*, 113.

30. Vivek Dhareshwar and Tejaswini Niranjana, "*Kaadalan* and the Politics of Resignification," 191.

31. As cited in Prasad, *Ideology of the Hindi Film*, 88. Sumita Chakravarty also notes that the Indian censorship codes drew heavily on Hollywood's Hayes Production Code; *National Identity and Popular Indian Cinema*, 73.

32. Monika Mehta, "What Is Behind Film Censorship?"

33. Shohini Ghosh, "The Cult of Madhuri," 27.

34. Dwyer, *All You Want Is Money*, 113.

35. As Vijay Mishra writes, "the element of Bombay Cinema that circulates most readily is not the film as a complete commodity (which requires concentrated viewing for some three hours) but fragments from it," namely, in the song and dance sequences that are shown as discrete video clips and broadcast on cable television in the diaspora. Mishra, *Bollywood Cinema*, 261–62.

36. Lalitha Gopalan, however, cautions against labeling the song and dance sequence

as merely "extra-diegetic" and instead argues that it has a more complicated relation to the narrative. She argues that "song and dance sequences are not randomly strung together . . . but both block and propel the narrative in crucial ways." *Cinema of Interruptions*, 21. Nevertheless, the way in which song and dance sequences act as critical sites of narrative "interruption," to use Gopalan's term, allow them to function as spaces within the cinematic text that are particularly available to queer viewing strategies.

37. Chakravarty, *National Identity and Indian Popular Cinema*, 76.

38. Thomas Waugh, "Queer Bollywood, or 'I'm the player, you're the naïve one.'"

39. Prasad, *Ideology of the Hindi Film*, 83–84.

40. Staiger, *Perverse Spectators*, 32.

41. There is an established body of work on the relation between Indian national identity and popular cinema. See in particular Chakravarty, *National Identity and Indian Popular Cinema*, and Prasad, *Ideology of the Hindi Film*.

42. White, *unInvited*, 15.

43. Ibid., 14.

44. Sumita Chakravarty defines "parallel" cinema, also termed "new" cinema, as follows: "More generally, the new cinema has shared an interest in linear narrative 'realistic' mise-en-scène, psychological portrayal of character, the 'motivated' use of songs and dances (as and when required by the context of the film), explicit scenes of sexuality, and a disenchantment with the workings of the Indian political system." *National Identity and Indian Popular Cinema*, 267.

45. For a feminist analysis of the courtesan film genre, see Chakravarty, *National Identity and Indian Popular Cinema*, 269–305.

46. Ibid., 284.

47. My thanks to Juana María Rodríguez for suggesting this reading to me.

48. Veena Talwar Oldenburg, "Lifestyle as Resistance." Mary John and Janaki Nair have usefully critiqued such recuperative accounts of courtesanal cultures as positing an overly linear "golden age narrative" that traces the decline of sexual freedom with the advent of British colonialism. See *A Question of Silence?*, 12.

49. Rosemary M. George, *The Politics of Home*, 133.

50. The use of the English word to name female homoeroticism renders it implicitly alien and inauthentic to Indian national culture.

51. Antoinette Burton, *Dwelling in the Archives*, 66.

52. Malek Alloula, *The Colonial Harem*, 95–104.

53. Ibid.

54. The intertextuality of *Razia Sultan* and *Mughal-e-Azam* is underscored by the fact that the director of *Razia Sultan*, Kamal Amrohi, wrote the screenplay for *Mughal-e-Azam* some twenty-five years earlier. See Ashish Rajadhyaksha and Paul Willeman, *Encyclopaedia of Indian Cinema*, 42.

55. White, *unInvited*, 8.

56. Mehta, "What Is Behind Film Censorship?," section 30.

57. See Eve K. Sedgwick, *Between Men*, 21–27.

58. In one paradigmatic instance of the fate of female gender-crossing characters in Bollywood, *Mera Naam Joker* (My Name is Joker, dir. Raj Kapoor, 1970) featured the actress Padmini as a cross-dressing vagabond and circus performer named Minoo Master. Minoo Master's butch toughness, however, prefigures the inevitable revelation scene, where she is exposed as Mina, a curvaceous beauty who dons a sari, grows her hair, and eventually becomes the hero's wife. Minoo Master's domestication as Mina points to the ways in which masculine women in film are not allowed to exist more than momentarily and are inevitably feminized in order to be drawn back into heterosexuality.

59. White, *unInvited*, 47.

60. To cite just a few examples: *Moulin Rouge* (dir. Baz Luhrmann, 2001); British playwright Andrew Lloyd Weber's collaboration with Indian composer A.R. Rahman in the play *Bombay Dreams* (2003); *The Guru* (dir. Daisy Von Scherler Mayer, 2003).

61. The most visible examples are *Monsoon Wedding* (dir. Mira Nair, 2000), *Bollywood/Hollywood* (dir. Deepa Mehta, 2001), and *Bend It Like Beckham* (dir. Gurinder Chadha, 2002).

62. See Vijay Prashad, *The Karma of Brown Folk*, 11–20, for an explication of U.S. Orientalism.

63. This widespread misreading of *Monsoon Wedding* as a Bollywood film was usefully pointed out by Alexandra Schneider, "Bollywood." In a telling instance of this misreading, Michael Giardina comments in an otherwise excellent article that "in recent years Bollywood films such as *Monsoon Wedding* have become wildly popular commercial successes in Britain"; see "Bending It Like Beckham," 80, n. 10.

64. *Monsoon Wedding* production notes.

65. Waugh, "Queer Bollywood," 285.

66. Shohini Ghosh, "*Hum Aapke Hain Koun . . . !,*" 84.

67. Patricia Uberoi, "Imagining the Family," 320.

68. *Monsoon Wedding* production notes.

69. Ibid.

70. Roger Ebert, "Monsoon Wedding."

71. See Tejaswini Ganti, "And Yet My Heart is Still Indian," for an account of how Bombay film producers indigenize Hollywood films and construct an "Indian audience" in the process.

72. See, for instance, Uberoi, "Imagining the Family," 309–52. See also Rustom Bharucha, "Utopia in Bollywood."

73. Arjun Appadurai and Carole Breckenridge, "Public Modernity in India."

74. Vijay Mishra, *Bollywood Cinema*, 218.

75. A significant exception is Shohini Ghosh's reading of the film in *"Hum Aapke Hain Koun . . . !"*

76. Ghosh, *"Hum Aapke Hain Koun . . . !,"* 87.

77. Ibid.

78. Uberoi, "Imagining the Family," 319.

79. Ibid., 317.

80. Burton, *Dwelling in the Archive,* 7.

81. Ibid., 67.

82. Ibid., 14.

83. Ibid., 69.

84. *Monsoon Wedding* production notes. Nair's self-presentation as the quintessential elite cosmopolitan consumer subject is blatantly apparent in a full-page spread in the magazine *Travel and Leisure.* The piece, entitled "Business Class," features a profile of Nair and details the products that she uses (Prada shoes, Dell laptop, pashmina shawl, bouquets of flowers "in *Monsoon Wedding* colors") in order to make time on the road feel like "home." The copy reads: "Splitting her time among three continents—her production company is in Manhattan, her family lives in Uganda and New York, and she spends at least one month a year in Delhi—Mira Nair leads a dizzying jet-set life." The article renders transparent the class privilege required to traverse national border and cultural spaces with ease. Lucie Young, "Business Class," 102. My thanks to Valerie Larsen for bringing this article to my attention.

85. Tejaswini Niranjana, *Siting Translation,* 3.

86. Vishal Jugdeo, e-mail correspondence, November 11, 2002.

87. *Monsoon Wedding* production notes.

88. Ghosh, *"Hum Aapke Hain Koun . . . !,"* 84.

89. Ibid.

90. White, *unInvited,* 141.

91. Karen Leonard, "Identity in the Diaspora."

92. Michael Giardina, "Bending It Like Beckham," 71.

93. Ibid., 78.

94. Ibid.

95. The success of *My Big Fat Greek Wedding* (dir. Nia Vardalos, 2002), or Chadha's own earlier film *What's Cooking* (2000), speaks to the unthreatening multicultural ethos and palatability of ethnic comedies that invariably mobilize a number of limited, recurring motifs, such as the family, generational conflict, weddings, and food.

96. Gurinder Chadha, production notes to *Bend It Like Beckham.*

97. My thanks to Tammy Ho for this insight.

98. The heavy-handed heteronormativity of *Bollywood / Hollywood* may speak to a

strategic decision on Mehta's part to avoid the controversy that greeted both *Fire* in 1998 and her next venture, *Water*, in 1999. The film shoot of *Water*, set in Varanasi and dealing with the question of Hindu widowhood, was successfully shut down by Hindu nationalists in 1999, whereupon Mehta returned to Toronto to begin shooting *Bollywood / Hollywood*. Aseem Chhabra, "*Bollywood / Hollywood* is not a Bollywood Film."

5 Local Sites / Global Contexts

1. Shohini Ghosh, "From the Frying Pan to the Fire," 16.

2. "Deepa Mehta's *Fire.*"

3. Madhu Kishwar, "Naïve Outpourings of a Self-Hating Indian."

4. Shoma Chatterjee, "One Sita Steps Beyond the Lakshmanrekha." See Ismat Chughtai, *The Quilt and Other Stories.*

5. "Ismat Chughtai on *Lihaf.*"

6. Geeta Patel, "Homely Housewives Run Amok," 10. I thank the author for sharing her unpublished manuscript with me.

7. Susie Tharu and K. Lalita, "Empire, Nation and the Literary Text," 214. For a critique of obscenity law in India, see Ratna Kapur, "The Profanity of Prudery."

8. Ratna Kapur, "Too Hot to Handle," 183–84.

9. Kumkum Sangari and Sudesh Vaid, "Introduction," in *Recasting Women,* 10. This collection sought to bring a gender analysis to bear on the Subaltern Studies Collective's project of renarrativizing Indian history "from below," that is, from the vantage point of peasant struggles and other movements that fell beneath the threshold of elite colonial, bourgeois, and nationalist histories. See the foundational work of Ranajit Guha, "On Some Aspects of the Historiography of Colonial India," and "The Prose of Counter-Insurgency."

10. As Lata Mani argues, the nineteenth-century debates on the status of Indian women among colonial officials, missionaries, and the indigenous elite "are in some sense not primarily about women but about what constitutes authentic cultural tradition." "Contentious Traditions," 90.

11. Sangari and Vaid, *Recasting Women,* 11.

12. Amrita Chhacchi, "Identity Politics, Secularism and Women," 82.

13. Chhachhi, "Identity Politics," 94.

14. Paola Baccheta, "Communal Property / Sexual Property," 194.

15. Ritu Menon and Kamla Bhasin, "Abducted Women, the State, and Questions of Honour."

16. Inderpal Grewal, *Home and Harem,* 7.

17. Other recent feminist collections to engage (to a limited extent) with the ques-

tion of sexuality include Rajeswari Sunder Rajan, ed., *Signposts*; Patricia Jeffery and Amrita Basu, eds., *Resisting the Sacred and the Secular*; Ratna Kapur, ed., *Feminist Terrains in Legal Domains*. Much of this scholarship, however, fails to fully explore the linkages between the production of heterosexuality and concomitant "perverse" or "abnormal" sexualities within colonial and nationalist frameworks.

18. See Mrinalini Sinha, "Nationalism and Respectable Sexuality in India." For an exemplary study of heterosexual masculinity and colonialism, see also Sinha, *Colonial Masculinity*.

19. Sinha, "Nationalism and Respectable Sexuality in India," 34.

20. Ibid., 44.

21. Ibid., 45. See Sinha, *Selections from Katherine Mayo's Mother India*, 277.

22. See Sinha, *Selections from Katherine Mayo's Mother India*, 277.

23. Ibid.

24. Sinha, "Nationalism and Respectable Sexuality in India," 45–46.

25. Ibid., 45.

26. Mary John and Janaki Nair, eds., *A Question of Silence?*

27. John and Nair, *A Question of Silence?*, 9.

28. Ibid., 19.

29. Ibid., 33.

30. Ibid., 36.

31. Mark Chiang, "Coming Out into the Global System," 375.

32. For example, one critic writes that "*Fire* is a plea for women's self-determination that . . . will probably strike viewers in this country as a bit obvious" (Walter Addeago, "*Fire* Cool to State of Marriage in India"). Similarly, other critics describe the film as taking place within the "suffocatingly masculine" and "pre-feminist" culture of contemporary India (see, e.g., Owen Gleiberman, "Take My Wife").

33. Roger Ebert, "*Fire* Strikes at Indian Repression."

34. See Margaret McGurk, "Tradition Broken in Indian Tale of Forbidden Love," and Bill Morrison, "Women on the Verge of a Cinematic Breakthrough."

35. Ashish Rajadhyaksha and Paul Willeman, *Encyclopaedia of Indian Cinema*, 180.

36. For further contextualization of Chughtai's work in relation to the Progressive Writers Association and Urdu literature more generally, see Ismat Chughtai, trans. M. Asaduddin, *Lifting the Veil*, xi–xxiv. See also Chughtai, trans. Tahira Naqvi, *My Friend, My Enemy*, vii–xi.

37. Chughtai, *The Crooked Line (Tehri Lakir)*.

38. Like many writers involved in the Progressive Writers Association, Chughtai intermittently worked as a scenarist and producer in the Bombay film industry from the 1940s to the 1970s, where she further explored these questions of class, gender, and

familial relations in the context of post-Independence India. Her husband, Shahid Latif, was a well-known Bombay film director and producer. Rajadhyaksha and Willeman, *Encyclopaedia of Indian Cinema*, 80.

39. Chughtai, *My Friend, My Enemy*, 174.

40. Avtar Brah, *Cartographies of Diaspora*, 209.

41. See Chandra Mohanty's now-classic essay, "Under Western Eyes: Feminist Scholarship and Colonial Discourses," for a critique of hegemonic discourses of Third World women's oppression, passivity, and victimization.

42. Eve K. Sedgwick, *Epistemology of the Closet*, 71. Of course, Sedgwick very deliberately limits her field of inquiry to Euro-American texts and makes claims only about these. Nevertheless, her formulations of the closet and concurrent tropes of silence and invisibility have become totalizing narratives in theorizing queer existence. Little attention has been paid to the different tropes of spacialization at work among differently raced lesbian and gay subjects within, say, a U.S. context. Martin Manalansan, for instance, has argued that notions of coming out and the closet are inadequate in narrativizing queer identity among gay Filipino men both in New York City and in the Philippines, where sexuality is always refracted through experiences of immigration. See Manalansan, "In the Shadows of Stonewall."

43. Chughtai, "The Quilt," 7.

44. Ibid.

45. Ibid., 8.

46. Ibid.

47. Ibid., 9.

48. Ibid., 13.

49. Ibid., 19.

50. Ibid., 10.

51. For instance, the narrator comments, "I can say that if someone touched me continuously like this, I would certainly rot," and later, "imagining the friction caused by this prolonged rubbing made me slightly sick." Chughtai, "The Quilt," 11.

52. Chughtai, "The Quilt," 16.

53. See Susie Tharu and K. Lalitha, eds., *Women Writing in India, Vol. 2*, 135.

54. As Elizabeth Grosz and others have argued, psychoanalytic discourse as articulated by Freud and Lacan has seen "desire, like female sexuality itself, as an absence, lack, or hole, an abyss seeking to be engulfed, stuffed to satisfaction." See Grosz, "Refiguring Lesbian Desire," 71.

55. As Geeta Patel comments, "the women in ['The Quilt'] do not 'become' lesbians even though they engage in physical activities with each other. This form of not being a lesbian . . . raises the question about where (in what national/cultural/historical sites)

performance needs to be located in order for it to produce 'identity.'" See Patel, "Homely Housewives Run Amok," 10.

56. Chughtai, "The Quilt," 11.

57. Ibid., 16.

58. Ibid., 11.

59. See Valerie Traub, "Ambiguities of Lesbian Viewing Pleasure," 311.

60. A number of theorists have explored the linkages in Euro-American medico-moral and other discourses between various paradigmatic figures of female sexual transgression, such as the prostitute, the "lesbian" or female invert, and the working-class female. See, for example, Judith Walkowitz, *The City of Dreadful Delight*.

61. Chughtai, "The Quilt," 10. The way in which Chughtai's masculinization of desiring female subjects is informed by colonial-era Western sexological discourse on Indian female sexuality remains to be further examined. Havelock Ellis, for instance, noted that sex between women, which he deemed particularly prevalent in India, was practiced by women endowed with the penetrative power of enlarged clitorises. See Ellis, *Studies in the Psychology of Sex*, 208.

62. D. A. Miller, "Anal *Rope*," 130.

63. Chughtai, "The Quilt," 19.

64. "A certain naming" is Judith Butler's phrase in *Bodies That Matter*, 162.

65. "Ismat Chughtai on *Lihaf*."

66. See Ginu Kamani, "Interview with Deepa Mehta."

67. Kaushalya Bannerji, "No Apologies."

68. Outside the confines of the middle-class North Indian home depicted in *Fire*, female homoerotic desire may manifest itself in forms other than that of hyperbolic or queer femininity. As Geeta Patel has noted in her discussion of the controversy around the 1987 "marriage" of two policewomen in central India, the police barracks in which the two women lived constituted a site of complicated and explicitly gendered erotic relations between women. See Patel, "Homely Housewives Run Amok," 14–22.

69. See Judith Halberstam's *Female Masculinity* for a theorization of "masculinity without men."

70. Esther Newton, "The Mythic Mannish Lesbian."

71. See Newton, "The Mythic Mannish Lesbian," for a critique of nineteenth-century "romantic friendships" as proto-lesbian/feminist relationships.

72. Clearly, a Euro-American bourgeois space of "home" is not akin to the domestic space represented in *Fire*, given that the latter is marked by a history of British colonialism, anticolonial nationalism, and contemporary Indian (and Hindu) nationalist politics.

73. See Peter Stack, "Review of *Fire*."

74. Patel, "Homely Housewives Run Amok," 13–14. Partha Chatterjee, for instance, argues that the anticolonial nationalist elite of pre-Independence India created

an "inner" sphere as its hegemonic space, one that existed outside the workings of the colonial state. The figure of the woman came to embody this space of an essential, immovable Indian identity or tradition. See Chatterjee, *The Nation and its Fragments*, 133. Patel holds that Chughtai's critique of the notion of women as desexualized and static markers of "tradition" had much to do with the charges of obscenity leveled against "The Quilt" upon its publication.

75. Patel, "Homely Housewives Run Amok," 7.

76. "Hindu Militants Stage Lesbian Film Attacks."

77. "Attacks on *Fire* Due to Lack of Vision, Says Sathyu." See also the Campaign for Lesbian Rights, *Lesbian Emergence*, 17–19, for an account of the progressive, leftist framing of the *Fire* controversy in terms of "freedom of expression" and not sexuality.

78. Premiere of *Earth* (dir. Deepa Mehta, 1998), Asia Society, New York, December 1998.

79. "Deepa Mehta on *Fire.*"

80. "Thackeray's Terms." Radha and Sita, are, as noted, names drawn from Hindu mythology while Shabana and Saira function in Thackeray's statement as generic Muslim names as well as specific references to Shabana Azmi, the star of the film, and to Saira Banu, the wife of actor Dilip Kumar, who was vocal in his support of the film. Eventually, Mehta did agree to change "Sita" to "Neeta" in the Hindi version of the film.

81. *BBC News Online*, December 9, 1998. http://www.bbc.co.uk.

82. George Lipsitz, *Dangerous Crossroads*, 7.

83. Sukthankar, Ashwini, et al., eds., *Lesbian Emergence*, 24.

84. For a critique of the cultural essentialism inherent in CALERI's stance, see Ratna Kapur, "Too Hot to Handle."

85. South Asian Lesbian and Gay Association, "Take a Stand in Support of Secularism, Freedom of Expression and Lesbian Rights in India."

86. South Asian Lesbian and Gay Association, "*Fire* in New York," 34.

87. As Vinay Lal comments, "The Ram Janmabhoomi Movement, which led to the destruction of the . . . Babri Majid, received considerable support from Hindus settled overseas, and the funding of Hindu institutions, temples and other purportedly 'charitable' enterprises by diaspora Hindus, particularly those from the United States, can be established beyond doubt." "The Politics of History on the Internet," 150.

6 Nostalgia, Desire, Diaspora

1. See Jocelyne Guilbault, "Racial Projects and Musical Discourses in Trinidad," for an analysis that usefully situates the debates around chutney and chutney soca in the context of the particularities of racialization and national identity in Trinidad.

2. As quoted in Peter Manuel, *East Indian Music in the West Indies*, 184.

3. Manuel, *East Indian Music in the West Indies*, 186.

4. Ibid., 171.

5. Tejaswini Niranjana, "Left to the Imagination."

6. Ibid., 128.

7. "Wining" refers to an Afro-Caribbean dance move that stresses pelvic rotation. See Manuel, *East Indian Music in the West Indies*, 174.

8. Manuel, *East Indian Music in the West Indies*, 175.

9. Ibid., 171.

10. Ibid., 174.

11. Ibid., 175.

12. See Rob Nixon for a discussion of the different valences of various terms used to describe displacement, such as exile, emigrant, expatriate, and refugee, in *London Calling*, 17–28. See Rosemary George for a useful distinction between exile literature and "the immigrant genre" in *The Politics of Home*, 174–75.

13. George, *The Politics of Home*, 175.

14. Shyam Selvadurai, *Funny Boy*.

15. Selvadurai, *Funny Boy*, 5.

16. Shani Mootoo, *Cereus Blooms at Night*.

17. Avtar Brah, *Cartographies of Diaspora*, 181.

18. For an excellent account of the historical split between Asian and Asian American studies, see Sucheta Mazumdar, "Asian American Studies and Asian Studies."

19. Ibid., 41.

20. For recent work on South Asian American cultural politics, see, for instance, Vijay Prashad, *The Karma of Brown Folk*; Amitava Kumar, *Passport Photos*; Matthew and Prashad, *Satyagraha in America*; Sunaina Maira, *Desis in the House*.

21. Prashad, *The Karma of Brown Folk*, 183.

22. See Prashad, *The Karma of Brown Folk*, 185–204, for a discussion of progressive South Asian organizing in New York City.

23. Rajiv Shankar, "Foreword: South Asian Identity in Asian America," ix-x.

24. The critiques that feminist and queer Asian American scholars have leveled, over the past two decades, at the groundbreaking anthology *Aiiieeeee!*, edited by Frank Chin et al., come to mind. See, for instance, Elaine H. Kim, *Asian American Literature*; Sauling Cynthia Wong, *Reading Asian American Literature*; Russell Leong, "Introduction: Home Bodies and the Body Politic"; David L. Eng and Alice Y. Hom, eds., *Q&A*; David L. Eng, *Racial Castration*.

25. See, for instance, Bharati Mukherjee, *Jasmine*; Chitra Banerjee Divakaruni, *Arranged Marriage*. For a critique of the racial and gender politics of *Jasmine*, see Susan Koshy, "The Geography of Female Subjectivity."

26. For an analysis of the creation of "inner" and "outer" spheres in anticolonial nationalist discourse in India, see Partha Chatterjee, "The Nationalist Resolution to the Woman's Question."

27. See Judith Halberstam, *The Drag King Book*, for a discussion of masculine non-performativity in the context of female drag king performances.

28. Selvadurai, *Funny Boy*, 19.

29. Ibid., 39.

30. Ibid., 262.

31. See Robert McRuer, "Boys' Own Stories and New Spellings of My Name," for a critique of the coming out narrative as "necessary for understanding one's (essential) gay identity"(267) and of Edmund White's novel in particular.

32. Selvadurai, *Funny Boy*, 5.

33. Dorinne Kondo suggests this formulation of "home" in her essay on Asian American negotiations of community and identity, "The Narrative Production of 'Home,' Community and Political Identity in Asian American Theater," 97.

34. Martin Manalansan, "Diasporic Deviants/Divas."

35. However, the flier's use of Hindi (rather than Tamil or Sinhala) even when referencing a Sri Lankan text points to the ways in which (North) Indian hegemony within South Asia may be replicated within queer South Asian spaces in the diaspora.

36. Selvadurai, *Funny Boy*, 302.

37. Ibid., 309–10.

38. Fredric Jameson, "Third World Literature in an Age of Multinational Capitalism."

39. Ibid., 69.

40. Aijaz Ahmad, *In Theory*, 95–122.

41. George, *The Politics of Home*, 91.

42. Madhavi Kale, *Fragments of Empire*, 5.

43. Indira Karamcheti, "The Shrinking Himalayas," 264.

44. Rhoda Reddock, "Freedom Denied."

45. M. Jacqui Alexander, "Erotic Autonomy as a Politics of Decolonization."

46. Patricia Mohammed, "Writing Gender into History."

47. Madhavi Kale, "Projecting Identities."

48. Prabhu Mohapatra, "Restoring the Family." Cited in Niranjana, "Left to the Imagination," 133.

49. Kale, *Fragments of Empire*, 174.

50. Ibid., 167.

51. Ibid., 36–37.

52. Ibid., 112.

53. George, *The Politics of Home*, 50.

54. Ibid., 51.

55. Mootoo, *Cereus Blooms at Night*, 51.

56. For a reading of how Mootoo's novel reframes questions of trauma and the incest narrative, see Ann Cvetkovich, *An Archive of Feelings*, 140–55.

57. Anne McClintock, *Imperial Leather*, 358.

7 Epilogue

1. Purnima Mankekar, "Brides Who Travel."

2. Indeed, in December 2003, the Indian congress passed a bill that was to smooth the way to dual citizenship for "Persons of Indian Origin" from particular nations in the West. A person holding this new form of "citizenship," however, would not be entitled to work or vote in India but could buy property and invest in its markets.

3. See the transnational Bollywood hit, *Kabhi Khushi Kabhie Gham* (dir. Karan Johar, 2001) for another, particularly egregious example of this new genre of Bollywood films set in the diaspora. The film similarly relies on the diasporic female as the embodiment of national tradition and culture, invariably figured as Hindu. Here the diasporic woman is always shown dressed in the markers of respectable Hindu femininity (in a sari, *bindi*, and *mangalsutra*, the gold chain worn by married Hindu women) and becomes the most ardent advocate for Indian identity and familial loyalty in the film.

4. Within the logic of the film, this success only comes at the expense of other communities of color: the Indian diner is only able to succeed when it lures customers away from the Chinese restaurant across the street. This narrative of Indian versus Chinese immigrant success betrays Indian nationalist anxieties over China's ascendance to world power status in the battle for regional hegemony in Asia.

5. Thomas Waugh, "Queer Bollywood," 285.

6. This genre was solidified in the 1970s with a series of films starring the Bollywood icon Amitabh Bhacchan partnered with a male sidekick. See Bhacchan's films from the 1970s and early 1980s celebrating male friendship, such as *Zanjeer* (dir. Prakash Mehra, 1973), *Sholay* (dir. Ramesh Sippy, 1975), and *Dostana* (dir. Raj Khosla, 1980).

7. Waugh, "Queer Bollywood," 286.

8. José Rabasa, "Of Zapatismo," 421.

9. Cherry Smyth, "Out of the Gaps," 110. I thank Cherry Smyth for bringing Sekhon's work to my attention, and for initially giving me the opportunity to write about it for *Diva Magazine*. I am most grateful to Parminder Sekhon for permission to discuss and reproduce her work.

BIBLIOGRAPHY

Addeago, Walter. "Fire Cool to State of Marriage in India." *San Francisco Examiner* (September 26, 1997): C7.

Ahmad, Aijaz. *In Theory: Classes, Nations, Literatures.* Delhi: Oxford University Press, 1994.

Alexander, Claire. *The Asian Gang: Ethnicity, Identity, Masculinity.* Oxford: Berg Press, 2000.

———. "(Dis)Entangling the 'Asian Gang': Ethnicity, Identity and Masculinity." In *Un/Settled Multiculturalisms: Diasporas, Entanglements, Transruptions,* edited by Barnor Hesse. London: Zed Books, 2000.

Alexander, M. Jacqui. "Erotic Autonomy as a Politics of Decolonization: An Anatomy of Feminist and State Practice in the Bahamas Tourist Economy." In *Feminist Genealogies, Colonial Legacies, Democratic Futures,* edited by M. Jacqui Alexander and Chandra T. Mohanty. New York: Routledge, 1997.

Ali, Monica. *Brick Lane.* London: Doubleday, 2003.

Alloula, Malek. *The Colonial Harem.* Minneapolis: University of Minnesota Press, 1986.

Anzaldúa, Gloria. *Borderlands/La Frontera.* San Francisco: Spinsters/Aunt Lute, 1987.

Appadurai, Arjun. "Disjuncture and Difference in the Global Cultural Economy." *Theory, Culture and Society* 7 (1990): 295–310.

Appadurai, Arjun, and Carole Breckenridge. "Public Modernity in India." In *Consuming Modernity: Public Culture in a South Asian World,* edited by Carole Breckenridge. Minneapolis: University of Minnesota Press, 1995.

Appiah, K. Anthony. "Foreword." In *Globalization and Its Discontents,* edited by Saskia Sassen. New York: New Press, 1998.

Asian Dub Foundation. "Black White." *Rafi's Revenge.* London Records, 1998.

———. "Hypocrite." *Rafi's Revenge.* London Records, 1998.

———. "Jericho." *Facts and Fictions.* Nation Records, 1995.

"Attacks on Fire Due to Lack of Vision, Says Sathyu," *Times of India* (February 3, 1999): A3.

Baccheta, Paola. "Communal Property/Sexual Property: On Representations of Muslim Women in Hindu Nationalist Discourse." In *Forging Identities: Gender, Communities and the State*, edited by Zoya Hassan. New Delhi: Kali for Women, 1994.

———. "When the (Hindu) Nation Exiles its Queers." *Social Text* 61 (Winter 1999): 141–61.

Bakrania, Falu. "Re-Fusing Identities: British Asian Youth and the Cultural Politics of Popular Music" (PhD Dissertation: Stanford University, 2003).

———. "Roomful of Asha: Gendered Negotiations of the Asian Underground," paper presented at South Asia Studies Conference, Berkeley, February 12, 2001.

Banerjea, Koushik. "Sounds of Whose Underground? The Fine Tuning of Diaspora in an Age of Mechanical Reproduction." *Theory, Culture and Society* 17, no. 3 (2000): 64–79.

Banerjea, Koushik, and P. Banerjea. "Psyche and Soul: A View from the South." In *Dis-Orienting Rhythms: The Politics of New Asian Dance Music*, edited by A. Sharma et al. London: Zed Press, 1996.

Bannerji, Kaushalya. "No Apologies." In *A Lotus of Another Color: An Unfolding of the South Asian Gay and Lesbian Experience*, edited by Rakesh Ratti. Boston: Alyson, 1993.

Bend It Like Beckham production notes, www2.foxsearchlight.com/benditlikebeckham.

Bhabha, Homi. "Are You a Man or a Mouse?" In *Constructing Masculinity*, edited by Maurice Berger et al. New York: Routledge, 1995.

———. *The Location of Culture.* New York: Routledge, 1994.

Bharucha, Rustom. "Utopia in Bollywood: *Hum Aapke Hain Koun . . . !*" *Economic and Political Weekly* (April 15, 1995): 801–904.

Bhattacharjee, Annanya. "The Habit of Ex-Nomination: Nation, Woman, and the Indian Immigrant Bourgeoisie." *Public Culture* 5, no. 1 (Fall 1992): 19–46.

———. "The Public/Private Mirage: Mapping Homes and Undomesticating Violence Work in the South Asian Immigrant Community." In *Feminist Genealogies, Colonial Legacies, Democratic Futures*, edited by Jacqui Alexander and Chandra Mohanty. New York: Routledge, 1997.

Biswas, Moinak. "The Couple and Their Spaces: *Harano Sur* as Melodrama Now." In *Making Meaning in Indian Cinema*, edited by Ravi S. Vasudevan. New Delhi: Oxford University Press, 2000.

Bobo, Jacqueline. *Black Women as Cultural Readers.* New York: Columbia University Press, 1995.

Brah, Avtar. *Cartographies of Diaspora: Contesting Identities.* London: Routledge, 1996.

Braziel, Jana Evans, and Anita Mannur. "Nation, Migration, Globalization: Points of Contention in Diaspora Studies." In *Theorizing Diaspora*, edited by Jana Evans Braziel and Anita Mannur. Malden, Mass.: Blackwell, 2003.

Burton, Antoinette. *Dwelling in the Archives: Women Writing House, Home and History in Late Colonial India*. London: Oxford University Press, 2003.

Butler, Judith. *Bodies That Matter: On the Discursive Limits of "Sex."* New York: Routledge, 1993.

——. "Imitation and Gender Insubordination." In *Inside / Out: Lesbian Theories, Gay Theories*, edited by Diana Fuss. New York: Routledge, 1991.

Chakravarty, Dipesh. *Provincializing Europe: Postcolonial Thought and Historical Difference*. Princeton: Princeton University Press, 2000.

Chakravarty, Sumita. *National Identity and Indian Popular Cinema, 1947–1987*. Austin: University of Texas Press, 1993.

Chander, Anupam. "Diaspora Bonds." *New York University Law Review* v.76 (October 2001): 1005–99.

Chatterjee, Partha. "The Nationalist Resolution to the Woman's Question." In *Recasting Women: Essays in Colonial History*, edited by Kumkum Sangari and Sudesh Vaid. New Delhi: Kali for Women, 1989.

——. *The Nation and Its Fragments: Colonial and Postcolonial Histories*. Princeton: Princeton University Press, 1993.

Chatterjee, Shoma. "One Sita Steps beyond the Lakshmanrekha." *Calcutta Telegraph* (January 12, 1997): B1.

Chhabra, Aseem. "*Bollywood / Hollywood* Is Not a Bollywood Film." http://www.rediff.com

Chhacchi, Amrita. "Identity Politics, Secularism and Women." In *Forging Identities: Gender, Communities and the State*, edited by Zoya Hassan. New Delhi: Kali for Women, 1994.

Chiang, Mark. "Coming Out into a Global System: Postmodern Patriarchies and Transnational Sexualities in *The Wedding Banquet*." In *Q&A: Queer in Asian America*, edited by David Eng and Alice Hom. Philadelphia: Temple University Press, 1998.

Chin, Frank, et al., eds. *Aiiieeeee! An Anthology of Asian American Writers*. New York: Meridian, 1997.

Chughtai, Ismat. *The Crooked Line*. Translated by Tahira Naqvi. London: Heinemann, 1995.

——. *The Heart Breaks Free*. Translated by Tahira Naqvi. New Delhi: Kali for Women, 1993.

——. *Lifting the Veil: Selected Writings of Ismat Chughtai*. Translated by M. Asaduddin. New Delhi: Penguin Books, 2001.

——. *My Friend, My Enemy: Essays, Reminiscences, Portraits*. Translated by Tahira Naqvi. New Delhi: Kali for Women, 2001.

——. *The Quilt and Other Stories*. Translated by Tahira Naqvi and Syeda Hameed. New Delhi: Kali for Women, 1992.

Connelly, Clara, and Pragna Patel. "Women Who Walk on Water." In *The Politics of Culture in the Shadow of Capital*, edited by Lisa Lowe and David Lloyd. Durham: Duke University Press, 1998.

Cvetkovich, Ann. *An Archive of Feelings: Trauma, Sexuality and Lesbian Public Cultures.* Durham: Duke University Press, 2003.

Dawson, Ashley. "Desi Remix: The Plural Dance Cultures of New York's South Asian Diaspora." *Jouvert* 7, no. 1 (2002). http://www.social.chass.ncsu.edu/jouvert/v7is1/desi.html.

———. "Dub Mentality: South Asian Dance Music in Britain and the Production of Space." *Social Semiotics* 12, no. 1 (April 2002): 27–44.

"Deepa Mehta on *Fire.*" BBC *News Online*, December 9, 1998. http://bbc.co.uk.

"Deepa Mehta's *Fire.*" *The Hindu*, editorial page, February 16, 1997. http://www.hindu.com/1997/02/16.

Dhareshwar, Vivek, and Tejaswini Niranjana. "*Kaadalan* and the Politics of Resignification: Fashion, Violence and the Body." In *Making Meaning in Indian Cinema*, edited by Ravi Vasudevan. New Delhi: Oxford University Press, 2000.

Divakaruni, Chitra Banerjee. *Arranged Marriage.* New York: Anchor Books, 1995.

Duggan, Lisa. *Sapphic Slashers: Sex, Violence and American Modernity.* Durham: Duke University Press, 2000.

———. *The Twilight of Equality? Neoliberalism, Cultural Poltics and the Attack on Democracy.* Boston: Beacon, 2003.

Dwyer, Rachel. *All You Want Is Money, All You Need Is Love: Sex and Romance in Modern India.* London: Cassell, 2000.

Ebert, Roger. "*Fire* Strikes at Indian Repression." *Chicago Sun Times* (September 17, 1997): 38.

———. "Monsoon Wedding." *Chicago Sun Times* (March 8, 2002). http://www.suntimes.com/ebert/ebert-reviews/2002/03/030801.html.

Ellis, Havelock. *Studies in the Psychology of Sex.* New York: Random House, 1908.

Eng, David. L. "Heterosexuality in the Face of Whiteness." In *Q&A: Queer in Asian America*, edited by David Eng and Alice Hom. Philadelphia: Temple University Press, 1998.

———. *Racial Castration: Managing Masculinity in Asian America.* Durham: Duke University Press, 2001.

Fanon, Frantz. *Black Skin, White Masks.* New York: Grove Press, 1967.

Ferguson, Roderick. *Aberrations in Black: Toward a Queer of Color Critique.* Minneapolis: University of Minnesota Press, 2003.

Fiol Matta, Licia. *A Queer Mother for the Nation: The State and Gabriela Mistral.* Minneapolis: University of Minnesota Press, 2002.

Fortier, Anne Marie. "Coming Home: Queer Migrations and Multiple Evocations of Home." *European Journal of Cultural Studies* 4 (2001): 405–24.

Fuglesang, Minou. *Veils and Videos: Female Youth Culture on the Kenyan Coast.* Stockholm: Studies in Anthropology, 1994.

Ganti, Tejaswini. "And Yet My Heart Is Still Indian: The Bombay Film Industry and the (H)Indianization of Hollywood." In *Media Worlds: Anthropology on New Terrain*, edited by Faye Ginsburg et al. Berkeley: University of California Press, 2002.

George, Rosemary. *The Politics of Home: Postcolonial Relocations and Twentieth-Century Fiction*. Cambridge: Cambridge University Press, 1997.

Ghosh, Munmun. "Abida Parveen." http://music.indya.com/reviews.

Ghosh, Shohini. "The Cult of Madhuri." *Gentleman Magazine* (October 1998): 26–28.

——. "From the Frying Pan to the Fire." *Communalism Combat* (January 1999): 16–19.

——. "*Hum Aapke Hain Koun . . . !*: Pluralizing Pleasures of Viewership." *Social Scientist* 28:2–3 (March–April 2000): 83–90.

Giardina, Michael. " 'Bending It Like Beckham' in the Global Popular: Stylish Hybridity, Performativity and the Politics of Representation." *Journal of Sport and Society* 27, no. 1 (February 2003): 65–82.

Gilroy, Paul. *The Black Atlantic: Modernity and Double Consciousness*. Cambridge: Harvard University Press, 1993.

——. *Small Acts: Thoughts on the Politics of Black Cultures*. New York: Serpent's Tail, 1993.

Gleiberman, Owen. "Take My Wife: *Fire*, a Tale of Illicit Lesbian Love in India, Evokes the Early Days of American Feminism." *Entertainment Weekly* (September 12, 1997): 110.

Gopalan, Lalitha. *Cinema of Interruptions: Action Genres in Contemporary Cinema*. London: BFI, 2003.

Gopinath, Gayatri. "Bombay, U.K., Yuba City: Bhangra Music and the Engendering of Diaspora." *Diaspora* 4, no. 3 (Winter 1995): 303–30.

Gorra, Michael. *After Empire: Scott, Naipaul, Rushdie*. Chicago: University of Chicago Press, 1997.

Grewal, Inderpal. *Home and Harem: Nation, Gender, Empire and the Cultures of Travel*. Durham: Duke University Press, 1996.

Grosz, Elizabeth. "Refiguring Lesbian Desire." In *The Lesbian Postmodern*, edited by Laura Doane. New York: Columbia University Press, 1994.

Guha, Ranajit. "On Some Aspects of the Historiography of Colonial India." *Subaltern Studies: Writings on South Asian History and Society* 1 (1982): 1–8.

——. "The Prose of Counter-Insurgency." *Subaltern Studies: Writings on South Asian History and Society* 2 (1983): 1–42.

Guilbault, Jocelyne. "Racial Projects and Musical Discourses in Trinidad." In *Music and the Racial Imagination*, edited by Ronald Radano and Philip V. Bohlman. Chicago: University of Chicago Press, 2000.

Halberstam, Judith. *The Drag King Book*. London: Serpent's Tail, 1998.

——. *Female Masculinity*. Durham: Duke University Press, 1997.

Hall, Stuart. "Cultural Identity and Diaspora." In *Theorizing Diaspora*, edited by Jana Evans Braziel and Anita Mannur. Malden, Mass.: Blackwell, 2003.

——. "Racism and Reaction." In *Five Views of Multi-Racial Britain*, edited by John Rex et al. London: Commission for Racial Equality, 1978.

Harper, Philip Brian. *Are We Not Men? Masculine Anxiety and the Problem of African American Identity*. London: Oxford University Press, 1998.

Hassan, Zoya, ed. *Forging Identities: Gender, Communities and the State.* New Delhi: Kali for Women, 1994.

Helmreich, Stefan. "Kinship, Nation and Paul Gilroy's Concept of Diaspora." *Diaspora* 2 (1992): 245.

Hesmondhalgh, David. "International Times: Fusions, Exoticism and Antiracism in Electronic Dance Music." In *Western Music and Its Others: Difference, Representation, and Appropriation in Music,* edited by Georgina Born and David Hesmondalgh. Berkeley: University of California Press, 2000.

"Hindu Militants Stage Lesbian Film Attacks," *BBC News Online,* December 3, 1998. http://news.bbc.co.uk.

Huq, Rupa. "Asian Kool? Bhangra and Beyond." In *Dis-Orienting Rhythms: The Politics of New Asian Dance Music,* edited by Sanjay Sharma et al. London: Zed Books, 1996.

Hutnyk, John. *Critique of Exotica: Music, Politics and the Culture Industry.* London: Pluto Press, 2000.

Hutnyk, John, and Sanjay Sharma. "Music and Politics: An Introduction." *Theory Culture and Society* 17, no. 3 (2000): 59.

"Ismat Chughtai on *Lihaf.*" *Manushi* 109 (November/December 1998). http://www.free.freespeech.org/manushi/127.

Jeffery, Patricia, and Amrita Basu, eds. *Resisting the Sacred and the Secular: Women's Activism and Politicized Religion in South Asia.* New Delhi: Kali for Women, 1999.

John, Mary, and Janaki Nair, eds. *A Question of Silence? The Sexual Economies of Modern India.* New Delhi: Kali for Women, 1998.

Kabeer, Naila. *The Power to Choose: Bangladeshi Women and Labour Market Decisions in London and Dhaka.* London: Verso, 2000.

Kale, Madhavi. *Fragments of Empire: Capital, Slavery and Indian Indentured Labor Migration in the British Caribbean.* Philadelphia: University of Pennsylvania Press, 1998.

——. "Projecting Identities: Empire and Indentured Labor Migration from India to Trinidad and British Guiana, 1836–1885." In *Nation and Migration: The Politics of Space in the South Asian Diaspora,* edited by Peter Van Der Veer. Philadelphia: University of Pennsylvania Press, 1994.

Kalra, Virinder. "*Vilayeti* Rhythms: Beyond Bhangra's Emblematic Status to a Translation of Lyrical Texts." *Theory, Culture and Society* 17, no. 3 (2000): 94–95.

Kamani, Ginu. "Interview with Deepa Mehta." *Trikone Magazine* 4, no. 4 (October 1997): 11–13.

Kaplan, E. Ann. *Looking for the Other: Feminism, Film and the Imperial Gaze.* New York: Routledge, 1997.

Kapur, Ratna, ed. *Feminist Terrains in Legal Domains.* New Delhi: Kali for Women, 1996.

——. "The Profanity of Prudery: The Moral Face of Obscenity Law." *Women: A Cultural Review* 8, no. 3 (1997): 293–302.

——. "Too Hot to Handle: The Cultural Politics of *Fire.*" In *Translating Desire: The*

Politics of Gender and Culture in India, edited by Brinda Bose. New Delhi: Katha, 2002.

Karamcheti, Indira. "The Shrinking Himalayas." *Diaspora* 2 (1992): 261–76.

Khan-Din, Ayub. *East is East: A Screenplay.* New York: Talk Miramax Books-Hyperion, 1999.

Kidwai, Saleem. "Introduction: Medieval Materials in the Perso-Urdu Traditions." In *Same-Sex Love in India: Readings from History and Literature*, edited by Ruth Vanita and Saleem Kidwai. New York: St. Martin's Press, 2000.

Kim, Elaine H. *Asian American Literature: An Introduction to the Writers and their Social Context.* Philadelphia: Temple University Press, 1982.

King, Bruce. *V. S. Naipaul.* New York: St. Martin's, 1993.

Kishwar, Madhu. "Naïve Outpourings of a Self-Hating Indian." *Manushi* 109 (November/December 1998). www.free.freespeech.org/manushi/127.

Kondo, Dorinne. "The Narrative Production of 'Home,' Community and Political Identity in Asian American Theater." In *Displacement, Diaspora and Geographies of Identity*, edited by Smadar Lavie and Ted Swedenburg. Durham: Duke University Press, 1996.

Koshy, Susan. "The Geography of Female Subjectivity: Ethnicity, Gender and Diaspora." *Diaspora* 3, no. 1 (Spring 1994): 69–84.

Kumar, Amitava. *Passport Photos.* Berkeley: University of California Press, 2000.

Kun, Josh. "Rock's *Reconquista.*" In *Rock over the Edge: Transformations in Popular Music Culture*, edited by Roger Beebe et al. Durham: Duke University Press, 2002.

——. "Sayuri Ciccone." *San Francisco Bay Guardian.* February 1999. http://www.sfbg.com.

Lal, Vinay. "The Politics of History on the Internet: Cyber-Diasporic Hinduism and the North American Hindu Diaspora." *Diaspora* 8, no. 2 (1999): 137–72.

Larkin, Brian. "Indian Films and Nigerian Lovers: Media and the Creation of Parallel Modernities." *Africa* 67, no. 3 (1997): 406–39.

Leonard, Karen. "Identity in the Diaspora: Surprising Voices." In *Cultural Compass: Ethnographic Explorations in Asian America*, edited by Martin Manalansan. Philadelphia: Temple University Press, 2000.

Leong, Russell. "Introduction: Home Bodies and the Body Politic." In *Asian American Sexualities: Dimensions of the Gay and Lesbian Experience*, edited by Russell Leong. New York: Routledge, 1996.

Liechty, Mark. "Media, Markets and Modernization: Youth Identities and the Experience of Modernity in Kathmandu, Nepal." In *Youth Cultures: A Cross-Cultural Perspective*, edited by Vered Amit-Talai and Helena Wulff. London: Routledge, 1994.

Linmark, Zamora R. *Rolling the R's.* New York: Kaya, 1995.

Lipsitz, George. *Dangerous Crossroads: Popular Music, Postmodernism and the Poetics of Place.* London: Verso, 1994.

Lorde, Audre. *Zami: A New Spelling of My Name*. Freedom, Calif.: Crossing Press, 1982.

Lowe, Lisa. *Immigrant Acts: On Asian American Cultural Politics*. Durham: Duke University Press, 1996.

——. "Work, Immigration, Gender: Asian 'American' Women." In *Immigrant Acts: On Asian American Cultural Politics*. Durham: Duke University Press, 1996.

Lowe, Lisa, and David Lloyd. "Introduction." In *The Politics of Culture in the Shadow of Capital*, edited by Lisa Lowe and David Lloyd. Durham: Duke University Press, 1997.

Maira, Sunaina. *Desis in the House: Indian American Youth Culture in New York City*. Philadelphia: Temple University Press, 2002.

Malavé, Arnaldo Cruz, and Martin Manalansan, eds. *Queer Globalizations*. New York: New York University Press, 1999.

Manalansan, Martin. "Diasporic Deviants/Divas: How Filipino Gay Transmigrants 'Play With the World.' " In *Queer Diasporas*, edited by Cindy Patton and Benigno Sanchez-Eppler. Durham: Duke University Press, 1997.

——. *Global Divas: Filipino Gay Men in New York City*. Durham: Duke University Press, 2003.

——. "In the Shadows of Stonewall: Examining Gay Transnational Politics and the Diasporic Dilemma." In *The Politics of Culture in the Shadow of Capital*, edited by Lisa Lowe and David Lloyd. Durham: Duke University Press, 1997.

Mani, Lata. *Contentious Traditions: The Debate on Sati in Colonial India*. Berkeley: University of California Press, 1998.

——. "Contentious Traditions: The Debate on *Sati* in Colonial India." In *Recasting Women: Essays in Colonial History*, edited by Kumkum Sangari and Sudesh Vaid. New Delhi: Kali for Women, 1989.

Mankekar, Purnima. "Brides Who Travel: Gender, Transnationalism, and Nationalism in Hindi Film." *positions* 7, no. 3 (1999): 731–61.

Manuel, Peter. *East Indian Music in the West Indies: Tan Singing, Chutney and the Making of Indo-Caribbean Culture*. Philadelphia: Temple University Press, 2000.

Martin, Biddy, and Chandra Talpade Mohanty. "Feminist Politics: What's Home Got to Do with It?" In *Feminist Studies/Critical Studies*, edited by Teresa de Lauretis. Bloomington: Indiana University Press, 1986.

Matthew, Biju, and Vijay Prashad, eds. *Satyagraha in America*. Special issue of *Amerasia* 25, no. 3 (1999/2000).

Mayne, Judith. "Paradoxes of Spectatorship." In *Viewing Positions: Ways of Seeing Film*, edited by Linda Williams. New Brunswick: Rutgers University Press, 1994.

Mazumdar, Sucheta. "Asian American Studies and Asian Studies: Rethinking Roots." In *Asian Americans: Comparative and Global Perspectives,* edited by Shirley Hune et al. Pullman: Washington State University Press, 1991.

McCann, Ian. "Bhangramuffin." *ID: The Sound Issue* (Fall 1993): 18.

McClintock, Anne. *Imperial Leather: Race, Gender and Sexuality in the Colonial Contest*. New York: Routledge, 1995.

McGurk, Margaret. "Tradition Broken in Indian Tale of Forbidden Love." *Cincinnati Enquirer* (January 16, 1998): W26.

McRuer, Robert. "Boys' Own Stories and New Spellings of My Name: Coming Out and Other Myths of Queer Positionality." *Genders* 2, no. 1 (1994): 260–83.

Mehta, Monika. "What Is behind Film Censorship? The *Khalnayak* Debates." *Jouvert* 5, no. 3 (2001): section 7. http://social.chass.ncsu.edu/jouvert/v5i3/mehta.html.

Menon, Ritu, and Kamala Bhasin. "Abducted Women, the State, and Questions of Honour: Three Perspectives on the Recovery Operation in Post-Partition India." In *Embodied Violence: Communalising Women's Sexuality in South Asia*, edited by Kumari Jayawardena and Malathi de Alwis. New Delhi: Kali for Women, 1996.

Menon, Ritu, and Kamala Bhasin, eds. *Borders and Boundaries: Women and India's Partition*. New Delhi: Kali for Women, 1998.

Mercer, Kobena. *Welcome to the Jungle: New Positions in Black Cultural Studies*. New York: Routledge, 1994.

Miller, D. A. "Anal *Rope*." In *Inside/Out: Lesbian Theories, Gay Theories*, edited by Diana Fuss. New York: Routledge, 1991.

Mishra, Vijay. *Bollywood Cinema: Temples of Desire*. New York: Routledge, 2002.

——. "The Diasporic Imaginary: Theorizing the Indian Diaspora." *Textual Practice* 10, no. 3 (1996): 421–47.

Mitter, Swasti. *Common Fate Common Bond: Women in the Global Economy*. London: Pluto Press, 1986.

——. "Industrial Restructuring and Manufacturing Homework: Immigrant Women and the UK Clothing Industry." *Capital and Class* 27 (Winter 1986): 37–80.

Mohammed, Patricia. "Writing Gender into History." In *Engendering History: Caribbean Women in Historical Perspective*, edited by Verene Shepherd et al. New York: St. Martin's Press, 1995.

Mohanty, Chandra. "Under Western Eyes: Feminist Scholarship and Colonial Discourses." *Feminist Review* 30 (Fall 1988): 65–88.

Mohapatra, Prabhu. "Restoring the Family: Wife Murders and the Making of a Sexual Contract for Indian Immigrant Labour in the British Caribbean Colonies, 1860–1920." Cited in Tejaswini Niranjana, "Left to the Imagination: Indian Nationalisms and Female Sexuality in Trinidad." In *A Question of Silence? The Sexual Economies of Modern India*, edited by Mary John and Janaki Nair. New Delhi: Kali for Women, 1998.

Monsoon Wedding production notes, www.monsoonweddingmovie.com.

Mootoo, Shani. *Cereus Blooms at Night*. Toronto: Press Gang, 1996.

Moraga, Cherrie. *Loving in the War Years: Lo que nunca paso por sus labios*. Boston: South End Press, 1983.

Moraga, Cherrie, and Gloria Anzaldúa, eds. *This Bridge Called My Back: Writings by Radical Women of Color*. New York: Kitchen Table, 1983.

Morrison, Bill. "Women on the Verge of a Cinematic Breakthrough." *News and Observer* (November 12, 1997): WUP10.

Mosse, George. *Nationalism and Sexuality: Middle-Class Morality and Sexual Norms in Modern Europe.* Madison: University of Wisconsin Press, 1985.

Mukherjee, Bharati. *Jasmine.* New York: Grove Weidenfeld, 1988.

Mulvey, Laura. "Visual Pleasure and Narrative Cinema." In *Issues in Feminist Film Criticism,* edited by Patricia Erens. Bloomington: Indiana University Press, 1990.

Muñoz, José. *Disidentifications: Queers of Color and the Performance of Politics.* Minneapolis: University of Minnesota Press, 1999.

——. "Gesture, Ephemera, Queer Feeling." In *Dancing Desires,* edited by Jane Desmond. Madison: University of Wisconsin Press, 1998.

Naipaul, V. S. *A House for Mr. Biswas.* New York: Vintage, 1984.

——. *The Mimic Men.* New York: Macmillan, 1967.

Nandy, Ashish, ed. *The Secret Politics of Our Desires: Innocence, Culpability and Indian Popular Cinema.* London: Zed Press, 1998.

Neal, Mark Anthony. *Soul Babies: Black Popular Culture and the Post-Soul Aesthetic.* New York: Routledge, 2002.

Newton, Esther. "The Mythic Mannish Lesbian: Radclyffe Hall and the New Woman." In *Hidden from History: Reclaiming the Gay and Lesbian Past,* edited by Martin Duberman et al. New York: Meridian, 1989.

Niranjana, Tejaswini. "Left to the Imagination: Indian Nationalisms and Female Sexuality in Trinidad." In *A Question of Silence? The Sexual Economies of Modern India,* edited by Mary John and Janaki Nair. New Delhi: Kali for Women, 1998.

——. *Siting Translation: History, Post-Structuralism and the Colonial Context.* Berkeley: University of California Press, 1992.

Nixon, Rob. *London Calling: V. S. Naipaul, Postcolonial Mandarin.* London: Oxford University Press, 1992.

Obejas, Achy. *Memory Mambo.* Pittsburgh: Cleis Press, 1996.

Oldenburg, Veena Talwar. "Lifestyle as Resistance: The Case of the Courtesans of Lucknow, India." *Feminist Studies* 16, no. 2 (1990): 259–87.

Ong, Aiwha. "The Gender and Labor Politics of Postmodernity." In *The Politics of Culture in the Shadow of Capital,* edited by Lisa Lowe and David Lloyd. Durham: Duke University Press, 1997.

Parker, Andrew, ed. *Nationalisms and Sexualities.* New York: Routledge, 1992.

Patel, Geeta. "Homely Housewives Run Amok: Lesbians in Marital Fixes." Unpublished manuscript.

Povinelli, Elizabeth, and George Chauncey, eds. "Thinking Sexuality Transnationally." Special issue, *GLQ* 5, no. 4 (1999).

Powell, Michael. *A Life in Movies: An Autobiography.* London: Faber and Faber, 2001. Quoted in Arthur Pais, "Sabu's Daughter Scripts the Second Coming of 'The Thief of Baghad,'" http://www.rediff.com/news/1999/jul.

Prasad, Madhava. *Ideology of the Hindi Film: A Historical Construction.* New Delhi: Oxford University Press, 1998.

Prashad, Vijay. *The Karma of Brown Folk.* Minneapolis: University of Minnesota Press, 2000.

Quiroga, José. *Tropics of Desire: Interventions from Queer Latino America.* New York: New York University Press, 2001.

Rabasa, José. "Of Zapatismo: Reflections on the Folkloric and the Impossible in a Subaltern Insurrection." In *The Politics of Culture in the Shadow of Capital,* edited by Lisa Lowe and David Lloyd. Durham: Duke University Press, 1997.

Rajadhyaksha, Ashish, and Paul Willeman. *Encyclopaedia of Indian Cinema.* London: BFI, 1999.

Rashid, Ian Iqbal. "Passage to England." *Trikone Magazine* 16, no. 3 (July 2001): 10–12.

Reddock, Rhoda. "Freedom Denied: Indian Women and Indentureship in Trinidad and Tobago, 1845–1917." *Economic and Political Weekly* 20, no. 43 (1985): 79–87.

Reid-Pharr, Robert. *Black Gay Man: Essays.* New York: New York University Press, 2001.

Roach, Joseph. *Cities of the Dead: Circum-Atlantic Performance.* New York: Columbia University Press, 1996.

Rodríguez, Juana María. *Queer Latinidád: Identity Practices, Discursive Spaces.* New York: New York University Press, 2003.

Rodriguez, Nice. *Throw It to the River.* Toronto: Women's Press, 1993.

Rubin. Gayle. "Thinking Sex: Notes for a Radical Theory of the Politics of Sexuality." In *Pleasure and Danger: Exploring Female Sexuality,* edited by Carole Vance. New York: Routledge, 1984.

Rushdie, Salman. *Midnight's Children.* London: Jonathan Cape, 1981.

Sangari, Kumkum, and Sudesh Vaid, eds. *Recasting Women: Essays in Colonial History.* New Delhi: Kali for Women, 1989.

Sardar, Ziauddin. "Dilip Kumar Made Me Do It." In *The Secret Politics of Our Desires,* edited by Ashish Nandy. London: Zed Press, 1998.

Schneider, Alexandra. "Bollywood: A World of Proximity and Difference," paper presented at the Society for Cinema Studies Conference, Minneapolis, March 7, 2003.

Sedgwick, Eve K. *Between Men: English Literature and Male Homosocial Desire.* New York: Columbia University Press, 1985.

——. *Epistemology of the Closet.* Berkeley: University of California Press, 1990.

Selvadurai, Shyam. *Funny Boy.* Toronto: McClelland and Stuart, 1994.

Shah, Nayan. *Contagious Divides: Epidemics and Race in San Francisco's Chinatown.* Berkeley: University of California Press, 2001.

Shankar, Rajiv. "Foreword: South Asian Identity in Asian America." In *A Part Yet Apart: South Asians in Asian America,* edited by Lavina Shankar and Rajini Srikanth. Philadelphia: Temple University Press, 1998.

Sharpe, Jenny. "Cartographies of Globalisation, Technologies of Gendered Subjectivities: The Dub Poetry of Jean 'Binta' Breeze." In *Gender and History,* forthcoming.

Shohat, Ella, and Robert Stam. *Unthinking Eurocentrism.* New York: Routledge, 1998.

Simons, Jon. "Spectre over London: *Mary Poppins*, Privatism and Finance Capital." *Scope: An On-Line Journal of Film Studies* (January 2000). http://www.nottingham .ac.uk/film.

Sinha, Mrinalini. *Colonial Masculinity: The "Manly Englishman" and the "Effeminate Bengali" in the Late Nineteenth Century.* Manchester: Manchester University Press, 1995.

——. "Nationalism and Respectable Sexuality in India." *Genders* 21 (1995): 30–57.

——. *Selections from Katherine Mayo's Mother India.* New Delhi: Kali for Women, 1998.

Sivanandan, A. *A Different Hunger: Writings on Black Resistance.* London: Pluto Press, 1982.

Smith, Anna Marie. *New Right Discourse on Race and Sexuality: Britain 1968–1990.* Cambridge: Cambridge University Press, 1994.

Smith, Barbara, ed. *Home Girls: A Black Feminist Anthology.* New York: Kitchen Table Press, 1983.

Smyth, Cherry. "Out of the Gaps: The Work of Parminder Sekhon." In *Red Threads: The South Asian Queer Connection in Photographs,* edited by Poulomi Desai and Parminder Sekhon. London: Diva Books, 2003.

South Asian Lesbian and Gay Association (SALGA). "*Fire* in New York: A Report." In *Lesbian Emergence: A Citizen's Report,* edited by Ashwini Sukthankar et al. New Delhi: Campaign for Lesbian Rights, 1999.

——. "Take a Stand in Support of Secularism, Freedom of Expression and Lesbian Rights in India." Press release. January 1999.

Stacey, Jackie. *Star Gazing: Hollywood Cinema and Female Spectatorship.* New York: Routledge, 1994.

Stack, Peter. "Review of *Fire.*" *The San Francisco Examiner* (September 26, 1997): C6.

Staiger, Janet. *Perverse Spectators: The Practices of Film Reception.* New York: New York University Press, 2000.

Straayer, Chris. *Deviant Eyes, Deviant Bodies: Sexual Re-Orientations in Film and Video.* New York: Columbia University Press, 1996.

Sukthankar, Ashwini, et al., eds. *Lesbian Emergence: A Citizen's Report.* New Delhi: Campaign for Lesbian Rights, 1999.

Sunder Rajan, Rajeswari, ed. *Signposts: Gender Issues in Post-Independence India.* New Delhi: Kali for Women, 1999.

"Thackeray's Terms." *The Hindu* (December 14, 1998): B24.

Thadani, Giti. *Sakhiyani: Lesbian Desire in Ancient and Modern India.* London: Cassell, 1996.

Tharu, Susie, and K. Lalita. "Empire, Nation and the Literary Text." In *Interrogating Modernity: Culture and Colonialism in India,* edited by Tejaswini Niranjana et al. Calcutta: Seagull Books, 1993.

——, eds. *Women Writing in India, Volume 2: The Twentieth Century.* New York: Feminist Press, 1993.

Traub, Valerie. "The Ambiguities of 'Lesbian' Viewing Pleasure: The (Dis)Articulations of *Black Widow.*" In *Body Guards: The Cultural Politics of Gender Ambiguity*, edited by Julia Epstein and Kristina Straub. New York: Routledge, 1991.

Uberoi, Patricia. "Dharma and Desire, Freedom and Destiny: Rescripting the Man-Woman Relationship in Popular Hindi Cinema." In *Embodiment: Essays on Gender and Identity*, edited by Meenakshi Thapar. Delhi: Oxford University Press, 1997.

———. "Imagining the Family: An Ethnography of Viewing *Hum Aapke Hain Koun . . . !.*" In *Pleasure and the Nation: The History, Politics and Consumption of Public Culture in India*, edited by Rachel Dwyer and Christopher Pinney. London: Oxford University Press, 2001.

Vanita, Ruth, ed. *Queering India: Same-Sex Love and Eroticism in Indian Culture and Society.* New York: Routledge, 2002.

Vasudevan, Ravi. "Addressing the Spectator of a 'Third World' National Cinema: The Bombay 'Social Film' of the 1940s and 1950s." *Screen* 36, no. 4 (1995): 305–24.

Vasudevan, Ravi, ed. *Making Meaning in Indian Cinema.* New Delhi: Oxford University Press, 2000.

Visweswaran, Kamala. "Diaspora by Design: Flexible Citizenship and South Asians in U.S. Racial Formations." *Diaspora* 6, no. 1 (1997): 5–29.

Walkowitz, Judith. *The City of Dreadful Delight: Narratives of Sexual Danger in Late-Victorian London.* Chicago: University of Chicago Press, 1992.

Warner, Michael. "Publics and Counterpublics." *Public Culture* 14, no. 1 (2002): 49–90.

———. *The Trouble with Normal: Sex, Politics and the Ethics of Queer Life.* New York: Free Press, 1999.

Waugh, Thomas. "Queer Bollywood, or 'I'm the player, you're the naïve one': Patterns of Sexual Subversion in Recent Indian Popular Cinema." In *Keyframes: Popular Cinema and Cultural Studies*, edited by Matthew Tinkcom and Amy Villarejo. New York: Routledge, 2001.

White, Patricia. *unInvited: Classical Hollywood Cinema and Lesbian Representability.* Bloomington: Indiana University Press, 1999.

Wong, Sau-ling Cynthia. *Reading Asian American Literature: From Necessity to Extravagance.* Princeton: Princeton University Press, 1993.

Young, Lucie. "Business Class." *Travel and Leisure* (May 2003): 102.

Zuberi, Nabeel. *Sounds English: Transnational Popular Music.* Urbana: University of Illinois Press, 2001.

FILMOGRAPHY

Bend It Like Beckham (2002), directed by Gurinder Chadha.

Bollywood / Hollywood (2001), directed by Deepa Mehta.

Brimful of Asia (1996), directed by Pratibha Parmar.

Bringing It All Back Home (1987), directed by Chrissie Stansfield.

Chaudvin Ka Chand (1960), directed by M. Sadiq.

Dostana (1980), directed by Raj Khosla.

Earth (1998), directed by Deepa Mehta.

East Is East (2000), directed by Damien O'Donnell.

Fire (1996), directed by Deepa Mehta.

Hum Aapke Hain Koun . . . ! (1994), directed by Sooraj Barjatya.

I'm British but. . . (1989), directed by Gurinder Chadha.

The Jungle Book (1942), directed by Alexander Korda.

Kabhi Khushi Kabhie Ghum (2001), directed by Karan Johar.

Kal Ho Naa Ho (2003), directed by Nikhil Advani.

Khalnayak (1993), directed by Subhash Gai.

Khush (1991), directed by Pratibha Parmar.

Lagaan (2001), directed by Ashutosh Gowariker.

Mary Poppins (1964), directed by Robert Stevenson.

Mera Naam Joker (1970), directed by Raj Kapoor.

Monsoon Wedding (2000), directed by Mira Nair.

Moulin Rouge (2001), directed by Baz Luhrmann.

Mughal-e-Azam (1961), directed by K. Asif.

Mutiny (2003), directed by Vivek Renjen Bald.

My Beautiful Laundrette (1985), directed by Stephen Frears.

My Son the Fanatic (1997), directed by Udayan Prasad.

Pakeezah (1971), directed by Kamal Amrohi.

Razia Sultan (1983), directed by Kamal Amrohi.

Sholay (1975), directed by Ramesh Sippy.

Subhah / Umbartha (1981), directed by Jabbar Patel.

Surviving Sabu (1996), directed by Ian Iqbal Rashid.

Tongues Untied (1989), directed by Marlon Riggs.

Utsav (1984), directed by Girish Karnad.

Zanjeer (1973), directed by Prakash Mehra.

INDEX

Nair, Janaki, 138–39
Nair, Mira, 25, 188
Nation, 6–7, 9–12, 15, 17, 20, 22–23, 28,
41, 79, 97, 123, 128, 139; and disapora,
7, 11, 13, 31–32, 78, 144, 187, 191; and
exclusion of lesbian, 19; and feminist
cultural practices, 62; heterosexual, 10,
12, 16, 102, 113, 189; Hindu, 17, 159;
as home, 7, 15, 166, 179, 186; masculine, 25, 81; as original, 13; patriarchal,
16, 82–83; postmodern, 72; and public
culture, 85; and sexual repression, 13
National Federal of Indian Associations
(NFIA), 16–17
Nationalism, 6, 16, 28, 101, 167, 171,
176; anticolonial, 14, 135–36, 180;
Asian American, 168; Black, 38, 45,
47–48; bourgeois, 20, 136–37; and
diaspora, 4, 9, 21, 26–27, 56, 159, 164;
and discourse, 6–7, 9, 14, 17–22, 25,
86, 108; ethnic, 7, 20, 174–75; and
gender, 10, 18, 26, 197 n. 25; and heteronormativity, 16; and heterosexuality, 9–11, 19, 137; histories of, 3;
and home, 9, 17, 160; and ideology, 11,
16–17, 28, 87; Indian, 10, 25, 97, 134–
35, 137–38, 162; and morality, 9;
Pakistani, 81–82, 85; and patriarchy,
14, 18; postcolonial, 64; racist, 83;
religious, 7, 26, 136, 140, 196 n.19; and
sexuality, 9, 164, 197 n.31; South
Asian, 12, 134; and state, 7
Nation-state, 19, 79, 137, 139
Naxalbari, 42
Naxalite Movement, 42
Neal, Mark Anthony, 48
Newton, Esther, 155
Niranjana, Tejaswini, 9, 13, 100, 122,
162–64
Non-resident Indian (NRI), 10, 124, 196
n.18

Nostalgia, 4, 27, 39–41, 43, 104, 116,
174, 177

Oedipality, 5–6, 58, 63, 75, 91; and colonized men, 66; and male subjectification, 71; and Naipaul and Rashid, 69
Oldenburg, Veena Talwar, 105
Ong Aiwha, 51
Orientalism, 87; and colonial fantasies,
67, 75; "millennial," 29–30, 43; in
South Asian diasporic, 38; and U.S.,
37–38, 70, 114, 167

Pakeezah (Kamal Amrohi), 64, 85–90,
207 n.60
Panjabi MC, 46
Parveen, Abida, 59–60
Patel, Geeta, 132, 156
Patel, Pragna, 47
Paternity, 5
Patriarchy, 5, 50, 135, 178; immigrant, 83;
nationalist, 14; state, 82
Pencha, Madhorama, 120
Politics: of class and race, 23; gay and lesbian transnational, 12; mainstream gay
and lesbian, 20
Popular culture, 12, 36, 38, 40–41, 43,
85
Prashad, Madhava, 97–98, 102
Prashad, Vijay, 8, 37–38, 70, 114,
167–68
Progressive Writers Association, 143
Public culture, 17, 30, 51, 76, 162, 199
n.53; counterpublic, 30, 96, 204 n.95;
definition of, 20; diasporic, 21, 29, 41,
43, 45, 48, 56, 58, 64–65, 85–86, 88,
122, 161, 164; national, 117; queer, 21,
59, 99, 140, 163–64, 171, 174, 187,
192; South Asian, 6, 12, 20, 59, 93;
transnational, 22, 42, 188, 191
Punjab, 31

Qawaali, 41, 57–58. *See also* Music
Queer: desire, 1–2, 25–27; diaspora, 3–6,
10, 12–17, 19–28, 192; race, 1, 3, 14
Queerness, 2, 13, 22, 83–84, 94, 106,
113, 123–25, 127–28, 152, 168, 185,
187; and colonialism, 184; and community, 158; diasporic, 78–79, 140;
and feminism, 6, 78, 157–58; and
home, 14–15, 17; as male, 129, 164;
and modernity, 194; and nationalist
ideologies, 11, 28; and racism, 69; of
texts, 13
Queer studies, 14
"The Quilt" (Ismat Chughtai), 13–14,
26, 130, 132–34, 142, 143–56, 159,
161, 164, 183
Quiroga, José, 60

Rabasa, José, 19, 192
Race, 23, 43, 66, 75–76, 185
Racialization, 27, 169; of body, 1; of
labor, 90; of queer desire, 3; of South
Asians, 8, 70–71; of space, 1, 15, 23
Racism, 2–3, 50, 90, 195 n.1; British, 89;
and masculine authority, 83; pan-
ethnic, anti-, 38; state-sponsored, 47,
82; white, 44
Rafi, Mohammed, 40
Ramayana, 117, 141
Rashid, Ian (*Surviving Sabu*), 15, 26, 64–
66, 71–73, 75–80, 83, 85, 87, 91–92,
94, 177, 194
Rashtriya Swayamsevak Sangh (RSS), 135
Razia Sultan (Kamal Amrohi), 104, 108–
13, 129, 148, 154
Reddi, Muthulakshmi, 137–38
Reddock, Rhoda, 179–80
Reid Pharr, Robert, 77
Roach, Joseph, 4, 21
Rushdie, Salman: *Satanic Verses*, 46; *Mid-
night's Children*, 72

Sagoo, Bally, 32, 40–41, 46
Sakhi, 17–18
Sangari, Kumkum, 134–35, 138
Sankofa film collective, 65
Sardar, Ziauddin, 93
Sarkar, Tanika, 135, 138
Sassen, Saskia, 43, 47–48, 60
Sati, 108
Sawhney, Nitin, 35
Sedgwick, Eve, 110, 145, 215 n.42
Sekhon, Parminder, 192–94
Selvadurai, Shyam (*Funny Boy*), 27, 165–
67, 170–77, 185–86
Sexuality, 23, 31, 114, 134, 140, 173, 177,
185; alternative and challenge to
nationalism, 9, 26, 150; and desire, 28;
deviant, 17, 137; and diaspora, 17, 20–
21, 179; discourses of, 3, 9–10, 17, 27,
88, 142; Eastern/Western, 137; female,
9–10, 100, 106, 110–11, 117, 122–23,
132, 135–36, 138, 148–49, 153, 161–
62, 179–80; and Hindu nationalism,
134; and home, 114; Indian, 137–39,
181, 183; Indo-Caribbean, 163; low-
class, 110; middle-class, 135; narrative
of gay, 27; "perverse," 2; queer, 2, 12,
113, 128–29, 155, 159, 172; and South
Asian American studies, 27; "Third
World" as premodern, 12; women's in
Bollywood cinema, 25
Sexual variance: gay and lesbian, 13
Shankar, Rajiv, 168
Sharma, Sanjay, 37, 39
Sharpe, Jenny, 8–9, 11
Shiv Sena, 131–32, 157, 159
Shohat, Ella, 68
Sholay (Flames; Ramesh Sippy), 101
Simon, Jon, 89
Singh, Talvin, 35–36, 39
Singh, Udham, 42
Sinha, Mrinalini, 72, 137–38

131; and home, 9, 14, 18; Indian, 9, 18, 162, 179–80; in nationalist discourse, 15, 18

Women Against Fundamentalism (WAF), 47

Women's Health Action Mobilization (WHAM), 192

Youth culture: British Asian, 49; South Asian, 18, 35

Zapatistas, 19–20

Zee, Johnny, 33

Zenana, 103, 108–9, 121–22, 156

Zuberi, Nabeel, 45–46

GAYATRI GOPINATH

is Assistant Professor of Women and Gender Studies

at the University of California, Davis.

Library of Congress Cataloging-in-Publication Data

Gopinath, Gayatri.
Impossible desires : queer diasporas and South Asian
public cultures / Gayatri Gopinath.
p. cm.
Includes bibliographical references and index.
ISBN 0-8223-3501-8 (cloth : alk. paper)
ISBN 0-8223-3513-1 (pbk. : alk. paper)
1. Gays in popular culture. 2. South Asians—Foreign
countries—Social conditions. 3. South Asians in literature. 4. South Asians in mass media. 5. Homosexuality
in motion pictures. 6. Homosexuality in literature.
7. Homosexuality in music. I. Title.
HQ76.25.G67 2005
306.76'6'089914—dc22   2004027163